Political Education
and
Stability

Political Education and Stability

Elite Responses to Political Conflict

Ted Tapper

School of Social Sciences,
University of Sussex

JOHN WILEY & SONS

London   New York   ·   Sydney   ·   Toronto

Library of Congress Cataloging in Publication Data:

Tapper, Edward.
Political education and stability.

1. Political socialization. 2. Political participation—Great Britain.
3. Political participation—United States. I. Title.
JA76.T35   301.5'92   75-30817

ISBN 0 471 01361 7

Set by Lightbown & Co.
72 Union Street, Ryde, Isle of Wight
Printed in Great Britain at The Pitman Press, Bath

To my mother

Jessie Tapper

and my late mother-in-law

Jean Howard

Preface

Following the publication of Herbert Hyman's text in 1959, political socialization expanded rapidly into a subdiscipline within the study of politics. Today this particular research boom is at end and perhaps it would be more appropriate to write an obituary regretting its demise rather than yet another book covering such a well-worn topic. Although I do not specifically discuss why political socialization research blossomed in the 1960s, nor the reasons for its decline, I do attempt to trace some of its major developments while it was a flourishing subdiscipline. I also use some of its central assumptions to provide a coherent theme with which to analyse certain contemporary socio-political movements within the Anglo-American democracies. As such this is a book which tries to accomplish a number of different things. It is a text on comparative government which examines the changing character of the Anglo-American political culture. At a time when we are about to celebrate the bicentenary of the American Revolution this seems to me to be both timely and of importance. The political culture is re-evaluated through an assessment of movements that have threatened the stability of the two polities. So it represents the attempt of a political sociologist to use contemporary history for his own purposes. The book, therefore, is a blend of contrasting ingredients and, although the final product may not be to everyone's taste, it reflects a tradition in social science that I admire.

Daniel Bell's *The End of Ideology* was a preview of political life in the modified capitalist democracies during the era of the advanced industrial state. This is another view of that political life, written of course with the benefit of over a decade of further historical experience. The 1960s witnessed the decline of consensus politics and the resurgence of ideology. But in comparative terms Britain and the United States remain stable polities and, although some have expressed their fears or hopes to the contrary, neither presidential nor parliamentary government is yet at an end. While disagreeing with Bell's analysis I do not concur with his many critics on the political left. The capitalist state is not simply a set of arrangements for the domination of one class by another class. At the same time class divisions are just one of the potentially divisive forces in the modern industrial state, and not necessarily the most important. In fact the socio-political movements examined in this book are remarkable as examples of non-class conflict.

The first five chapters examine some of the central problems within the traditional political socialization literature. Chapter 1 discusses the relationship between socialization processes and the character of the polity, while Chapter 2 shows that the way behaviour is acquired has consequences not only for the individual but also for the political system. In the third chapter I argue that formal education, the major instrument of political education available to the state, has been used in Britain and the United States to create, and has attempted to legitimize, inegalitarian forms of citizenship. In the fourth and fifth chapters patterns of political participation and elite recruitment are the focus of attention for they represent well-established forms of role socialization. The second part of the book is based on case material drawn from contemporary socio-political movements. These movements are essentially revolts against prevailing patterns of inequality. The purpose is to see what implications they hold for the process of political learning and how this impinges upon our understanding of the Anglo-American political culture. The chapter on working-class Tories is a different type of case study, for it considers individuals who have apparently accepted the status quo. It is included because it is a well-researched area of political role socialization and because, in spite of being a totally different kind of case study, it has been understood in remarkably similar terms by social scientists.

Many people assisted me in the preparation of this book, Bruce Graham and Robert Dowse read an early draft in its entirety; while Kevin McCormick, Robert Benewick, Brian Salter, Susannah Handley, Mari Warner, Nigel Bowles, Alan Gray, Tony Davison, Marcus Cunliffe and Rupert Wilkinson provided comments on specific chapters. Kevin McCormick and Andy Reid were kind enough to pass on to me material on the conflict in divided Ulster. For some years I have taught a course on political education at the University of Sussex and successive students have provided me with many valuable insights and comments on all aspects of this book. The University of Sussex gave me a leave of absence from teaching duties and provided me with funds which speeded the completion of the writing. Finally I would like to thank the Publisher, John Wiley and Sons, for their kindness and professionalism. Of course I assume full responsibility for the final contents.

TED TAPPER

University of Sussex
July 1975

Acknowledgements

The author wishes to thank the following for granting permission to reproduce extracts from their publications.

George Allen & Unwin Ltd.
Page 45 (Tawney, *Secondary Education for All*, Allen and Unwin, London, 1922).

American Sociological Association
Page 53 (Litt, 'Civic education, community norms and political indoctrination', *American Sociological Review*, 1963, **28,** p. 74).

Associated Book Publishers Ltd.
Pages 42, 43 and 50 (Maclure, *Educational Documents: England and Wales*, Chapman and Hall, London, 1965).

Cambridge University Press
Page 9 (Marsh, 'Political socialization: the implicit assumptions questioned', *British Journal of Political Science*, 1971, **1,** p. 64.
Page 110 (Jessop, 'Civility and traditionalism in English political culture', *British Journal of Political Science*, 1971, **1,** p. 14.
Page 114 (Goldthorpe *et al.*, *The Affluent Worker: Political Attitudes and Behaviour*, Cambridge University Press, Cambridge, 1968).

Daedalus
Page 169 (Rainwater, 'Crucible of identity: the Negro lower-class family', *Daedalus*, 1966, p. 176).

Doubleday
Page 134 (From *The Berkeley Student Revolt*, copyright © 1965 by Seymour Martin Lipset and Sheldon S. Wolin. Reprinted by permission of Doubleday & Company Inc.).

Faber and Faber Ltd.
Page 23 (Tapper, *Young People and Society*, Faber and Faber, London, 1971).
Pages 222–223 (Rose, *Governing Without Consensus*, Faber and Faber, London, 1971).

Harvard Educational Review
Page 55 (Hess, 'Discussion: Political Socialization in the Schools', *Harvard Educational Review*, 1968, **38,** pp. 532–533).

Massachusetts Institute of Technology Press
Page 177 (Glazer and Moynihan, *Beyond the Melting Pot*, MIT Press, Cambridge, Mass., 1963).

New Republic Inc.
Page 146 (Brzezinski, 'Revolution and counter revolution', *New Republic*, 1 June 1968, p. 24).

The Observer Ltd.
Pages 221–222 (Wilby, 'Ulster at school', *Observer Review*, 18 August 1974, p. 21).

Oxford University Press
Page 137 (Beloff, 'Universities and violence', *Survey*, 1968, **69**, p. 39).

Penguin Books Ltd.
Pages 83–84 (Blondel, *Voters, Parties and Leaders*, Penguin Books, Harmondsworth, 1963).

Prentice-Hall Inc.
Page 194 (Amundsen, *The Silenced Majority: Women and American Democracy*, Prentice-Hall, Englewood Cliffs, New Jersey, 1971).

Princeton University Press.
Pages 11, 12, 191 and 204 (Selections from Gabriel A. Almond and Sidney Verba, *The Civic Culture: Political Attitudes and Democracy in Five Nations* (copyright © 1963 by Princeton University Press, pp. 397–497. Reprinted by permission of Princeton University Press)).

Random House Inc.
Page 10 (Sigel (ed.), *Learning about Politics*, Random House, New York, 1970).
Page 83 (Matthews, *The Social Background of Political Decision-makers*, Random House, New York, 1954).

Routledge & Kegan Paul Ltd.
Page 60 (Kornhauser, *The Politics of Mass Society*, Routledge & Kegan Paul, London, 1960).
Page 110 (Runciman, *Relative Deprivation and Social Justice*, Routledge & Kegan Paul, London, 1966).
Page 111 (Parkin, 'Working-class Conservatives: A theory of political deviance', *British Journal of Sociology*, 1967, **18**, p. 289).
Page 140 (Lipset, *Rebellion in the University: A History of Students Activism in America*, Routledge & Kegan Paul, London, 1972).

Sage Publications Inc.
Page 80 (Excerpt from 'The Comparative Study of Elite Socialization' by Donald D. Searing, reprinted from *Comparative Political Studies* Vol. I, No. 4 (Jan. 1969) p. 495 by permission of the Publisher, Sage Publications, Inc).

Teachers College Press, Columbia University.
Page 52 (Bereday in Merriam (ed.), *The Making of Citizens*, Teachers College Press, New York, 1966).

Contents

Chapter 1

The Theory of Socialized Support

Understanding political stability

A central interest in the study of politics is to account for the stability of the political order. It is an interest with a long and honourable heritage and as such the answers have been both numerous and diverse.[1] One of the major branches of modern sociology provides an answer that relates individual behaviour to the structure of the polity. The essential ingredient in this relationship is the support of the citizenry for the established order. Citizen support is not something that nation states can take for granted, so institutions have been established and processes instigated that have as their goal the building of support. These processes are invariably referred to as socialization and the institutions as the socializing agents. On the basis of this theory political stability is thus a consequence of socialization processes that are effective in creating citizen support. Past research into political socialization has generally credited Plato with initiating this theory. To Plato may belong the honour of initiation but political scientists owe a more direct and greater debt to Talcott Parsons.[2] Besides discussing the various theoretical problems that flow out of a socialization explanation of stability, Parsons has also attempted to relate the theory to varying shifts in contemporary American society. His concern with the ingredients of the learning process is matched, for example, by an interest in the implications of the changing nature of American education or the vociferous demands of Afro-Americans.

The major bridge between Parsons' grand theory and the more mundane empirical findings in the field of political socialization has been constructed by David Easton. This is not surprising in view of their common interest in applying systems analysis to the study of social phenomena. In the late 1950s Easton wrote, 'Once we adopt the idea that political life constitutes a system of behavior, however, we are led to inquire into the conditions that make it possible for the system to maintain itself or to change, that is, to fail to maintain itself'.[3] By the middle of the 1960s the part that political socialization has to play in establishing stability is made explicit: 'Fundamentally, the theoretical significance of the study of socializing processes in political life resides in its contribution to our understanding of the way in which political systems are able to persist, even as they change, for more than one generation'.[4]

There is a common structure to most of the models of the political system. The polity is conceived of as a number of outputs and inputs with some interaction between them thanks to the way in which outputs feedback to reshape inputs.[5] The two input variables are demands and support which can each be subdivided into a number of component parts. Support is usually thought of as both mass socialized support, and elite recruitment and socialization. Demands are the opposite of support in the sense that they have to be either met, deflected or opposed, all of which is likely to involve the use of scarce resources. But if support is determined by socialization processes so then is the pattern of demands. Socialization is likely to influence the kinds of demands that are made, the intensity with which they are held and the way in which they are presented. The distinction between demands and support may not therefore be that clear-cut, for the stability of a polity can be as much a consequence of limited demands as of high support. An important difference between the two concepts is the extent to which they can be regulated by elite manipulation. It is much easier to control or stimulate demands than it is to build or destroy support. Demands, therefore, are more likely than support to be influenced by factors other than socialization. Governments continuously use legislation as a means of channelling demands and in many cases it has an almost instantaneous impact. It is more difficult to conceive of regulating support by passing legislation, although this may redirect the institutions and procedures that shape the pattern of support. It may be quite some time, however, before this actually changes behaviour.

When political scientists talk of elite recruitment and socialization they are invariably thinking in terms of political activists and more especially the institutionalized political elites. The central premise is that to keep the political life of a society flourishing, and all that follows from that, there have to be individuals who are prepared to engage in political activity and to hold political office. In spite of the faith that democracies supposedly have in the capabilities of the average citizen, political elites have a special importance in democratic polities. Empirical evidence shows that democratic values are more faithfully adhered to by political elites than by most other citizens. Activists can be viewed as the custodians of the society's values. One theme in democratic theory is that political leaders can fulfil important educative functions because they are at the centre of political debate. The way they conduct themselves will influence not only how citizens regard them as individuals but also how citizens evaluate politics.[6]

The concept of socialized support raises a number of definitional problems that have associated theoretical implications. Easton and Dennis define support as ' . . . feelings of trust, confidence, or affection, and their opposites, that persons may direct to some object. If support is positive, a person favours an object; if support is negative, he withholds or withdraws his favour from the object'.[7] They subdivide support into two categories — diffuse and specific. Specific support is the individual's assessment of the rewards and disadvantages accruing to him from his belonging to the political system and more particularly it is his evaluation of the personal effects of governmental policies.[8] Diffuse support is much more relevant for socialization studies for it is ' . . . the generalized trust and confidence that members invest in the various objects of the system as ends in themselves'.[9] The assumption is that although individual citizens may on occasions withdraw specific support the stability of the polity is threatened only if there is a mass withdrawal of diffuse support.

Support is a strong word in the sense that it suggests positive action on the part of the individual who is giving or withholding it. It is not often that citizens express themselves in concrete behavioural terms either on behalf of, or in opposition to, the established order. For the most part they merely accept things as they are, or, if you like, they simply comply. The problem then is to ascertain whether compliance can indeed be interpreted as support for the status quo, or is it rather latent hostility waiting to be galvanized into action? There is no straightforward answer to this question but in that most empirical of political science research areas — the voting studies — the non-voters have generally been described as positive compliers. Indeed, abstaining from voting has been elevated into an act of positive support, for some have argued that if the voting turn-out is too high this is a likely sign of political instability.[10] These distinctions are important: it is essential to know whether political stability in a particular case is grounded on positive support rather than token acceptance or passive compliance.

Easton suggests three ways of expressing support — in relation to the political community, or to the authorities, or (most importantly) to the regime. British and American citizens can usually disapprove of current holders of political office with impunity and still be considered loyal subjects and good democrats. By the political community Easton appears to mean the nation state, and the loyal citizen would be one who identifies himself as American, British, or what have you. To some extent Easton takes support at this level for granted, and it is fair to say that if there is no overall notion of common citizenship then the prospects for political stability are indeed slim.[11] The regime is the institutionalized structure and the rules of the game that govern the community's political life.[12] It can be argued that a citizen is to be more valued if he understands and approves of the rules of the political system than if he is excessively and uncritically unpatriotic. This would make political stability dependent upon a consensus of political values of which an adherence to the procedures governing the conduct of political life would be the most important.[13]

A potential danger in stressing the importance of citizen support for regime norms is that the norms can assume an undeserved sanctity while the behaviour of citizens is always interpreted in ways that suggest that the norms are supported, or at least not threatened. This can be illustrated with reference to the dilemma facing those who examined American voting behaviour. The initial tacit belief was that voting patterns were being observed in a democratic polity (i.e. the United States), and when levels of unawareness and apathy were discovered which suggested the United States did not match the precepts of democratic theory then it was the theory that had to be adjusted rather than the conditions that gave rise to the empirical realities. This avoided the challenging alternative response of suggesting ways of increasing citizen involvement in politics. In a similar way, if the regime norms of the assumed democratic polity are not supported by some citizens then there is a temptation to explain this away rather than accept the possibility that perhaps the norms are undemocratic or that the basis of support is far from universal.

The actual areas of empirical investigation in the study of political socialization have tended to be both limited in scope and somewhat obvious in their direction. The majority of the research has looked at children's perceptions of political authority. A common theme has centred around the young child's idealization of political authority, especially as exemplified by the President of the United States. As the child grows older he comes to perceive political authority as residing in roles and institutions rather than as being personified by particular individuals.[14] It is interesting to note that in some of their cross-cultural studies American political scientists have replicated the pattern of their home-based research. This has caused them some difficulties in relation to the United Kingdom where the Queen, the official Head of State, reigns but does not rule.[15] This early idealization of political authority is seen as providing a long-term basis of support for the political system, but this depends upon accepting certain assumptions about learning processes; this I will consider further in the next chapter. Secondly, it is believed that if political authority can be conveniently personalized in the form of a prominent public figure then this provides the emerging citizen with an easily understood entrée into political life. Even if this is so it does mean there has to be a significant widening of experiences before the individual moves from the personal to the institutional aspects of politics, and this is a movement that has so far been taken for granted rather than carefully charted.[16]

The second most important area of empirical investigation concerns the acquisition of party loyalties. It is convenient to observe patterns of party affiliations because there is little difficulty in constructing appropriate questions and the resulting information can be readily quantified. It would be difficult to deny that this is a significant aspect of political behaviour, although one may dispute its precise meaning. Herbert Hyman suggests that party identifications act as a frame of reference for the citizen that can be superimposed upon a changing world. The party helps the individual to formulate his position on the many issues that are likely to cross his path.[17] If this is so then the political party acts as a constant reference-point in much the same way as early formulated attitudes towards political authority are meant to guide later behaviour.

The continuity of party affiliations makes them a powerful force working for political stability. It is part of the conventional wisdom of political science that party loyalties are socialized within the family and thus transferred from parents to children.[18] Although this may be essentially correct some qualifications are in order. The initial research was culture-bound, for Converse and Dupeux have show that the same transference of party loyalties cannot be taken for granted in France in quite the same way as in the Anglo-American context.[19] Apparently French children are less likely to know their parents' affiliations than American children and in any case there will be greater uncertainty when there are several, rather than two, major parties and when parties spring into prominence only to disappear almost as rapidly. Even in the two-party polities of Britain and the United States the family transference of party loyalties is far from guaranteed. Recent trends in the United Kingdom indicate an erosion of the two-party system and a considerable percentage of the electorate must be switching its allegiances. The end result is fewer stable preference patterns to pass on to children. In 1967 I conducted a small survey into the political attitudes of secondary-schoolchildren. At this time the fortunes of the Labour Government were at a nadir, and many of the children whose parents were supporters of the Labour party indicated that they either did not support a political party or they were not certain as to what party they would end up voting for.[20] What this suggests is that party loyalties are not especially viable as a permanent frame of reference but will be re-evaluated according to the pressure of the day and age. Jennings and Niemi have noted that American high-school students are much more likely than their parents to be political independents and that when they adhere to parental preferences their partisanship is less intense.[21]

A more rewarding field of empirical investigation is the attempt to trace the development of differing orientations towards the political system. If stability stems from socialized support it is not a form of support that is to be interpreted as blind, passive obedience to governmental authorities. In theory democratic polities encourage citizen participation in the political process and this implies some form of general involvement in the making of policy. In reality participation may be interpreted as little more than showing one's allegiance to and satisfaction with the status quo. This may be especially so when the major form of participation — voting — has such a ritualistic quality. But this is not how it should be; participation is meant to facilitate citizen control over policy alternatives, even if this may mean only making a choice between two not-so-very-different elites who have formulated two not-so-very-different programmes. The point about participation is the belief that the involved citizen is also the loyal citizen, for if the individual has a part to play in the policy-making process he also has a stake in the system.

Greenstein has divided the content of political learning into three parts: acquiring a subject role, learning a citizen role, and socialization into specialized political roles.[22] How subject roles are learnt has dominated the literature which would incorporate most of the material on the idealization of political authority. The citizen role centres around the individual's capacity to participate in the political process, and, given the fact that children are not political participants in any meaningful sense, it is not the easiest of fields in which to conduct research. The emphasis has been upon discovering patterns of predispositions that are likely to influence future participation.[23] Much of the research has been carried out under the rubric of 'political efficacy'. The most comprehensive measure of political efficacy has been formulated by Easton and Dennis, who suggest five possible ingredients: the extent to which the individual feels he is politically potent, his willingness to believe that governments will respond to his demands, his understanding of how political processes work, the adequacy of the means of influence the individual can employ and finally the extent to which he feels change is feasible.[24]

Leaving aside the very tricky problem of whether these measures of efficacy, their findings are fascinating — not so much because they are entirely unexpected but rather because they represent one of the few pieces of socialization reasearch not to exude overwhelming optimism.[25] As the child grows older he becomes more politically efficacious, but even as late as the eighth grade 17 per cent of their sample were classified as 'low' in efficacy and 29 per cent were only 'moderately' efficacious. Important sub-sample variations appeared, for those with lower IQs and those placed lower on the socio-economic scale were less politically efficacious. Although there were no consistent sex differences for political efficacy, females were remarkably less politically involved than males.[26] In spite of these mixed findings the two authors conclude with the usual optimistic comments: 'But for the inculcation of this norm [political efficacy] at an early and impressionable age, later adult political frustrations in modern mass societies might be less easily contained: disillusionment with this norm of democracy might well find more favorable conditions for growth'.[27] It is difficult to reconcile this with the fact that their own data show that less than half of the eighth-graders classified as low in socio-economic status are 'high' in political efficacy. If it does not exist in the first place then it is hard to see how political efficacy can contain later adult political frustrations.

Besides a considerable degree of uncertainty surrounding both the meaning and content of socialized support there is also controversy as to its consequences. There are few who make the connection between socialization and system stability in such bold terms as Morrison and McIntyre, who write, 'Political socialization can be seen as the processes by which political systems maintain themselves against breakdown or radical change'.[28] In contrast to this most of the more eminent figures in the discipline have proved themselves masters at hedging their bets. In 1957 Easton referred to the importance of formal education in securing system maintenance but at the same time he noted that the system could change, or, as he quaintly put it, 'fail to maintain itself'.[29] Since then Easton has been much more likely to talk of system persistence rather than system maintenance. In a 1965 article he linked persistence with change with the claim that we needed to know how political systems persisted even as they changed.[30] By 1969 he asserted neutrality for his definition, for political socialization could perpetuate either stability or instability depending upon the nature of the polity. In a stable political system it will tend to aid this stability, and likewise in an instable political system it will tend to reaffirm this instability.[31] By 1971 the two parts in the definition changed place; Dennis, one of Easton's main collaborators, described political socialization as a process that enables us to understand first of all change and then stability.[32]

This changing emphasis is reflected throughout the political socialization literature. Greenstein has argued that the criticism of the initial stress upon stability is partially a consequence of a definitional confusion, for to argue, as Greenstein himself has done, that political socialization is one of the ways of preserving the political order does not mean that individuals will always conform to societal norms.[33] This is a somewhat different line of reasoning from Easton's, who appears to be arguing that socialization transmits an environmental norm that may encourage political instability, rather than that individuals can fail to act upon norms. Easton's position implies a degree of rigidity that is very rarely likely to apply in reality. However, if Greenstein feels that citizens can escape societal norms then there is the problem of how to account for this. This is an issue that will form the theme of the second part of this chapter; now it is sufficient to comment that Greenstein's liberality has opened a true Pandora's box.

There is some considerable doubt as to whether the change in direction is more apparent than real. What are the distinctions between maintenance, persistence and change? Maintenance can be viewed as the perpetuation of a system in an unchanged form, while persistence represents a modification of that system over time. It is virtually impossible that a system could be totally static so it becomes difficult to distinguish between systems that are maintaining themselves and systems that are persisting. How much change does there have to be before systems can be said to have changed rather than have persisted? The definition of persistence can be made so broad that few systems will fail to persist.[34]

According to one theory, young people are more prone to rebellion against authority than older people, especially at that period in their lives where they have left their childhood family but still have not established a family and career in their own right. As children they were taught respect for authority by their parents; as adults they come to a renewed respect for authority when they have dependents and economic and professional rights to protect.[35] Roberta Sigel has summed up this perception of youthful radicalism most concisely: 'In part, the just-observed departure from familial values is merely temporary. Many young people are known to have adopted radically different ways of thinking about politics and other social matters during adolescence, only to revert to familial ways during adulthood'.[36] All this may be true but it also helps to cast doubts upon the belief that individuals can escape the stabilizing influence of political socialization. After all, if radical politics are associated with only a particular phase of the life cycle then this can hardly be taken too seriously.

There is some doubt, therefore, as to whether the apparent change in direction is in reality little more than a growth of terminological confusion. Some of the responsibility for this rests with the critique of the early literature as much as with the shortcomings within that literature. The possible consequences of the political learning process have been broadened considerably without any serious attempt to answer some of the important questions that follow from this. Kavanagh, a firm believer in the influence of adult — especially directly political — experiences, writes, 'The overall effect of the socialization process, then, may be to change or even recreate, as well as sustain, the political culture.[37] If ever a quotation served to illustrate that detail and precision have not yet replaced vagueness and confusion, here it is.

Given the difficulties involved in showing a relationship between individual behaviour and the character of the political system and the confusions surrounding the precise direction of that relationship —

stability, persistence or change — it is not too surprising that the effect of socialization on stability is now under sceptical scrutiny. David Marsh writes,

Political socialization involves the study of the development of political attitudes and behaviour. The problem of the relationship between the outcome of this process and the operation of the political system is one which is best considered separately. Indeed any relationship which exists between changes in the outcome of the political socialization process and changes in the political system is far from simple, and involves many complex intervening variables.[38]

Such an approach would limit the study of political socialization to an analysis of learning processes and as such would diminish its importance for political scientists.

One of the dangers inherent in socialization theory is that system characteristics will be seen as a consequence only of socialized behaviour and nothing else. This is patently absurd, but to go to the other extreme and suggest that citizen behaviour has no bearing upon the nature of the political system is equally ridiculous. It is true that the interconnection between socialization processes and the way in which the political system works may, as Marsh suggests, be extremely complex, but then most interesting problems have complex answers. Superficially it appears that stability is on a firmer basis if it rests on socialized support as distinct from other methods of control. This is especially so if the range of assumptions commonly associated with the theory of socialized support is also accepted. If what is learnt earliest stays with one longest, if support is learnt at a tender age, and if initial impressions of political authority are highly benevolent, then socialization is inevitably a powerful aid to perpetuating the established order. By definition socialization means the internationalizations of norms that structure behaviour. If the process has been successful then it should be possible to count on a reservoir of support for the status quo that does not depend upon the offering of bribes or the employment of sanctions. Most societies employ various methods of perpetuating their political systems. Citizens may be kept under control through the skilful use of coercion, the judicious meeting of certain demands or even by the total depoliticization of the mass of the population. Such methods may work very successfully for long periods of time but it is still difficult to believe that they provide a firmer basis for stability that the active support of the majority of the citizens.

Of course many political systems exist that cannot rely upon mass socialized support for their perpetuation for they simply do not have the means to achieve this. In other cases, even if the means did exist the chances of success would be slim for the internal social divisions are so great. In such circumstances it is necessary to look for other techniques of control. This could mean using resources to develop elite cadres to run the nation state almost in isolation from the populace.

Alternatively, political compromise might be arrived at whereby spoils are equitably divided amongst a number of potentially conflicting groups so that most parties think it worth their while to keep the political system going. Even in these cases support is not totally lacking but it is not the kind of general support central to socialization theory. Political instability is not the same thing as the destruction of a political order. Up to now successive British governments have agreed to the use of military force to help ensure that Northern Ireland remains a part of the United Kingdom. In spite of the destruction of the province's own parliament and executive, fundamental changes in the regime norms, and the overthrow of political authorities, ultimate power has continueed to reside in the Westminster Parliament and divided Ulster is still part of the United Kingdom. So some aspects of a political system can exist without general support, but when the complying citizens decide to overthrow the regime the price paid for the perpetuation of the old order is very high indeed.

The oversocalized conception of man[39]

Perhaps the single most controversial assumption in the theory of socialized support is that all citizens are exposed to universal learning experiences that attempt to inculcate in each of them the same standards of political behaviour. The only recognition of the need to vary this process is in the recruitment and socialization of political elites. This gives a simplified 'responsible elite/supportive mass' view of the relationship of citizens to the political order. This is seen in Easton's notion that citizens are socialized into societal norms and that as a result either stabilizing or disharmonious behaviour can be transmitted depending on the nature of the political system, or in Greenstein's belief that the good citizen is one who judiciously combines subject and citizen roles. As Roberta Sigel has written,

Another glaring omission lies in the fact that no selection addresses itself to an empirical test of the basic assumption behind political socialization thinking, namely that political socialization is essential to political stability. Is this in fact so? . . . Maybe the question ought to read, How many citizens (located where) must have internalized system's political norms for the system to operate smoothly and harmoniously?'[40]

This may necessitate an impossible degree of political quantification, but it does raise important questions about the individualistic focus of socialization theory.

One of the criticisms levelled at normative democratic theory by contemporary political scientists of the behavioural persuasion is that the theory has placed too much stress upon the qualities of the individual.[41] What is needed are theories that depend more upon the total range of citizen characteristics so that stability is as much a consequence of apparently undemocratic behaviour like political apathy as it is of those worthy traits of involvement and knowledge.[42] Even if this requirement is met it still raises the question of what are the ideal proportions of participation and apathy. Is stability *as much* a consequence of informed participation as it is of indifferent apathy? Surely if the polity is to be described as democratic this is a difficult premise to sustain. If apathy is indeed an aid to stability this still begs the question of its impact upon the distribution of status, income and power. What assists stability may also promote inequality and some would argue that the evils of the latter are greater than the blessings of the former.

Of greater interest to me is why these claims in favour of taking an overall view of the citizenry, that have been made in the very visible area of the voting studies, have not been widely considered by those working in the field of political socialization. This is partially a result of concentrating attention upon what is learnt rather than on the implications for the system of this. This is reinforced by the fact that the learning theories have a strong psychological, even psychoanalytical orientation. Furthermore, the socialization theorists were too sophisticated not to have recognized the implications of adopting a theory of differential citizenship. If stability depended upon a distribution of citizen characteristics then presumably the political elites who had most say in running the state machinery would attempt to promote this. The outcome would be the state sponsorship of apathy as well as other political qualities. But political qualities are not self-contained entities, for they have all kinds of social and economic implications. By and large the theory of socialization, and the related empirical research, were evolved on the basis of observing a supposedly proto-typical democracy, the United States. It would have been difficult to have worked with such premises without placing in serious jeopardy this view of the United States as an ideal type of democracy.

Almond and Verba show a characteristic uncertainty over whether the unit of analysis should be the individual or the total citizenry. They argue that in a democratic polity there is a delicate balance between governmental power and responsiveness which places conflicting demands upon its citizens:

Certain things are demanded of the ordinary citizen if elites are to be responsive to him: the ordinary citizen must express his point of view so that elites can know what he wants; he must be involved in politics so that he will know and care whether elites are being responsive, and he must be influential so as to enforce responsive behavior by elites . . . But if the alternate pole of elite power is to be achieved, quite contradictory attitudes and behavior are to be expected of the ordinary man. If elites are to be powerful and make authoritative decisions, then the involvement, activity, and influence of the ordinary man must be limited. The ordinary man must turn power over to elites and let them rule. The need for elite power requires that the ordinary citizen be relatively passive, uninvolved, and deferential to elites.[43]

Besides polarizing the community into ordinary people and elites these writers stress the importance of attitudinal conflicts within the individual, at least within the average citizen if not the elite member. But they stress that this personal internal division exists alongside a societal continuum of behaviour:

Our data suggest that in two broad ways the civic culture maintains the citizen's active influential role as well as his more passive role: on the one hand, there is in the society a distribution of individuals who pursue one or other of the conflicting citizen goals; on the other hand, certain inconsistencies in the attitudes of an individual make it possible for him to pursue these seemingly conflicting goals at the same time'.[44]

Within their book *The Civic Culture* there is little empirical evidence to support the claim that certain individuals are a balance of internal inconsistencies. Rather we find a sizeable minority of both the British and American citizens persuaded that they lacked the competence to influence either the national or local course of political events.[45] These are the passive citizens who appear to be outside the political system.

If each democratic citizen is an amalgam of the same political attitudes then the notion of a universal socialization process is given considerable support. If behaviour is essentially a product of socialization and all, or nearly all, citizens exhibit the same inconsistencies then they are all likely to have been exposed to the same socialization influences. This is a strong argument for concentrating upon the individual learning process, for if we are all going to end up in the same mould then we each represent the societal ideal. It is difficult to maintain such a thesis in the light of the harsh realities of this world. A possible defence is to maintain that there is a 'normal' or 'typical', perhaps even 'ideal', relationship between the citizen and the political order. This may be transgressed by some individuals who find themselves in 'special' socio-economic circumstances or even 'disturbed' psychological states. It is certainly possible to show significant correlations between both social and psychological variables and political attitudes. The problem then is that some citizens, described in both socio-economic and psychological terms, may be thought to be more desirable than others. How do we regard those who fail to conform to this societal model and what do we do about them?

In the revised 1969 edition of his famous political socialization text Herbert Hyman writes, 'The meaning [of political socialization] I intended was narrower, more traditional. I hoped to preserve the terms for those processes that most members of a society or of a sub-group experience, in contrast with learning that is idiosyncratic in character'.[46] There then follows a very revealing statement as to why he preferred this narrower focus: 'The former process produces the regularities, uniformities, that are directly relevant to the stability of political systems and that lend themselves to social and educational policy. The latter process produces endless variability, creates unpredictability, and defies institutional forms of control'.[47] The implication is not only that some behaviour is more relevant than other behaviour for political stability (thus perhaps denying that stability is a consequence of a balanced pattern of political behaviour) but also that some of us have more normal relations to the political order than others, and when the relationship is normal it assists stability and when it is not it results in disorder! According to this view political behaviour such as alienation and apathy are aberrations that work against stability, rather than socialized behaviour that is part of a balanced pattern of predispositions.

In the Parsonian view there are two different elements to the content of socialization.[48] In the first place socialization processes attempt to inculcate general societal norms. There is no guarantee that these norms will be acted upon in the same manner by each and every individual for they will be mediated by differing social positions. Some people will simply lack the resources to act upon them in the way that others, and perhaps the norms themselves, imply that they should do.[49] Running parallel to the inculcation of societal norms is the fact of role socialization. It is more usual to think of role socialization in economic and social rather than political terms, but the recognition of the special function of political elites indicates its broad applicability. The tendency to dichotomize citizens into either the mass or the elite has meant that the political socialization studies have largely ignored role socialization. More importantly they have overlooked the potential conflict between universal and role socialization patterns. This is partly because Parsons himself has been all too willing to point to harmony and turn a blind eye to tension. Indeed many American social scientists felt that as the post-Second World War years unfolded so harmony increased and conflict and tension declined. This was especially so in relation to class conflict; some concluded that distinctions between social classes were breaking down and that class had less of an influence upon shaping behaviour. In part this book is a survey of some of the crises that arose in the 1960s and the kind of challenge they posed to this conception of the Anglo-American democracies.

Although all kinds of socio-economic influences impinge upon political behaviour, democratic citizens in theory have equal political rights but socio-economic forces work in ways which undermine the rights of some citizens and bolster the power of others. The question then is to what extent this trend is reinforced by socialization processes so that individuals come to internalize this inequality and comply with its consequences. Furthermore, it is essential to ask what part the various institutions of the state play in attempting to perpetuate and legitimate this inequality. If citizens do indeed accept both political inequality and its consequences then the state may be assisting in the undermining of political rights. The gain could be peace and harmony but a tranquillity for which some pay a higher price than others. What I think the history of the 1960s showed was that there was no easy and permanent reconciliation between universal and role socialization patterns. In that decade several large groups challenged the implications of role socialization. They demanded that political elites should implement different distributions of scarce resources so the quality of their lives — in social, economic and political terms — could be changed. What is fascinating is that the attack upon role socialization was frequently made in the name of societal norms. Such norms may act as a constraint upon citizen behaviour in the sense that they have been accorded considerable respect and the individual is supposed to conform to them, but at the same time the citizen can reasonably expect the state to provide the conditions that make it possible for him to conform. Part of the demand for change emanating in this decade was that democracies paid only lip-service to their values, and as long as the instruments of the state did not treat people as if the values had some real meaning then these people could not be expected to behave as if they already had equal rights. The tension between the theoretical values and the realities of role socialization came to the fore and the former was used as an instrument to bring about changes in the latter.

In a situation of scarce resources a conflict between universal values and the implications of role socialization is inevitable. This is especially so in democratic polities that attempt to maximize, at least in theory, the fulfilment of the rights of citizenship. The conflict may not appear to exist, either because inequality in the exercise of those rights has been accepted or because those who refuse to accept it are not in a position to make their feelings known or to mobilize support for a change. Democratic polities are vulnerable to this tension not only because of the maximizing pressures of their ideology but also because of inconsistencies within this ideology. Egalitarian and libertarian strains push and pull in various directions, making it possible for different groups to clutch at different straws. The end result is at best a temporary and fragile harmony and not the smooth transitions within the broad framework posited by Parsons.

The Parsonian view of the socialization process has to a considerable extent been accepted by certain writers on the political left. In an assessment of a conventional definition of political socialization Ralph Miliband writes,

The weakness of this formulation, and of much of the discussion of 'political socialization' in relation to Western political systems, is that it tends to be rather coy about the specific ideological content of that socialization, and about the fact that much of the process is intended, in these regimes, to foster acceptance of a *capitalist* social order and of its values, an adaptation to its requirements, a rejection of alternatives to it; in short, that what is involved here is very largely a process of massive *indoctrination*.[50]

He then proceeds to discuss at length how the capitalist system, in particular the British capitalist system, successfully conducts its socialization machinations to produce a conforming citizenry.[51] This is an even more absurdly over-socialized conception of man that that emanating from the mainstream socialization literature, for besides assuming the same simple-minded model in which the individual is defined by the messages he receives (something, incidentally that Parsons does not do) Miliband also neglects to illustrate some of the socialization inconsistencies inherent within all advanced industrialized societies. These inconsistencies centre around the inequalities associated with a necessary division of labour and the need to spread skills (e.g. literacy) that make it possible for individuals to challenge this inequality. The important contradictions that exist in capitalism are not minor concessions to different ideologies, as Miliband would have us believe, but rather stem from these essentially opposing pressures that are part of the nature of industrial society, capitalist or otherwise. It is possible to evaluate socialization processes in political terms, i.e. as something you either 'approve' or 'disapprove' of according to what kind of society they are helping to preserve. This may partially account for the monolithic interpretations of socialization, with in one case the wicked capitalist system perpetuating the iniquities of the class structure and in the other a democratic polity gaining the allegiance of its citizens.

The initial bias in favour of a complementary view of universal and role socialization patterns was strongly aided by the restricted focus of the early empirical research, more especially the kinds of children who made up their samples. Hess and Torney write, 'The purpose of this project was to examine the most characteristic forms of political socialization in the United States. In order to focus on this objective, it was decided to defer consideration of subcultural groups in which political socialization might differ from the dominant culture'.[52] In order to achieve this goal, 'Testing was conducted, in so far as possible, in city neighbourhoods which were not primarily populated by ethnic groups'.[53] Hess' and Torney's major project was published in 1967; their sample is remarkably similar to that of the earlier Greenstein study (1965) and is identical to that of the later Easton and Dennis book (1969). In a nation as ethnically diverse as the United States it would surely be difficult to draw a line between those ethnic groups who experience 'characteristic forms of political socialization' and those who do not. Again these authors imply that a citizenship norm exists into which some have been better socialized than others.

In all fairness the political socialization research was progressively widened to incorporate a diverse range of groups. Jaros and Hirsch have shown that the children of Appalachia have socializing experiences that differ from those of white urban middle-class America, and not surprisingly these children view political authority in a less benevolent manner.[54] Greenberg has reached very similar conclusions about the black children of the urban ghettos, and even Easton and Dennis found that amongst high school seniors there was a large minority of white working-class students with 'low' political efficacy.[55] More telling evidence comes from the numerous studies of adult political behaviour, for so substantial are adult levels of political apathy and ignorance that some political scientists have been persuaded that these are essential prerequisites of system stability. Of course apathy and ignorance are not distributed randomly throughout the population but rather are concentrated heavily in the lower socio-economic and poorly educated sectors of the community.[56] This adult behaviour may not be a direct consequence of childhood experiences but it still suggests the presence of differential socialization processes. Even those citizens who have a degree of awareness and some meaningful interaction with the political system think more of their potential influence rather than their specific and direct impact upon policy-making.[57] They are the people who have learnt to be potential rather than actual activists.

This extension of the political socialization research could be viewed as a triumph for subcultural theory which assumes that there are groups within society that have evolved such distinctive life-styles that it is inevitable that their political behaviour should also deviate from the norm. It would be hard to say if the deviation was more a result of life-styles, including socialization processes, evolved within the group, or a lack of resources to act according to societal norms. This is another classic chicken-and-egg dilemma because a subculture may be developed in response to exclusion from the mainstream of society with the outcome that some subcultural traits then make it even more difficult to secure resources controlled by the wider society. My view is that to advocate the case for a differential socialization process is not the same as supporting subcultural theory. Rieselbach and Balch maintain,

Political socialization works not only to minimize conflict and thereby stabilize the system but to maintain existing divisions. Class and sex differences in political attitudes and orientations are apparent in early childhood. It is important to remember that not all segments of society share all values of the larger society.[58]

But it is equally important to remember that few individuals, let alone segments of society, are totally isolated from all the mainstream societal values. Furthermore, in political terms it is not at all easy to say what the subcultural pattern of behaviour has to be before it could be described as failing to conform to the values of the larger society. Perhaps the group merely exhibits a pattern of behaviour that helps to create a wider balance, assuming one accepts the need to examine total, rather than partial, societal characteristics.

If it were possible to define the boundaries of certain groups, and to describe the precise nature of the peculiar behavioural traits of their members and how internal group dynamics help to perpetuate, if not create, these, then the problem of evaluating what bearing this is likely to have upon system stability emerges. Social divisions are no threat to the stability of a political system as long as what flows from them is successfully ligitimized. It is when such legitimacy is not established, or it starts to crumble, that conflict is likely to ensue. Whether this is seen as a problem or not depends very much upon the evaluation of stability, as opposed to the evaluation of social divisions. Much the same could be said of political apathy. Its perpetuation may help the political order to persist, but is this its only consequence? If not, are the other outcomes such as to make the perpetuation of apathy unacceptable? Although it is meaningful, therefore, to think of a complex group structure and associated differential patterns of political behaviour, they cannot be assessed without reference to wider societal concerns and norms.

Miliband has rightly criticized the political socialization literature for failing to enunciate clearly the ideological predispositions that socialization processes attempt to perpetuate in capitalist society. However, it is an assumption of socialization theory that all societies — capitalist, socialist or what have you — will attempt to transmit a particular view of the world. A related and more substantive criticism is that the contemporary empirical literature has rarely attempted to illustrate how an ideology is transmitted. The focus has been upon the content of political learning — what has been internalized — rather than how people learn. This has a number of important consequences. It reinforces the individualistic approach to political socialization for there is little discussion of the structural context within which political behaviour is acquired. If there were not regular patterns related to the numerous social divisions one could almost be deluded into thinking that political behaviour was learnt at random. The role of the state, and those who have most control of the state machinery, in directing the process of political learning has been sadly ignored. This is surprising in view of the theoretical position that socialization occupies in systems theory — the primary means by which the system attempts to persist — and in the light of Charles Merriam's pioneering work into state-controlled patterns of political learning.[59] Finally, ignoring the structure of political learning lends greater credence to the notion that subcultures are free to devise their own life-styles. The fact that much of what is considered to be abnormal behaviour originates from societal patterns of discrimination is frequently ignored.

I accept the basic assumption of socialization theory that all societies attempt to structure the political learning process in ways that will aid their perpetuation. In spite of the dearth of empirical work on this issue, it must be recognized that this is far from a fortuitous process for institutions have been created and procedures established that attempt to superimpose a hierarchical pattern of political behaviour. But it is a programme fraught with uncertainty, and by no means is there any guarantee of success. Democratic polities enunciate universalistic values that contain a number of important internal conflicts, and yet they expect many of their citizens to occupy roles that seemingly contravene some of the implications of these societal values. The Anglo-American democracies are advanced industrial nations with egalitarian strains in their political ideologies and inegalitarian socio-economic and political orders. At the same time both values and necessity require a comparatively literate and articulate population. The stage is set for tension and conflict rather than consensus and harmony.

Notes

1. For example, Locke and Hobbes posed a differing contract theory as the basis of ordered government and society, while Rousseau stressed the need for the state to embody the General Will to best achieve the same ends. Marx saw instability, in all its forms, as an inevitable consequence of conflicting class interests and only when social classes were eradicated (in the higher phase of communism) could one expect harmony and tranquillity.
2. The debt to Parsons is especially dependent upon the function he ascribes to socialization processes in linking the individual personality and the social structure. See T. Parsons, 'Family structure and the socialization of the child', in T. Parsons and R. Bales, *Family, Socialization and interaction Process*, Free Press, Glencoe, Illinois, 1955, pp. 35–131.
3. D. Easton, 'The function of formal education in a political system', *School Review*, **65** (1957), 309.
4. D. Easton and J. Dennis, 'The child's image of government', *The Annals*, **361** (1965), 41.
5. G. A. Almond, 'Introduction: A functional approach to comparative politics', in G. A. Almond and J. S. Coleman, *The Politics of the Developing Areas*, Princeton University Press, Princeton, New Jersey, 1960, pp. 3–64, D. Easton, *A Systems Analysis of Political Life, Wiley*, New York, 1965, pp. 29–33.
6. For an analysis of the claim that elites are the custodians of democratic values see H. McClosky, 'Consensus and ideology in American politics', *American Political Science Review*, **58** (1964), 361–382. Although the survey evidence may suggest this is generally true, the Watergate affair is sufficient evidence to show that it does not necessarily apply in the specific case.
7. D. Easton and J. Dennis, *Children in the Political System*, McGraw-Hill, New York, 1969, p. 57.
8. Ibid., pp. 61–62.
9. Ibid., pp. 62–63.
10. Rapid increases in turn out, rather than high turn out *per se*, are a better measure of political instability. On this see pp. 60–61.
11. As is most dramatically illustrated in Northern Ireland. See pp. 212–218.
12. For a full discussion of what Easton understands by 'regime' see his *A Systems Analysis of Political Life*, pp. 190–211.
13. For the best analysis of what democracy is and is not see G. Sartori, *Democratic Theory*, Praeger, New York, 1965. For a penetrating discussion of democracy as a set of rules governing political competition see J. Schumpeter, *Capitalism, Socialism and Democracy*, Unwin, London, 1954 (4th edition), ch. 22, 23.
14. *Children in the Political System*, pp. 254–270.

15. F. Greenstein and S. Tarrow, *Political Orientations of Children: The Use of a Semi-Projective Technique in Three Nations,* Sage Publications, Beverley Hills, California, 1970.
16. Probably Easton and Dennis come closest to charting this transition but it requires more detailed observation than can be made in a general social survey.
17. H. Hyman, *Political Socialization,* Free Press, New York, 1969 (2nd edition), pp. 56–57.
18. B. Berelson *et al., Voting,* Chicago University Press, Chicago, 1954, p. 95. D. Butler and D. Stokes, *Politcal Change in Britain: Forces Shaping Electoral Choice,* Macmillan, London, 1969, p. 47. Of course one can go beyond this, as Butler and Stokes do, and explain the exceptions to the rule.
19. P. Converse and G. Dupeux, 'Politicization of the electorate in France and the United States', *Public Opinion Quarterly,* **26** (1962), 1–23.
20. E. R. Tapper and R. A. Butler, 'Continuity and change in adolescent political party preferences', *Political Studies,* **18** (1970), 390–394.
21. M. Kent Jennings and R. Niemi, 'The transmission of political values from parent to child', *American Political Science Review,* **62** (1968), 169–184.
22. F. Greenstein, 'Political socialization', *International Encyclopedia of the Social Sciences,* **14** (1968), 552.
23. In particular see D. Easton and J. Dennis, 'The child's acquisition of regime norms: Political efficacy', *American Political Science Review,* **61** (1967), 25–38.
24. Ibid., pp. 28–29.
25. It could be argued with some justification that the individual who feels he is politically impotent is not showing so much a low sense of efficacy as a high sense of reality.
26. Ibid., pp. 33–38.
27. Ibid., p. 38.
28. A. Morrison and D. McIntyre, *Schools and Socialization,* Penguin Books, Harmondsworth, 1971, p. 127.
29. 'The function of formal education in a political system', p. 309.
30. 'The child's image of government', p. 41.
31. *Children in the Political System,* p. 7.
32. 'A chief reason why the political socialization process has recently come under intense analytical scrutiny is the new recognition of its connection to the processes of fundamental change and stability in the political system'. J. Dennis *et al.,* 'Support for nation and government among English children', *British Journal of Political Science,* **1** (1971), 25.
33. F. Greenstein, 'A note of the ambiguity of "political socialization": Definitions, criticisms and strategies of inquiry', *Journal of Politics,* **32** (1970), 973.
34. For the scope of this definition of persistence see *Children in the Political System,* pp. 48–49.
35. This is undoubtedly true of Easton's and Dennis' view of the political learning processes. See *Children in the Political System,* pp. 305–307.
36. R. Sigel (ed.), *Learning about Politics,* Random House, New York, 1970, p. 412.
37. D. Kavanagh, *Political Culture,* Macmillan, London, 1972, p. 29.
38. D. Marsh, 'Political socialization: The implicit assumptions questioned', *British Journal of Political Science,* **1** (1971), 464.
39. D. Wrong, 'The oversocialized conception of man in modern sociology', *American Sociological Review,* **26** (1961), 183–192.
40. Op. cit., p. XIV.
41. Berelson *et al.,* op. cit., ch. 14.
42. This is one of the themes of Berelson's chapter 14. See also T. Parsons, ' "Voting" and the equilibrium of the American political system', in T. Parsons, *Sociological Theory and Modern Society,* Free Press, New York, pp. 223–263.

20

43. G. Almond and S. Verba, *The Civic Culture,* Princeton University Press, Princeton, New Jersey, 1963, p. 478.
44. Ibid., p. 479.
45. Ibid., p. 186. Their data show that 19 per cent of the British sample and 15 per cent of the American sample felt they lacked the necessary competence to affect either the national or local levels of government.
46. op. cit., p. VII.
47. Ibid. Sigel reiterates a very similar claim: 'The more disadvantaged the citizen, that is, the less access he is given to the values of society and the more he is treated as an inferior, then the more likely he will not become fully socialized into the ongoing political norms . . . ' op. cit., p. 496.
48. T. Parsons, 'The functional prerequisites of social systems', in T. Parsons, *The Social System,* Free Press, Glencoe, Illinois, 1951, pp. 26–36. T. Parsons, 'Role conflict and the genesis of deviance', ibid., pp. 280–283.
49. On this see R. K. Merton, 'Social problems and sociological theory' in R. K. Merton and R. A. Nisbet (eds.), *Contemporary Social Problems,* Harcourt, Brace and World, New York, 1966 (2nd edition), pp. 775–823.
50. R. Miliband, *The State in Capitalist Society,* Weidenfeld and Nicolson, London, 1969, p. 182 (emphasis in original text).
51. ibid., ch. 7, 8.
52. R. Hess and J. Torney, *The Development of Political Attitudes in Children,* Aldine, Chicago, 1967, p. 229.
53. ibid., p. 230.
54. H. Hirsch, *Politicization and Poverty,* Free Press, New York, 1971. D. Jaros *et al.,* 'The malevolent leader: Political socialization in an American subculture', *American Political Science Review,* **62** (1968), 564–575.
55. E. S. Greenberg, 'The political socialization of black children', in E. S. Greenberg (ed.), *Political Socialization,* Atherton Press, New York, 1970, pp. 178–190. For a comment on Easton's and Dennis' findings see p. 6.
56. On this see pp. 60–69.
57. See Almond and Verba, op. cit., pp. 480–482.
58. L. Rieselbach and G. Balch (eds.), *Psychology and Politics: An Introductory Reader,* Holt, Rinehart and Winston, New York, 1969, p. 74.
59. C. Merriam, *The Making of Citizens: A Comparative Study of Methods of Civic Training,* Chicago University Press, Chicago, 1931.

Chapter 2

Learning Political Behaviour

The process of political learning

Although it is self-evident that political behaviour is learnt behaviour, when Hyman wrote his pioneering political socialization text in 1959 he could write, 'One seeks far and wide for any extended treatment of political behaviour as learned behaviour, despite the fact that this is patently the case . . . '[1] This apparent reluctance of political scientists to observe a learning process is not altogether unexpected. The kinds of skills this involves are much more likely to have been acquired by psychologists than political scientists, and Greenstein has actually hinted that it is a task that political scientists would be wise to leave alone.[2] Part of the reluctance to come to terms with political-learning is because it is a process, and as such raises both difficult methodological and theoretical problems.[3]

The fact that political learning occurs over time makes its observation a complex undertaking. Observation requires the commitment of various scarce resources of which time is probably the most important.[4] Robert Lane, amongst others, found a way around some of the problems by conducting lengthy, in-depth interviews with adults.[5] The sample size, however, is inevitably small and the reliance upon the accuracy of the subject's recall is high. Naturally there is no analysis of the learning process as it takes place but rather an attempt to piece together a series of snapshots, some more faded than others, in order to throw as much light as possible upon the acquisition of political behaviour. To his credit Lane has tried to fit the odd pieces of information together to make a total personality structure. The more usual technique is to correlate a series of independent variables (especially socio-economic status, sex, religion, residence and age) with a series of dependent variables (for example, party loyalties, levels and forms of participation and numerous attitudinal scales). The conclusion to be made is obvious, that is, in some way or other the independent variable has caused the dependent variable, but rarely are we informed as to how or why this has taken place. Correlations of varying complexity are offered in place of an analysis of a dynamic process.

In 1970 Roberta Sigel wrote, 'Finding sections from political science literature for this chapter [on political learning] was particularly difficult because political scientists, for the most part, have not been very much concerned with the learning process and have instead concentrated on the output (what is learned)'.[6] So in spite of an additional 10 years of flourishing research she is able to reinterate the complaint of Herbert Hyman. Although there may not be a great deal of literature that looks at the political learning process in a systematic way, in the sense that it has a theory of how individuals learn their political behaviour and then empirically tests derivative hypotheses, many political scientists have made numerous assertions about how behaviour is learnt. From the point of view of learning theory these assertions may leave a great deal to be desired, but they have a bearing upon how the relationship between the citizen and the polity has been conceived.

The study of political learning can be divided into four areas: who learns, from whom we learn, how we learn and what we learn. The previous chapter, in its analysis of the theory of socialized support, very broadly covered the area of what is learnt, so what now remains is to examine the three other topics. The links between these facets of the learning process are obvious. Looking at individuals at a particular stage of their life-cycle (who learns) partially determines what socializing agents (from whom we learn) have to be taken into consideration. In many societies formal education does not commence until the child is at least five years old, so if the sample consists of under-five-year-olds formal education is at best only an anticipatory socialization agent. In a similar vein, age can determine both how we learn and what is learnt. Physical or mental skills may be necessary before the child can understand certain learning procedures, and at the same time it may be impossible to grasp some concepts until more elementary information has been acquired.

Who learns?

Who learns can be understood in different ways. The subjects can be defined exclusively by their age or by various social criteria. One of my criticisms of the theory or socialized support was that the empirical evidence was by and large obtained from samples that would be most inclined to substantiate its major premises. In other words there was too narrow a definition of who learns. In this chapter I will restrict my focus to the alternative understanding of who learns, that which defined the subjects by their age, with the intention of seeing if a parallel criticism emerges.

Most survey research will attempt to legitimate the sample upon which the data and interpretations are based, even if this should only make the usual apologies for its limitations. A prominent legitimation in the political socialization research is to claim that the sample is composed of an age group which is at an especially sensitive stage in the learning process. Up to the mid-1960s most of the studies emphasized the centrality of the early years, which meant the age range 3 to 13. In 1962 Easton and Hess, expressing the consensus, wrote, 'The truly formative years of the maturing member of a political system would seem to be the years between the age of 3 and 13. It is this period when rapid growth and development in political orientations take place, as in many areas of non-political socialization'.[7] They arrived at this conclusion having first conducted a pilot study of high-school students (with an age range of approximately 14 to 18) which led them to comment: 'While there was some evidence of some change during the high school years, the magnitude of accumulated attitudes apparent in the freshmen classes indicated that the process of political socialization had been under way for some time and was nearing completion'.[8] Given this kind of evidence the future research focus was obvious — concentrate upon pre-high-school students — and indeed most American political socialization studies have been based upon samples, stratified according to age, of 7 to 14-year-olds.[9]

Without denying the importance of the early years others have staked a claim for adolescence, which has been variously defined as commencing with puberty and ending in the early twenties! This claim is based upon the special stresses and strains the individual experiences in the adolescent years. This flows from the interaction of internal personal development and the need to form various adult social roles. I used such an argument to justify the selection of a sample of 14- to 15-year-olds:

This is an interesting stage in the life cycle; on the verge of leaving behind them the family and the school, and preparing to enter the job market . . . They are also at one of the crucial points in the development of their personalities. Erik Erikson considers this age as the time when the adolescent struggles to form a meaningful identity, by searching to establish a satisfying role within his society.[10]

In fact nearly all the political socialization research conducted in the United Kingdom has concentrated upon adolescents in secondary schools.[11] It is difficult to avoid the suspicion that this is because such subjects are readily available in concentrated numbers rather than because of any pertinent theoretical reasons.

From the mid-1960s one of the growth areas in political sociology, which has only recently petered out, has been the study of students in higher education.[12] For a short period of time something approaching the dimensions of a subdiscipline emerged and blossomed. It seemed as if every political scientist, sociologist and indeed psychologist of note wanted to explain (or should it be explain away) the phenomenon of student radicalism.[13] Given what was taking place in many universities across the world this was a natural development. Some have argued that student radicalism — with many a pampered white middle-class student in the forefront of the movement — has undermined the findings of the early political socialization research. The image of students in rebellion against society did not fit very well with that of compliant and conforming children. The events were used to support the claim that important developments can take place in political learning after adolescence. The presumption was that the students were rebelling against contemporary society, and their current circumstances — especially the university context — had a significant bearing upon how they behaved.

As a later chapter deals specifically with student rebellion in the 1960s a few comments will suffice here. Much of the research into student behaviour has shown that the radicals tend to come from rather special family environments. Kenneth Keniston, a very sympathetic and sensitive observer, has pointed to the high incidence of mother dominance, the political awareness and liberality of the family backgrounds, and the opportunities the students had to participate in the making of family decisions while they were growing up.[14] Central to Keniston's thesis is the interaction between these early experiences and later realities, so that the radical is one who is concerned at society's failure to fulfil its values. In passing it should be noted that Keniston glosses over the point that perhaps radicals have a misconception of societal values, especially some of the internal value conflicts, and the kinds of compromises that may be necessary to reconcile competing claims. Another, less favourable, view of students is that they are in a period of extended adolescence and this gives them more time to resolve their identity crisis for they can delay the choice of a confining adult role.

A final, and almost inevitable, progression was to extend the study of political socialization into the adult years. Sigel has devoted a section of her political socialization reader to a discussion of 'socialization in adulthood',[15] and Dennis Kavanagh has maintained that some adult experiences are more influential than childhood socialization.[16] This contention is given substantial backing by the earlier findings of Almond and Verba. They found a closer correlation bettween certain political attitudes and participation in decisions reached at work than between the same attitudes and participation in decision-making within the family and school.[17] On the basis of this they concluded: 'Therefore, those institutions closer to the political realm in which authority patterns become more similar in kind to authority patterns in the political system may be more crucial for the formation of political attitudes'.[18] Unfortunately two separate elements are somewhat confused here. There is the proximity in time between the socializing experience (in this case participation in decision-making) and what they call the political realm, and the similarity of authority patterns within the socializing institutions and within the political system. Presumably it is the latter that is more responsible for forging the link between political attitudes and experiences in the work place. However, no guarantee exists that authority patterns in these two spheres will converge. Many families are likely to have more democratic decision-making procedures than many firms, but while the child is being socialized within the family he is still some way from participation in the political system, and in many other respects there may be less congruity between the family and the political system than between the work place and the political system. When it comes to specifying why adult learning experiences should be more important than others the logic of the case is perhaps less secure than first impressions suggest.

In each case the focus for who learns is justified on the grounds that the age group is at a crucial stage in the learning process: the early years are a formative period in which basic orientations are acquired, adolescence is the time in which the individual starts to assume adult roles, during student days the fortunate undergraduate is in a position to question societal values, and adults engage in activities — including political events — that are closer to politics and thus much more relevant for the acquisition of political behaviour. In spite of this widening of the research scope to encompass older age groups, few would be willing to deny the powerful influence of the early years; this is as true of Sigel and Kavanagh as of those who have studied the growing political awareness of children.[19]

A relevant question is why research should have expanded to incorporate older age groups. This was partly a simple consequence of the rapid expansion of the political socialization research field. Once growth was under way it was almost inevitably that the theoretical and empirical scope of the subdiscipline would expand. The spectacle of increasing student radicalism on the university campuses naturally invited comment, especially when this seemed to contradict so many of the earlier research findings. Furthermore, those who advocated the claims of the early years had made sufficiently sweeping generalizations as to almost invite rebuttal. In a bold statement James Davies has written, 'And most of the individual's political personality — his tendencies to think and act politically in particular ways — have been determined at home, several years before he can take part in politics as an ordinary adult citizen or as a political prominent'.[20] This not atypical statement makes several important claims: that the most influential aspects of political personality are acquired in the early years, that what is learnt earliest stays with the individual longest, and that this initial experience has a crucial bearing upon later political behaviour.

The attack on the above position has taken various forms. It may be generally agreed that in the Anglo-American democracies certain aspects of political learning, for example a party identification, may be acquired at a comparatively tender age, but there is considerable questioning of the precise significance of this behaviour. Many would question the assumption that party identifications, to give an example, have an all-powerful bearing upon the formation of political values, beliefs and expectations.[21] Some evidence has been forthcoming that challenges Easton's and Hess' claim that no political learning of any significance takes place during the high-school years. Jennings and Niemi argue that their sample showed the following shifts during these years: political interest increased, 'independent' party allegiances declined, there was a growth in the knowledge of the differences between the two major parties, the good citizen came to be evaluated more in political rather than personal terms and political cynicism increased.[22]

Behind these conflicts regarding the precise nature of reality, and what interpretations can be made of data patterns, lies a more fundamental issue. In general those political scientists who stressed the centrality of the early years in the socialization process also maintained that young people showed a high degree of support for the established political order. If what is learnt earliest stays with the individual longest and shapes his later political behaviour then this is a recipe for political stability, even stagnation. What was the political scientist who was not enamoured of the American political system to do? He could either show, as certain writers on the political left have done, how an essentially corrupt political system managed to seduce citizens into giving their allegiance, or alternatively he could challenge the theoretical assumptions and empirical findings of the published research. Besides being more within the tradition of empirically oriented social science, the latter approach held out greater hope in the sense that it was possible to show that many citizens were still aware that the polity had severe shortcomings. If this was indeed so then it was realistic to think of making changes within the system for there were still some who could show the way.

A willingness to look at other stages in the life cycle besides the child-hood years parallels the shift in socialization theory away from systems maintenance to systems persistence. This is not surprising, for if the individual is influenced by a wider range of learning experiences, which a longer period of socialization would certainly entail, then it will be more difficult to predict behaviour and that behaviour is more likely to fluctuate. In a theory that still links individual and system characteristics persistence is a much safer bet than maintenance. This longer view of the learning process is another aspect of the attack upon universal socialization patterns. If the all-important political learning took place in the early years then within any one cultural context all budding citizens would be exposed to much the same set of stimuli. Once the time scale is lengthened then the variation in potential socialization influences is enormous. A pattern of comparative continuity in the experiences of one individual will stand in sharp contrast to those who have known social and geographic mobility. Even if what is internalized in the early years is exceedingly influential the extent to which it can retain this hold will vary widely from one subject to the next.

As with the changing emphasis seen in the move from systems maintenance through persistence and then on to change, this inclusion of almost the entire life cycle in the socialization process has its drawbacks as well as advantages. It is now possible to apply the label of socialization to a vast range of research so it perhaps becomes a rather handy, but somewhat meaningless, catch-all phrase. Concentration upon the early years meant that attention was restricted to those who were in the process of being inducted into the political mores of the community. This restriction resulted in a specific empirical focus as well as a limited range of theoretical problems, and it could be argued that social science research is at its best when it is working within such boundaries.

The socializing agents

In view of the widespread acceptance that the early years are paramount in shaping political behaviour, it follows that the nuclear family must be the central socializing agent. Even with the move away from the childhood years there are few who would discount the influence of the family entirely. The trend is away from descriptions that use adjectives like 'foremost', 'central' or 'most important' to ones which employ 'very important', 'the first' or 'influential'.[23] Common sense suggests the family must retain its function as a critical socializing agent. In western industrialized societies the majority of citizens are raised within the nuclear family, so it exercises its hold on the maturing individual. This does not mean that the child is a *tabula rasa* or even completely helpless throughout childhood, but he or she is entirely dependent upon parental help and guidance. There is a greater power discrepancy in the family between socializer (parents) and socialized (child) than in almost any other situation in which the individual is likely to find himself. The power discrepancy exists with respect to many variables and it occurs over a protracted period of time. It is this helplessness that makes the child so vulnerable. In extreme circumstances some adults can find themselves in parallel situations to the maturing child and, although they may act like automatons in response to the dictates of their circumstances, they have a past set of experiences to draw upon. These experiences may not serve as much of a defence mechanism in the new order, in fact they may even hinder survival, but they are a likely barrier against individual internalization of the values implicit in the environment.[24] The very young child has drives rather than a memory and as such he is much more likely to internalize parental values, especially if this will ease the path to fulfilling drives. The family has come to share many of its functions with the state, and the state superimposes some constraints upon those tasks regulated by the family alone, but these are no more than small inroads into parental hegemony. The family remains an honoured societal institution.

The family has rightly been seen as exercising an essentially conservative influence for it helps to perpetuate traditional values, attitudes and behavioural patterns. It is difficult for the state, at least in the short run, to control family patterns of socialization. This problem is critical for those nations that want to introduce radical societal changes and see established mores as an obstacle to those plans. In these circumstances the family comes under pressure. The Soviet Union, for example, in its early years attacked the family as a 'bourgeois institution' and tried to undermine its influence by making marriage and divorce comparatively simple to obtain.[25] In the drive for change other socializing agents can be used to transmit the new messages. These are institutions that are more amenable to elite manipulation and thus can be relied upon to impart the correct messages. The instruments of control will vary but schools, political parties, armies, youth organizations and communes have all helped to serve this purpose in one situation or another. However, unless the family is going to be eliminated as a societal institution — and this is exceedingly difficult given the various problems involved in the procreation and raising of children — then the regime has, sooner or later, to come to terms with it. Once the new way of life has been flourishing for a period of time this is less of a problem for the family can perhaps be relied upon to teach the correct way of life. It is no longer a 'bourgeois' institution but rather a 'socialist', or what have you, defence against counter-revolutionary forces. The Soviet Union provides an example of this startling transition from a negative to a positive perspective.

The notion that the good democratic citizen has to learn both subject and citizen roles has led Hess and Torney to the conclusion that the school is the most influential socialization agent. They write,

From the point of view of the totality of socialization into the political system, these results indicate that the effectiveness of the family in transmitting attitudes has been over-estimated in previous research . . . It is our conclusion from these data that the school stands out as the central, salient and dominant force in the political socialization of the young child.[26]

This sweeping conclusion is substantiated empirically by the rather flimsy evidence that as the students grow older so their attitudes come to more closely resemble those of their teachers than those of their parents.[27] A more interesting observation concerns their exceedingly convenient view of the socialization process. The good citizen has to learn two somewhat contradictory roles, and behold, two different socializing agents shape, in the correct sequence, the appropriate perspectives!

Once political socialization was expanded into a lifelong experience it was inevitable that socializing agents other than the family should come under scrutiny. Occasionally the impression is given that the author has sat down and listed every possible influence that could have an effect upon political learning. Besides the family and the school attention is now directed towards peer groups, the mass media, the factory floor, political activity *per se,* cataclysmic events and even the spirit of the times.[28] Associated with this trend is a parallel development; the stress is no longer upon what is the most influential socializing agent but rather their relative importance. This would not be unedifying if the search for relative influence flowed out of theories that attempted to relate the agents of socialization to one another. By and large, however, it is ascertained by examining the strength of correlations between varying independent and dependent variables, so that the study of socialization becomes as much an exercise in statistical virtuosity as a field of political analysis.[29]

Assessing the relative impact of socializing agents became a poor substitute for showing how they interconnected to influence one another in the making of political behaviour. How does the school relate to the family, or the peer group to the school, to modify early patterns of political learning? Why do certain school experiences apparently have an impact upon some individuals but not others? In what circumstances does the mass media exert an influence? Questions such as these—directed at analysing a socialization pattern — have largely been ignored.[30] The fact that some variables may be more pertinent than others in helping to form political behaviour has a theoretical and practical importance which centres around the question of political stability versus political change. If nearly all political learning of importance takes place within the framework of the family then it is difficult to think of introducing political change through the socialization process. Family centred socialization experiences also suggest an implicit and indirect quality to the process, i.e. what the child learns is either based upon using his parents as a model or information acquired about non-political events is transferred to the political arena. With other socializing agents it is more realistic to think of a degree of state control; for example, most educational systems are run by the state and have well-formulated goals that have strong political overtones. With this level of explicitness it is more feasible to think of socialization as an instrument of control employed either to create a new political order or to buttress one with shaky foundations. In these cases we may be more inclined to describe the process as indoctrination rather than socialization.

The nature of the learning process

In spite of the fact that the way in which individuals acquire their behaviour is not a direct concern of the political scientist, except in as much as the form of acquisition may effect the way the individual behaves politically, there have been a number of attempts by political scientists to create models of the political learning process.[31] Rather than examining each of the models separately and in detail, I will attempt to analyse some of their more general and important assumptions. To a certain extent this means highlighting several points that have already been touched upon, but it is hoped that their synthesis in this section will bring greater clarity to the literature's view of how people acquire their political behaviour.

Many of the notions surrounding the early phases of the political learning process have a distinctly Freudian flavour, and Easton and Dennis have gone so far as to suggest that some of their arguments are in a Freudian vein.[32] Although there are different interpretations of the many aspects of Freud's work, there is general agreement on the importance he gave to the first five years in the formation of personality, and the centrality of the interaction of mother, father and child in this process. What the political socialization theorists have tended to do is to co-opt some of the convenient aspects of his work rather than attempt to apply his theory as a whole to the nature of political learning. At times the occasional references to 'mother dominance' or 'identity crisis' gives the impression that use is being made of Freudian bric-à-brac.

An important stage in political learning has to be the initial contacts with things political. Given the fact that this will occur while the child is young, and thus still a dependent member of a family, the parents must exercise considerable influence over how this will take place. I have already pointed out the prevalence of the assumption that this is a point of indirect political contact. This is inevitable in the sense that the family is not regarded, at least in most societies, as a political institution and the child is at some considerable distance from direct contact with the political system. However, some political scientists have taken the matter further than this by suggesting that there is either no political content, or at best hidden political content, in the initial messages. Whether or not there is political content in a message depends very much on what is understood by the term political. The empirical examples quoted invariably centre around the parents (nearly always the father!) transmitting the idea that a superior authority structure exists (and this can be personalized in the form of the policeman) that they all have to obey.[33] To me this is the epitome of a political message because it is meant to convey the idea that established power structures organize our lives, and if we should choose to disobey then we risk sanctions being applied to us. It is not necessarily a well-developed political message for it is unlikely to contain very coherent statements about the nature of the power structure, how it came into being, and what controls we can exercise over it, but this lack of sophistication does not rule it out as a political message.

If political content exists in the early messages then the assumption is that this casts politics, and more especially politicians, in a very favourable light. It is as if the young child views the world of politics through rose-tinted spectacles worn by his parents. It is true that adults may have a negative image of politicians — and many American citizens certainly do[34] — but they take care not to mention this in front of the children. It is difficult to understand why this should be so, but it is believed that parents recognize the frailty of their children and their need for security and stability so they are at pains to protect them from the harsh political realities of this world. The best one can say for this is that it is an exceedingly culturally biased view of the way parents bring up their children. It almost implies that in relation to their children parents are above political partisanship, which appears to contradict the evidence that political loyalties are acquired within the family. Of course parents may separate for the child the notions of role and personality but this would contradict one of the other assumptions, i.e. that the personalization of authority provides an easy route into the world of politics.

In the American political system the President supposedly acts as a bridge between the personal and political spheres of life. This is because political power is symbolized in the shape of one man, which makes it easier for the child to grasp the concept of political power and all that is associated with it. Easton and Dennis go so far as to hint that other political systems, lacking 'a personalized power point', may experience difficulties in politically socializing children.[35] Part of the puzzle is the system's need to build support, and apparently if power is personalized this presents fewer obstacles. Easton and Dennis write, 'If the President is indeed the living symbol of the political system — "our government" — for the young child, the main conduit through which a child moves into the full stream of political life in the United States, we may suspect that support for the regime arises easily and naturally'.[36] This symbolic role of the Presidency has been reinforced and extended by Greenstein, who argues that the President fulfils a number of psychological functions: he simplifies the perception of government and politics, he provides an outlet for emotional expression, he serves as a symbol of unity, in crisis situations he provides citizens with a vicarious means of taking political action, and finally he is a reassuring symbol of social stability.[37] These are all functions that can be interpreted as helping to build citizen support for the political order.

There is the empirical point that it is hard to see how such a controversial political figure can readily be transferred into a symbol of national unity. Obviously the image of President Nixon changed as he became more and more embroiled in the Watergate fracas. Transcending this is the understanding as to why the President is able to perform these particular functions. The President appears to act as a super-surrogate father figure, for he is the child's own father writ large, wiser, more powerful and more benevolent. Greenstein, writing significantly, in the *American Journal of Psychiatry,* maintains, 'Finally there is some scattered clinical evidence that at least for a portion of the population the President is the unconscious symbolic surrogate of childhood authority figures'.[38] Later he adds to this, 'For example, when President Roosevelt died a number of psychoanalysts reported that their patients responded to his death in ways which indicated that they symbolically equated the President with one or both of their parents'.[39] Putting to one side the obvious comment that it is presumably rather dangerous to generalize about the total American population on the basis of those undergoing some form of psychoanalytic treatment, the underlying assumption is that the individual transfers a model image of his father onto a powerful political figure, in this case the President. This transference may indeed occur, but for it to have an outcome that is beneficial for political stability the child has to perceive parental authority in benign terms. This is yet another aspect of the cultural bias of the mainstream political socialization literature, for it takes for granted that children are raised in a stable family environment with understanding parents. Although most evidence points to the influence of the family, it is not always quite the family model that Greenstein, Easton and indeed Parsons appear to have in mind.[40]

It is possible to make a more limited case for some of these assumptions, which in all fairness Greenstein himself appears to favour.[41] The data are *not inconsistent* with some of the central themes. White middle-class American schoolchildren, at least when the surveys were conducted, did have a favourable image of both parental and presidential authority. It was inevitable, therefore, that intelligent and imaginative people should link the two, especially as they were navigating uncharted seas. Perhaps the case was presented in a way that suggested tentative hypotheses were proven facts, but at least certain lines of investigation were laid down for subsequent researchers as well as a challenge for those who were less than happy with some of its implications.

'The Freudian vein', evident in much of the literature on how the young child learns about politics, coalesces uneasily with the idea that political learning relates to general cognitive development. Initially political authority is seen in purely personal and affective terms and it is only as the child grows older that he has the capacity to understand the idea that power resides in institutions and roles rather than in persons. In specific terms the child is less inclined to think of a benevolent President and much more likely to talk about the power of the office of the Presidency. This change in direction is marked by a distinct decline in the President's benevolent image, although feelings of trust remain remarkably high. At this stage other socializing agents, besides the family, start to play a greater part in the political learning process. For example, once the child's cognitive capacities are sufficiently developed the school can use explicit instruction to teach its pupils about the nation's governmental structure. A cognitive developmental model assumes that the learning process is dependent upon the evolution of the individual's capacity to absorb and understand information. An ability to comprehend the political world would then relate to a general maturation of the individual's cognitive skills. The amount of research in this particular field is negligible and the point at which cognitive capacity takes over from the transference of images from parents to political figures, or even how the two approaches relate to one another, remains to be explored.[42]

⏤ Over time perceptions of the political learning process have changed rapidly. The initial emphasis upon the early years and the family has been replaced by a perspective which appears to embrace the totality of life's experiences. This has meant that a process seen as stable, internally harmonious and complete in all its important essentials by the age of thirteen, is now viewed as *potentially* instable, internally inconsistent and life long. These changes match a parallel development in both the content of what is learnt and the implications this holds for the political system. No longer is it felt that citizens will inevitably be socialized into supporting the established political order so that the outcome of political socialization is systems maintenance. This catholic viewpoint may indeed be in closer touch with reality but it raises the very pertinent question of what precisely then is the theoretical significance of political socialization. Parsons, followed by Easton and Almond, saw socialization as one of the inputs into the political system, the central means by which a certain set of political arrangements were to be kept going. If this is now in doubt then what is to replace it? The only serious answer to this question has been to take refuge in a verbal confusion by alluding to the likelihood of systems persistence as opposed presumably to either stagnation or revolution.

There have been fewer parallel developments in political learning models — i.e. how people learn their political behaviour — for the simple reason that no such models exist. However, some of the learning assumptions that buttressed the notion that political socialization was a means to political stability have come under attack. To maintain that so much of political behaviour was acquired implicitly suggested that the status quo was secure for it apparently had no need of explicit propaganda. The major socializing agent was an essentially non-political institution, the family. But, as I have argued, this conception of the process depends very much upon what is meant by both 'political' and 'implicit'. In the western democracies the family is an honoured institution because it can be relied upon to fulfil its socialization functions within certain accepted parameters. The state, therefore, has less need to resort to crude tactics that smack more of propaganda than socialization. More specifically, political scientists have worked with simple-minded notions of what family structures look like and have failed to substantiate how images of parental authority are transferred to political figures or in what ways a growing awareness of roles and institutions relates to cognitive development.

Perhaps the major weakness in the assumptions made about political learning was the way in which they neatly, and too conveniently, related a particular understanding of what the individual should learn with the process itself. It was not simply a question of the end product, the democratic citizen, resembling a careful blend of subject and citizen roles, but rather how at each particular stage of the learning experience the individual was exposed to the kinds of influences that would teach him what he had to know at that point in his life cycle. It was almost as if the future citizen was moving along a carefully controlled assembly line with all the appropriate parts being added at the correct point in time. Although there is now a widespread recognition that as much variety as conformity exists within the political learning process, it is still possible to maintain that an ideal model can be created if one has a clear understanding of how the democratic citizen should behave. Even if this were possible or desirable, it presumes the need for a degree of consistency to the learning process if the world is 'to be made safe for democracy'. This would be extremely difficult to achieve in reality and raises the spectre of a very fine regulation of life-styles.

Some of the assumptions about political learning remain intact in spite of a changed understanding as to its content and functions. The content and functions may not be a result of the way that political behaviour is acquired but rather a consequence of the circumstances within which the learning process is placed. These could be individual circumstances such as the absence of a father, the presence of a dominant mother or considerable family instability; or alternatively societal circumstances such as the poverty of a region, the ethnic composition of a city or the socio-economic structure of a town. But regardless of what the content and functions are, political behaviour is learnt in response to individual and social pressures, and it is because these differ that citizens end up with contrasting perspectives, and not because the behaviour has been learnt in an essentially different way. For example, the family remains a consistently powerful socializing agent but it will impart differing messages according to its precise structure, internal procedures and societal context, and it is the nature of these messages that determine whether or not it will help to build political stability. I accept the substance of this argument but would like to add that it is not simply a question of ascertaining whether a socializing agent is influential or not but also how it exerts its influence, for this can determine not only the messages that are learnt but also with what strength they are held, the likelihood of their being acted upon and the form this action will take. What this suggests is that learning experiences have a meaning over and above the kinds of messages that are being taught and that an ostensibly identical socialization agent (for example the family) will vary in the kind of influence it exerts according to how it is structured. Thus it is too simple-minded to say that the family can transmit either malevolent or benevolent images of political authority dependent on whether the father is absent or not, the parental view of political authority or simply the child's empathy for his parents. What we need to know in addition is the way in which family structure, procedures and attitudes actually shape the child's behaviour for without this we cannot ascertain the form this behavioural pattern will take.

One of the most important modifications to our understanding of how political behaviour is learnt is the notion that experiences acquired at one stage of the life cycle can clash with those accumulated at a different time and place. Hess and Torney, for example, felt that learning experiences were both accumulative and harmonious, leading, in the United States, to the well-rounded democratic citizen.[43] Keniston, however, has maintained that one of the forces motivating student radicals was their perception of a clash between values internalized during childhood and the realities of American society of which they became increasingly aware as they grew older. In an ironic way the student radical was the over-socialized American and not the political deviant.[44] My own concept of a differential socialization process adds to the potential instability of learning experiences. Like the subcultural theorists it accepts that citizens are being socialized into different political roles, and that various social criteria — for example, socio-economic status, ethnic background and sex — will have a strong influence upon determining the kind of role the individual will occupy, but like Parsons I believe there are wider societal values and these may well conflict with some of the implications of role differentiation. This was a conflict that Parsons was inclined to devalue until some of the events of the 1960s forced him to think otherwise. Some individuals, therefore, may well experience *continuous* contradictory socialization pressures but, like Keniston, I believe that these are sharper at some points of the life cycle than at others.[45] The end result is contradictory learning experiences that impart contradictory messages, and one of the fascinating questions is how the conflict is perceived and reconciled, or perhaps found to be irreconcilable.

Langton has pointed out that such terms as 'teaching', 'inculcation', 'training', 'transmission' and even 'socialization' conceive of the individual as a passive recipient of messages from the external environment which he internalizes and acts upon.[46] I have not put forward a view of the political socialization process that is essentially different from this, and in the phrase of Wrong's, 'the oversocialized conception of man' persists. This is because I believe that man is in essence a product of his environment, but it is not an environment that contains a totally harmonious view of the world and whose influence is pervasive enough to ensnare all its unsuspecting victims. Societal values may exist, and there may be elaborate and sophisticated attempts to inculcate them, but the values themselves are likely to contain serious internal inconsistencies and in a situation of scarce resources it is difficult to maximize their implementation. Role socialization is a consequence of this failure and its inegalitarian implications have to be legitimated. As long as the legitimations prevail so will stability, but once they start to break down the likely outcome is conflict. It is especially difficult to legitimate some of the inegalitarian implications of role socialization in democratic polities that have strong egalitarian streaks in their ideologies. Of course the ideology may be reinterpreted to justify inequality but this is a fragile process, and in fact within both Britain and America there have been continuous debates as to the precise meaning of their value systems. If to some of these more basic inconsistencies is added the vagaries of most personal life-styles, then the idea that behaviour can be controlled, and its meaning predicted, is indeed very tenuous.

Notes

1. op. cit., p. 17.
2. 'A note on the ambiguity of "political socialization": Definitions, criticisms and strategies of inquiry', p. 971.
3. These are points made by Greenstein, but he provides a rather confused answer as to what should be done about the problem. On the one hand he seems to suggest that the different theoretical orientations of psychologists and political scientists make it unlikely that grounding political socialization research in developmental psychology will increase our understanding of the political world, but on the other hand he maintains that research is most promising . . . when one's theoretical concerns are with a phenomenon that is critically dependent upon psychological determinants'. ibid., p. 975. To a great extent it depends on the research objectives, and Greenstein appears to be more interested in the political learning process *per se* than in its societal implications.
4. The two most important other restrictions probably being money and the problem of finding subjects with such a sustained commitment to the project.
5. R. Lane, *Political Ideology: Why the Common American Man Believes What He Does,* Free Press, New York, 1962.
6. op. cit., p. XIII.
7. D. Easton and R. Hess, 'The child's political world', *Midwest Journal of Political Science,* **6** (1962), 235.
8. R. Hess and D. Easton, 'The role of the elementary school in political socialization', *School Review,* **70** (1962), 258–259.
9. This includes most of the research of D. Easton, F. Greenstein and R. Hess.
10. T. Tapper, *Young People and Society,* Faber and Faber, London, 1971, pp. 45–46.
11. Besides my own book see T. Nossiter, 'How children learn about politics', *New Society,* **14** (31 July, 1969), 166–167 (sample aged 11 to 16); R. Dowse and J. Hughes, 'The family, the school and the political socialization process', *Sociology,* **5** (1971), 21–45 (sample aged 11 to 17).
12. For a full discussion of this expansion see below chapter 7.
13. See pp. 134–145.
14. K. Keniston, *The Young Radicals: Notes on Committed Youth,* Harcourt, Brace and World, New York, 1968, ch. 2.
15. op. cit., ch. 7.
16. op. cit., p. 35.
17. op. cit., p. 365.
18. ibid., p. 328.
19. See Kavanagh, op. cit., p. 30 and R. Sigel, 'Assumptions about the learning of political values', *The Annals,* **361** (1965), 1 and 'In retrospect', p. 128 (her concluding comments to the edition of the journal).

20. J. Davies, 'The family's role in political socialization', *The Annals,* **361** (1965), 11.
21. For an example of the acceptance of this assumption see L. Froman and J. Skipper, 'An approach to the learning of party identification', *Public Opinion Quarterly,* **27** (1963), 473.
22. M. Kent Jennings and R. Niemi, 'Patterns of political learning', *Harvard Educational Review,* **38** (1968), 443–467.
23. A development which was very necessary if one was to incorporate other socialization agents.
24. See the pattern of survival in the Nazi concentration camps. B. Bettelheim, *The Informed Heart: Autonomy in a Mass Age,* Thames and Hudson, London, 1960, ch. 4, 5.
25. For an interesting interpretation of changing Soviet attitude towards the family see K. Millett, *Sexual Politics,* Rupert-Hart Davies, London, 1971, pp. 168–176.
26. R. Hess and J. Torney, op. cit., pp. 217–219.
27. ibid., p. 114.
28. For a good discussion of the variety of socialization agents see R. Dawson and K. Prewitt, *Political Socialization,* Little, Brown, Boston, 1969, Part III.
29. For an example of this statistical virtuosity see K. Langton, *Political Socialization,* Oxford University Press, New York, 1969, ch. 6.
30. Concentrating upon England, I attempted to build a simple macro-model of the socialization process. In spite of its severe limitations it is one of the few attempts known to me. see op. cit., pp. 30–44.
31. For the best such attempt see Hess and Torney, op. cit., pp. 19–22.
32. *Children in the Political System,* pp. 202–203.
33. The policeman is a central figure in Easton's and Dennis' work. See ibid., ch. 10, 11.
34. As is made perfectly clear by the Watergate fracas. See W. C. Mitchell, 'The ambivalent social status of the American politician', *Western Political Quarterly,* **12** (1959), 683–698. More specifically look at F. C. Arterton, 'The Impact of Watergate on children's attitudes toward political authority', *Political Science Quarterly,* **89** (1974), 269–288.
35. op. cit., p. 412.
36. ibid., pp. 196–197.
37. F. Greenstein, 'The psychological functions of the Presidency for citizens, in E. E. Cornwell (ed.), *The American Presidency: Vital Center,* Scott Foresman, Chicago, 1966, pp. 30–36.
38. F. Greenstein, 'Popular images of the President', *American Journal of Psychiatry,* **122** (1965), 527.
39. 'The psychological functions of the Presidency for citizens', p. 35.
40. For an example of the potential political impact of differing family structures see the work of Jaros and Hirsch on the Appalachian mountain people.
41. See F. Greenstein's 'A note on the ambiguity of "Political Socialization": Definitions, criticisms and strategies of inquiry', pp. 969–978.
42. It is difficult to fulfil this task through the social survey approach for this provides a snapshot of attitudinal patterns, perhaps at different points in time, rather than traces the dynamics of a process.
43. op. cit., pp. 20–22.
44. See p. 152.
45. I would argue that a crucial stage is about the time of entering full-time employment. Prior to this fateful day the individual may be perfectly aware of his particular place in the socio-economic hierarchy but finding, or perhaps not finding, a job concretizes this awareness. It is hard to maintain illusions in the face of this reality.
46. op. cit., pp. 162–163.

Chapter 3

Education and Political Behaviour

Formal education as an agent of political socialization

It is generally accepted that formal schooling is a central agent of political socialization, perhaps second in importance only to the family. But formal education differs from the family in as much as it is more readily controlled by the state. It is, therefore, a direct rather than an indirect agent of political socialization and as such transmits its political messages in an explicit rather than an implicit fashion. Although this sweeping generalization is essentially correct, it has to be modified by a member of important clauses. In the first place there has to be an educational system. This may seem an obvious point, but in many parts of the world formal schooling is of recent origins and still quite fragmentary in scope and structure. It is in such circumstances that the state is most likely to face the problem of how to allocate its scarce resources. Is the stress to be upon the development of elementary education with perhaps the objective of eliminating mass illiteracy? Or will there be an attempt to train a home-based elite which has the necessary skills to run the state? Not all nation states have to make such harsh choices but they reflect the kind of problem faced by many of the poorer nations in the Third World. This graphically illustrates the point that education can be a divisive social, if not political force.

If the state lacks a well-structured educational system then in the short run stability has to rest on another basis. Even in some of the advanced industrial nations trying to solve conflict through a manipulation of the educational system can be an exceedingly risky enterprise. The racial integration of American schools, which was to follow from the Supreme Court's 1954 decision in the Brown versus the Board of Education of Topeka case, was a direct attempt to stimulate social change by tampering with the ethnic composition of student bodies. In the long run it may be hailed as a great landmark in the amelioration of racial relations, but in the short run it has generated considerable political conflict and even twenty years later some of its repercussions can still be felt.[1] Some bold spirits have suggested that the conflict between the two religious communities in Northern Ireland could be mitigated by integrating the schools, but other more timid souls feel that in the present climate this could merely extend the number of conflict arenas rather than produce more understanding inter-communal attitudes.[2]

No educational system is simply an agent of political socialization and nothing else. In fact many people, including some of those most intimately involved in formal schooling, would argue that as far as it is possible politics and education should be separated. For some years now a campaign has been under way in Britain to replace the selective secondary schools by a comprehensive system. Frequently the cry has been heard that this has resulted in bringing politics into education; the advocates of comprehensive schools are supposedly as interested (if not more interested) in socio-political goals as in seeing the schools pursue their more normal function of maximizing academic attainment.[3] The counter-argument is that the selective secondary system likewise has its socio-political biases, for there is substantial evidence to show that those who obtain the best academic qualifications, and the greatest share of scarce educational resources, tend to come from particular socio-economic backgrounds. The implication of this, therefore, is of the impossibility of separating formal schooling from wider societal pressures. Although I accept this, I would argue that these pressures do not automatically point in the same direction and indeed they may make conflicting demands on the schools. For example, the need to train manpower for an established occupational structure may run counter to the demand that the schools should be an instrument of social mobility.

Education is not an entity that assumes its shape and form simply in response to societal pressures. In both Britain and the United States the educational systems are composed of large numbers of people, most of whom have a very definite stake in what course the educational institutions should pursue. Furthermore, an ideology exists as to the way in which schools should educate their pupils. The assumption is that they develop enquiring minds and, although they may fail dismally to live up to this ideal, it is still a principle that from time to time can have considerable repercussions. As we shall see, not all looked with favour upon the expansion of education in nineteenth century England, for some felt that an educated working class would perhaps challenge the structure of the established order. Formal education, therefore, can act as an instrument of social enquiry as well as social control and elites may not have it all their own way in deciding what course to follow.

Both the United States and Britain are stable, well-established polities with free and universal state schools that have been in existence for a comparatively long period of time. In view of this it is natural to expect them to rely partially upon the schools to inculcate in their budding citizens appropriate forms of political behaviour. In his classic text on civics education Charles Merriam wrote. ' . . . everywhere the formal educational system is an outstanding agency of civic training'.[4] It is reasonable to assume that in the meantime this function has increased, for more individuals are now exposed to more formal education than ever before, and the school has made inroads into some of the tasks previously undertaken exclusively by the family. However, the mere fact that they are neither new nor revolutionary nation states means that they have less need of explicit agents of socialization; so, in contrast with most other educational systems, British and American schools are likely to be more implicit and indirect in pursuing their socialization functions. Because they exist within contrasting societal contexts British and American schools will differ somewhat in this respect, but these differences should be kept in perspective.

Because implicit and indirect socialization techniques are employed, disputes may arise as to whether they have a political content and, if so, what is the precise nature of this content. In the United Kingdom, for example, a selective educational system has been legitimated on pedagogical grounds, but does this mean that the selection exists to serve only pedagogical ends? It is hard to give a straight answer to this question, but even if there are only pedagogical intentions the side consequence is a considerable and well-directed degree of social inequality. It is legitimate therefore, to make a case on the basis of actual outcomes especially when there is evidence to suggest that intentions are somewhat murky. As a final point it is pertinent to note that pedagogical reasons inevitably contain certain ideas as to what man and his society should aim for.

The case for considering the political consequences of pedagogical legitimations is strengthened by the fact that these are, by and large, controlled by the state. In relation to selection in British education T. H. Marshall writes,

The first point to note is that, in this matter of selection for secondary education, the state is in full command of the whole situation. It provides the primary schools that prepare the children for the examinations, it designs the secondary system for which they are being selected, and therefore determines the categories into which they are to be sorted, and it invents and administers the tests.[5]

Whether we approve or disapprove of the direction this control has taken will probably determine our attitude to Marshall's subsequent stricture, 'Such power is dangerous!'.

One of the most difficult problems associated with the analysis of formal education as a socializing agent is ascertaining how it is to be measured. Most research either makes hypotheses about the influence of the content of formal education or examines the strength of a correlation between length and/or type of education and a particular aspect of political behaviour. Those looking at content have concentrated upon the more explicitly political aspects of the curriculum, especially civics programmes. Both Britain and American studies conclude that these have little influence upon those exposed to them. Langton, writing with an air of finality, claims, ' . . . there is a lack of evidence that the civics curriculum has a significant effect on the political orientations of the great majority of American high school students'.[6] This assumes that it is possible to define the goals of a civics curriculum and to separate out, from all other variables, its specific influence. In a technical sense the latter task may be possible, but it runs counter to my own notion of a socialization process in which influences interact with one another as opposed to a model in which discrete variables exert their hold in an accumulative fashion. A wider version of Langton's assessment of civics education is to be found in the work of Coleman and Jencks, who have concluded that formal education (measured by an enormous variety of structural criteria) exerts little influence upon individual academic performance, income levels or occupational status.[7]

Defining formal education by its curriculum content has the advantage of excluding non-educational variables, although other school-based influences (for example the teacher's interpretation of the curriculum content) may intrude. In other definitions extra-school influences are likely to intrude. For example educational attainment or the kind of school attended is heavily dependent upon socio-economic criteria, so without careful controls it is hard to say if educational or social differences are being measured. In this sense there is a real need for statistical expertise to separate the differential impact of the socializing agents, but what is also required is models that relate their integrative impact. After all, people do come from certain class backgrounds and they do attend schools, and so it is impossible to think of the end product without knowing how one relates to the other. In the rest of this chapter I want to examine certain features of the British and American educational systems, show how these features are interrelated, what their dependence is upon wider societal forces, and the kinds of influence all this is likely to exert upon patterns of political behaviour.

British and American schools

This is not meant to be a comprehensive view of formal education in Britain and the United States. From an enormous volume of material I have selected aspects pertaining to political education, and more especially, those ingredients that throw some light upon the process of role socialization and the inculcation of universal political values.

Educational values

The British commitment to education has traditionally been severely restricted. State intervention commenced in earnest only a hundred years ago with the passing of the 1870 Education Act, at which time the goal was to fill in the gaps left by the religious bodies, so perpetuating the nineteenth-century principle of *laissez-fair*. On the other hand, from the earliest days of the American Republic community opinion favoured the creation of schools.[8] By the mid-nineteenth century New England had a free and universal system of elementary schools, which was admired in some of the contemporary British educational reports. Although admiration was unstinting, the likely expense to the ratepayers was considered sufficient reason not to follow the same path in Britain.[9]

The British commitment to education has been limited in a number of different ways. A strong elitist principle has been one of the main guiding-posts, which has meant that education has been seen as a scarce resource to be doled out to the masses in sparing quantities. This has influenced both the structure and content of education, with the elite receiving a different kind of education, in separate institutions, from the masses. Indeed there was some fear that if the state expanded educational opportunities this could stimulate revolutionary fervour. Certain members of the British aristocracy and bourgeoisie dreaded that the excesses of continental revolutions would be transported to these supposedly idyllic isles. The solution was to educate individuals for their station of life, so the schools had the task of confirming a class structure by teaching the kind of behavioural patterns that a hierarchical set of class relations demanded. The dominant feeling may have been that only those from higher class backgrounds were capable of benefiting from the more elevated forms of education, but this was explicitly associated with the idea that different classes needed different kinds of education because of their future place in the hierarchy. This is beautifully illustrated by a snippet from the Rev. James Fraser's evidence to the Newcastle Commission of 1861: 'Even if it were possible, I doubt whether it would be desirable, with a view to the real interests of the peasant boy, to keep him at school till he was 14 or 15 years of age. But it is not possible. We must make up our minds to see the last of him, as far as the day school is concerned, at 10 or 11'.[10] Contrast this with the kind of values the Clarendon Report of 1864 felt the public schools exuded: ' . . . their capacity to govern others and to control themselves, their aptitude for combining freedom with order, their public spirit, their vigour and manliness of character, their strong but not slavish respect for public opinion, their love of healthy sports and exercise'.[11] All these values were admirably suited for the future members of a secure, governing elite.

Implicit in the notion that people are educated for a station in life is the idea that education serves various societal ends rather than the liberation of individuals. In fact the 1870 Education Act was a direct response to socio-economic and political pressures and not a sudden conversion to the belief that education was intrinsically worthwhile. Britain's industrial supremacy was threatened by the growing might of Germany and the

United States. The industrial structure was becoming more complex, thus creating a demand for increasing numbers of skilled workers and white-collar staff. In 1867 the franchise had been extended to male householders in the towns so that one sceptic was moved to comment on the need 'to educate our masters'.[12] These complementary forces were neatly summarized by W. E. Forster in his speech introducing the 1870 Act to the House of Commons:

Upon the speedy provision of elementary education depends our industrial prosperity . . . if we leave our work-folk any longer unskilled, notwithstanding their strong sinews and determined energy, they will become over-matched in the competition of the world. Upon this speedy provision depends also, I fully believe, the good, the safe working of our constitutional system. To its honour, Parliament has lately decided that England shall in future be governed by popular government . . . now that we have given them political power we must not wait any longer to give them education.[13]

This is a perfect view of the utilitarian function of education, with the calculating elite replacing Bentham's rational man and the end goal being not so much the greatest happiness of the greatest number but order, prosperity and efficiency.[14]

There is a quite explicit legacy, therefore, of a relationship between politics and education. Forster claimed that citizens needed to be educated if popular government was going to work properly. This is not the same thing as saying, however, that citizens require explicit political education, i.e. civics training, if parliamentary democracy is to be preserved. In much the same way Forster recognized a relationship between education and industrial efficiciency, but this did not mean workers would then receive a good grounding in technical education. In fact the British schools have been noteworthy for both their lack of explicit political training and their failings in the field of technical education. In spite of this it would be impossible to deny that the educational values flow out of a particular conception of what society should look like and suggest a structure and content to the schools that would help to perpetuate this conception.

In the United States the emphasis is less upon how education acts as an instrument of social control and more upon how it works to widen personal development and promote social mobility. Of course there are socio-political goals built into the educational system, but they are more dependent upon a standardized understanding of citizenship as opposed to the British notion of distinct strata of citizens. This is why the desegregation of educational facilities was considered to be so important, for the schools were supposed to be the melting-pot from which the ideal American citizen emerged, and why the claims that schools in fact have little influence have been met with such incredulity. The conception of a common citizenship is reflected in the fact that until the turn of the twentieth century the classics — the key to self-enlightenment — dominated the high-school curriculum. The classics formed the core of a common curriculum that was not eroded until the classics themselves were toppled from their pinnacle.[15] Although there was a class bias in the composition of high schools they were not exclusively institutions for the wealthy. Edward Krug writes,

> . . . the principal of a midwestern high school . . . contended in 1887 that the majority of the graduates were 'the children of those whom some were pleased to class the common people', half the pupils representing families who were not householders and less than one-quarter being 'from homes where wealth abounds'.[16]

The parallel would be English working-class schoolchildren receiving a classics education at a late nineteenth-century grammar school — perhaps not a miracle but hardly a common occurrence.

In both countries central values have either been eroded or placed on different foundations. In Britain there is a contemporary battle over the perpetuation of selection in secondary education, but for quite some time now elitism has been based upon a combination of class and 'merit' rather than simply class. Defenders of the status quo would argue that, although class biases may be present in the educational system, no one of ability is prevented from reaching the highest rungs of the ladder. Furthermore, in a society with such a precarious economic base it is essential to allow ability to flourish free from the trammels of the less able. Even if this claim is accepted the problem still remains of how the able are to be distinguished from the less able, for the class biases of the IQ tests which legitimated selective secondary education, have been exposed for all to see. The major opponents of selection are not egalitarians in the sense that they believe everyone should be exposed to a common course, but rather they are fighting for a common, or comprehensive, structure within which differentiation will take place. In a sense they are the true merito-crats, for the aim is to maximize equality of opportunity within a uniform structure. To what extent this will succeed in evolving a common concep-tion of citizenship, or escaping the pervasive influence of social class, remains to be seen.[17]

As the nineteenth century progressed American schools were subjected to the pressures of industrialization and mass immigration. This resulted in the expansion of vocational studies, the introduction of standard certification techniques, the growing separation of students destined for college and the work-a-day world, and more explicit programmes of civic training. In the phrase of the educationalists, the schools were turned into instruments of 'social efficiency', reflected in both structural and curriculum changes. The schools inevitably became instruments of social control rather than vehicles of personal development. In spite of these changes, however, a strong idealistic streak is retained in American educational values. This is highlighted when comparisons are made with Britain, where there is still a wide belief in a narrow concept of merit, and an attempt is made to measure this; on the basis of this measurement young children are channelled into specific social, economic and indeed political directions.

This shift in American educational values has meant that the schools are more of an explicit agent of political education than is the case in Britain. Again this relates to the wider societal context, for the United States had to face the problem of socializing immigrants who not only did not speak English, but also came from countries with political traditions that were completely alien to the American way of life. The schools were allocated a central role in this process and they became community institutions in a way that has never been true of Britain. The school was not simply a place where the immigrant learnt to read and write English but also the centre at which he acquired the characteristics of citizenship. So formal education was seen increasingly as a direct socializer of new citizens, and in view of these kinds of influences, it is remarkable that American education has been able to retain so much of its liberal arts tradition.

Formal structure

The most important expression of educational values is the structure of the educational system. I would maintain that this has more bearing upon the shape of political behaviour than all the other aspects of formal education. However, structure is not something that can readily be separated from either other features of the educational system or wider societal forces. It is the link between both society's values and socio-economic relations and the kind of educational experience to which individuals are exposed. It is a two-way link, in the sense that it channels both values and class relations into the educational system and at the same time colours very significantly the kind of educational experience an individual can expect to receive.

In 1922 Tawney neatly summarized the guiding principle behind the structure of English education:

The organization of education on the lines of class, though qualified in the last twenty years, has characterized the English system of public education since its very inception, and has been a symptom, an effect and a cause of the control of the lives of the mass of men and women by a privileged minority.[18]

Although further substantial qualifications have been added since Tawney wrote this, England still has an elitist education system which separates children into different kinds of schools, on the basis of both academic and social criteria, with a view to training them for various niches in the socio-economic hierarchy. The complexity of the secondary school pecking order illustrates the point perfectly: the prestigious public schools and the more famous of the direct grant grammar schools, the smaller private and less illustrious direct grant grammar schools, the grammar schools that are controlled, to varying degrees, by the local authorities, the comprehensive schools (comprehensive in name if not in reality), and by general repute at the bottom of the status ladder, the secondary moderns. The evidence that attendance at a particular type of secondary school has a direct bearing upon many aspects of the individual's life chances is substantial: his school-leaving age, his academic success, his likelihood of pursuing higher education and above all his future occupational choice and thus his social class status.[19]

This hierarchial structure is even more complex than the classification based on school type alone would indicate. Within schools students are invariably further segregated by refined streaming arrangements. It is not sufficient to pass the 11-plus examination to go to university but this can be better ensured by being placed in the top grammar school stream. It may be possible to mitigate the damage bestowed by an 11-plus failure label, but it is that much more difficult to escape the stigma of being a D-stream pupil in a secondary modern school. The perpetuation, and possible elaboration, of streaming in the comprehensive schools is just one factor which could prevent them from fulfilling some of the more idealistic hopes that have been pinned on them.[20]

In spite of the claim, therefore, that political education is conducted in British schools in an implicit fashion, this elaborate structural differentiation would suggest a brutal confinement of socializing experiences upon those pupils of secondary-school age. Children from relatively similar backgrounds are placed within the same type of school and subjected to a specialized training designed to fit them for the station they will most likely occupy in later life. Throughout this century a scholarship ladder has tenuously bridged the gulf between the humblest of elementary schools and the grandest of universities. Ostensibly its purpose is to allow talent to rise to the top and it is the touchstone for those who maintain that British education is based as much on merit as on privilege. The scholarship ladder means that there is a certain amount of sponsored mobility and a potential consequence is conflict in socializing experiences. The extent to which prolonged conflict occurs is difficult to ascertain. It is clear that most pupils who do not accept the grammar school's values — the major educational vehicle of working-class mobility — gravitate to the lower streams and leave school as soon as the law permits. Colin Lacey has shown that the crucial battles between the student and the school ethos are completed by the end of the first year; by then the pecking order is established and the anti-school clique goes its own way.[21] Jackson and Marsden have gone further than this by claiming that in the pursuit of academic success the working-class grammar-schoolboy is apt to be turned into a conforming apolitical creature.[22]

In the past ten years a very haphazard movement towards a comprehensive system of secondary education has taken place. The very tentativeness of the change is the best proof that old ways die hard but, in spite of all its limitations, it represents one of the most significant modifications of the formal structure to have occurred in British education. The first problem is ascertaining whether the reforms will be broad enough to to affect substantially the overall structure of secondary education. In specific terms this means: will the prestigious public and direct-grant grammar schools succeed in remaining outside the new order and so preserve strong elements of elitism? Secondly, will the comprehensive school be able to avoid recreating the traditional structural differentiations within the new order? At the time of writing the answer to these two questions is far from clear but the evidence does not leave much room for optimism.[23]

First impressions would suggest that the best way to describe the structure of American education is as universal and unitary. Although the United States has a number of prestigious private schools, their influence is not as great as their public school equivalents in Britain. The vast majority of students flow through the grade schools and then on to the junior and senior high schools. There is a high-school 'dropout' problem but most students complete their secondary education, leaving at the age of seventeen or eighteen. Higher education is nowhere as exclusive as in Britain, and the student who graduates from high school can usually find a college place, perhaps in a junior or community college, if he or she should want one.[24] This standardization prevails throughout the United States in spite of the fact that education is still very much under the control of local school boards. The schools, therefore, act as a strong unifying and centralizing force in American society, in direct contrast to the differentiating function they fulfil in the United Kingdom.

This picture of uniformity is marred (although some would argue enhanced) by a number of noticeable cracks. I would agree with Floud and Halsey that the most pervasive influence on education is a nation's economic development,[25] and the United States is certainly no exception to this. A competitive industrial economy requires schools that will train people to meet its needs, so education becomes a certification process in which the end product — the graduating student — is carefully stamped and graded. Failure is not surrounded by the same explicit symbols as it is in the United Kingdom, for the refining process takes place within a uniform structure and this helps to perpetuate the myth that America is indeed the land of unlimited opportunities. So success and failure are ascribed to individual skill, character and luck and are not seen as consequences of the character of institutions.[26] But if success and failure are personalized this is a more sophisticated technique of socialization than placing them in an institutional context. It certainly deflects attention away from structural limitations and onto individual failings, and it serves the same function of legitimizing an inegalitarian social order.

The pressures of industrialization and the emergence of the high schools as mass educational institutions have led to some internal school cleavages. Prospective college entrants are channelled toward higher education in their high-school years by following college preparatory courses, while others undertake any one of a number of vocational programmes. This tracking, as the Americans call it, appears to be little different from streaming and certainly the guiding principle is the same: individuals are placed in a status hierarchy on the basis of their present and past performances, their interests and their future aspirations. It is true that a much higher percentage of an age group goes to college in the United States than in Britain, but this advantage is partially lost by placing the colleges in the mainstream of the certification process. The outcome is an elaborate hierarchy of colleges — both private and state institutions — a very fine measure of academic performance, and a high dropout rate. Obviously British universities have similar characteristics but not to the same degree. Americans refer to the barriers they erect against the fulfilment of aspirations as 'cooling out', whereas the British are more likely to use less euphemistic terms and talk of '11-plus failures' or 'grammar-school material'.[27]

Regional and local variations in the quality of education are another major qualification to the unified structure of American schools. James Coleman has written, 'These are the differences that make the job of evaluating high school records so exasperatingly difficult, differences which require that the upper quartile in one high school be considered equal to the third or bottom quartile in another'.[28] What Coleman is saying is that a high school in the decaying centre of a conurbation, or in the rural backwoods, will not offer the same educational experience as one in the respectable suburbs. The issue is further complicated by the class and ethnic composition of the student body. If the school's intake is from the immediate neighbourhood, and that neighbourhood suffers from various social problems, this will affect the quality of the educational experience the school can offer. This is not contradicted by Jencks' claim that schools have comparatively little influence on their students because what may be preventing the schools from having an impact is not so much features pertaining to themselves (e.g. facilities or teacher–pupil ratios) but rather the characteristics of their student body (e.g. the kind of families from which they are drawn).[29] I am claiming that you cannot separate the school from its societal context, because part of the definition of a school is this context, which in this particular case means the kind of children the school has to teach. The recent racial riots in Boston show the difficulty of tampering with the pupil intake of the schools, but bussing has met with resistance from the ethnic groups who wish to preserve their 'identity' as well as the whites who are ostensibly worried about 'academic standards'.

It is scarcely worthwhile having a uniform educational structure if there is a tendency for different schools to educate different social groups. This is another basic problem facing the comprehensive schools movement in Britain for, as in the United States, schools are neighbourhood institutions and thus tend to have differing social compositions. We are also certainly more aware than many Americans appear to be, if one is to judge by some of the post-Coleman Report research, that part of the definition of a school is the social composition of its student body. The major handicap the secondary moderns have had to suffer is that they received pupils who failed the 11-plus and, given the class biases built into the method of testing, this meant that a disproportionate number of their pupils were working-class children. All the other considerations were essentially irrelevant in the face of these facts, and the same, I would suggest, is true of a high school composed of an overwhelming majority of American students from deprived homes.

What the general and internal (i.e. intra-school) structural cleavages aim at achieving is a pattern of role socialization. In Britain an explicitly hierarchical education system directs pupils towards various adult roles and the evidence points to a close marriage of class and educational structures. This may be legitimated on the grounds that elitism, besides being inevitable in the long run, ('talent will out'), has all kinds of beneficial effects and, in any case, placement within the hierarchy is supposedly on objective criteria — intelligence testing. In the United States role socialization is more a consequence of the demands of the economy for specialist skills and the fact that schools of the same type — thanks to the neighbourhood principle — can be composed of entirely different social groupings. In the British case success and failure are institution-lized while in America they are personalized, but the end result is much the same; for the common goal is to legitimate an inegalitarian distribution of scarce resources.

The content of formal education

One would expect the content of formal education to reflect both societal values and structural constraints. But these forces can run in opposite directions. Some of the political and educational values are meant to be universal in their application, e.g. all citizens have basic political rights or education is everyone's birthright, but an inegalitarian structure is bound to limit this universal application. The content of formal education can be expected to mirror this basic division, for at one level it will stress the importance of common rights of citizenship but at another attempt to legitimize differentiation in the use of those rights. Of course there is no guarantee that the two levels will be successfully reconciled, or even that it is desirable to try to reconcile them.

As befits a nation state with a long history, a considerable degree of political stability and a comparatively homogeneous population, the amount of direct political education in British schools is limited. There is no continuous history of civics education but various subjects have strong political connotations. The churches have exercised a powerful hold over

British schools and, not surprisingly, religious instruction is an important part of the curriculum and daily rituals. Tradition states that working-class children should receive a Christian education, and in the nineteenth century religious instruction was seen as a means of preserving established forms of authority while expanding the system. Teaching the three Rs, accompanied by liberal doses of religion, was hardly likely to stimulate revolutionary thoughts, especially when the Bible formed the backbone of many of the reading and writing lessons. Some may have thought this necessary in order to achieve a wider moral perfection, but the fact that it also helped many to sleep easier at nights cannot be overlooked. As Maclure succinctly notes,

Religion and philanthropy were joined by utilitarian motives. The violence and poverty of the time, the sharpness of social distinctions, the prevalence of pauperism and the links between poverty, ignorance, and crime made it inevitable that the better-off classes should look for practical advantages from their benevolence. They expected much from religious instruction and Bible reading, including social peace, industrial skill, and the arts of self-government.[30]

One of the contemporary school rituals is the commencement of the day with an assembly composed of all the teachers and pupils. The religious content in this daily event is high: hymn-singing, prayers and a short sermon make up the staple diet. To induce patriotism and respect for authority may not be the only purpose associated with the singing of hymns, but it is surely more than a coincidence that 'All Things Bright and Beautiful' should resound so frequently throughout the length and breadth of the land between 9.00 and 9.30 a.m.[31] I know of no research that has quantified the themes of assembly sermons, but personal reflection suggests that a discourse on the need to maintain high moral standards or putting one's talents to the best use would figure quite prominently.

History is the subject that has the closest links with political education and its central function has been to build a sense of national loyalty. In his summary of history teaching in the British schools of the 1920s John Gaus concluded, 'As yet, however, the greatest attention in the schools is given to English history, with some attention to the development of the Empire'.[32] But his study revealed the emergence of a broader view: 'Undoubtedly the present trend in history teaching is for a wider outlook and a greater emphasis on social, regional, and international aspects of history'.[33] This wider focus has clearly increased; reality dictates that Britain can no longer regard herself as of such great importance that she can ignore the history of other nations, and social and economic history now has much more status within the profession. In spite of these worthwhile developments many schools continue to teach an elitist interpretation of history: it is the story of kings and queens, dukes, earls and barons, and more recently prime ministers and their immediate entourage. It is still common practice for teachers to subdivide history into distinct time periods with the boundaries defined by the births and deaths of monarchs.

The pupils are then taken on a long, probably monotonous journey as school-year by school-year they plough through the successive reigns.

It is possible to extend almost *ad infinitum* the list of subjects associated with the indirect political education of pupils, and certainly a good case could be made out for including geography, English literature and language. Some audacious spirits are prepared to state the case for 'The teaching of citizenship through domestic subjects!'[34] Pediodically the schools are urged to place the teaching of civics on a more formal basis. In the 1930s the Association for Education in Citizenship was active and, although from its publications it held an enlightened view of civics education it was very much concerned to preserve 'democracy', which it saw threatened by the spread of totalitarianism in Europe.[35] At present a version of the same demand is expressed by the Hansard Society's Politics Association through its journal, *Teaching Politics*. The aim is to see that trainee teachers receive more instruction in the teaching of politics, and that politics should be more widely taught as a subject in its own right in the schools.[36] In fact pilot studies are under way to discover good programmes of civics education and this has received some official blessing.[37] There appears to be a general feeling that with the lowering of the voting age to eighteen schools should impart some explicit political instruction, especially as some pupils will also be voters. This is perhaps reinforced by the apparent widespread rejection of traditional values and institutions on the part of young people. The more adventurous should be cautious in view of the evidence that civics courses are rarely effective and have also been widely castigated for what Philip Abrams describes as a surfeit of impartiality that results in a judicious blandness which neither informs nor stimulates.[38]

In direct contrast to Britain, civics education in the United States is an integral part of the school curriculum, with a comparatively long history behind it. There is almost unanimous agreement that the schools should conduct some form of civics training, and from time to time the professional associations of many academic disciplines have investigated what contribution their particular subject should make.[39] Although civics education may be widely accepted, that is about as far as the consensus goes with most controversy surrounding not so much its goals but how they are to be fulfilled.

Congress, in a report of the Senate Committee on Labour and Public Welfare, claimed that civics education should embody the following objectives:

... civics includes the function as well as the structure of American government at all levels, including the impact on government of current developments at home and abroad ... it is hoped it would include an understanding of the responsibilities of citizens in a democracy. Knowledge of these responsibilities of citizenship, the committee believes, is essential if we are to strengthen the intellectual and moral fibre of our nation.[40]

But how is this to be achieved? Strong pressure has been exerted in favour of a narrow and chauvinistic interpretation of civics education with, from time to time, various patriotic organizations (including the highly respected American Legion) trying to persuade the schools to toe their line. In a comment on Merriam's *The Making of Citizens,* George Bereday makes the following observation:

Specifically, American education, with its ritual salute of the flag, the insistence on one language instruction as a device of assimilation (denationalizing?) immigrants, and the conformist fears about 'the American way of life', rates very high on the scale of systems committed to teaching a nationalistic content.[41]

Bereday's own research led him to the conclusion that more similarities than differences exist between the American and Soviet patterns of political education.[42]

A contemporary criticism of American civics programmes is that, far from being super-patriotic, they are more inclined to adopt a neutral and sterile posture.[43] Content analyses have shown a marked tendency to avoid controversial topics such as race relations, the distribution of wealth, the structure of the economy and conflict within the policy-making process. Mark Krug has aptly summed up the critique: 'If one were pressed to single out the one most important weakness in the study of civics in high schools, it would be the almost complete exclusion of politics'.[44] The student is exposed to the formal and legal aspects of the American political system and the fear is often expressed that this could give him too great an expectation of individual political power, resulting in disillusionment in later life. This assumes the student fails to pick up the difference between theory and reality from other sources, and if he does, this could make the civics courses even more irrelevant.

If the first interpretation of civics education was to create super-patriots, and the second to avoid political controversy altogether, then the third has concentrated upon the promotion of 'informed political participation'. This has been the goal of liberal educationalists throughout American history, incorporating those, like Dewey, who are theorists on the grand scale, and others who are content to rest their case on the need to build more social science and conflict into the courses.[45] The 1960s, in which conflict between youth and the political order rose to unprecedented heights, witnessed an explosion of interest in this particular approach, and a trend towards a more enlightened course content was set in motion.

There is not a great deal of research on the relationship between course content and pupil characteristics. This could take three pure forms: different pupils would be taught different courses, the same courses would be interpreted in various ways according to the characteristics of the pupils, and all pupils would receive a common programme. Certainly by the secondary-school years common programmes are very much of a rarity in both countries. In Britain certain subjects — notably the classics — have been monopolized by the public and grammar schools. For a long time part of the hallmark of a well educated gentleman was his classical training, and the assumed virtues of a classics education is a legacy that dies hard in Britain. External examinations impose both uniformity and differentiation upon curriculum content, for while they bind all those who have entered the race for exam success they act as a barrier between those who have joined and those who have been excluded from the competition. In some respects this can link the curricula of secondary modern and public schools while placing pupils from the same secondary modern school in comparatively different educational worlds. Within many schools academic segregation and a common course will run parallel to one another, thus making the relationship between curriculum content and pupil characteristics more complex. Occasionally this has been accorded theoretical pretensions: pupils learn a common form of citizenship but at the same time can develop their own individual talents. The problem is the difficulty of disguising the fact that those who are creamed off for some subjects (invariably those with the highest academic status) are being prepared for a different life-style from the other pupils. In the light of this is it possible to maintain the notion that we have the same rights and duties as citizens?

Edgar Litt, on the basis of observing pupils in three contrasting school districts, has arrived at similar conclusions for the United States:

In sum, then, students in the three communities are being trained to play different political roles, and to respond to political phenomena in different ways. In the working class community where political involvement is low, the arena of civic education offers training in the basic democratic procedures without stressing political participation or the citizens' view of conflict and disagreement as indigenous to the political system. Politics is conducted by formal governmental institutions working in harmony for the benefit of citizens . . . In the lower middle class school system of Beta — a community with moderately active political life — training in the elements of democratic government is supplemented by an emphasis on the responsibilities of citizenship, not on the dynamics of public decision-making . . . Only in the affluent and politically vibrant community (Alpha) are insights into political processes and functions of politics passed on to those, who, judging from their socio-economic and political environment, will likely man those positions that involve them in influencing or making political decisions.[46]

Although one can only marvel at the highly convenient precision in the interaction between community, school and civics programme there is no doubting the general direction of Litt's findings.

Comparative perspectives

The central theme of this chapter has been that educational values, structure and curriculum content interrelate in such a way as to produce a carefully defined socialization process within which political predispositions are acquired. Other aspects — for example the role of the teaching profession — could have been included but this would have merely

reinforced the picture without adding to it substantially.[47] It is my conclusion that education is an important instrument of political socialization.
But so far I have not documented a clear relationship between the two
educational systems and the political behaviour of citizens, and this is a
task that remains for subsequent chapters. However, independent of this
relationship there is the question of what patterns of political behaviour
are likely to emerge given these kinds of values, structure and content.

What is surprising is the presence of striking similarities alongside
equally striking differences. At first sight the differences are more apparent
than the similarities: in Britain an elitist philosophy is reflected in a
class-based educational system that acts as an instrument of social differentiation, while American education is one of society's centralizing and
unifying forces for it espouses a common citizenship identity within a
comprehensive structure. The contrasts stem from opposing ideological
traditions working themselves out in very different societal milieux. In
spite of the conflicts, which do have substance, similar pressures force the
schools along parallel paths. In both countries success and failure have
to be legitimized. In the United States this is personalized while in Britain
it is placed on an institutional footing, but the end result is inequality.
Economic forces have resulted in the American schools increasing their
internal differentiation of pupils while in Britain economic arguments
have been used to justify the change-over from selective to comprehensive
secondary education. The end result may well be a united drive for equality
of educational opportunity within a uniform structure.

As the ethnic diversity of the United States increased there were fears
for the American way of life, so the schools became explicit instruments
of citizenship training. In Britain the same process has been accomplished
in a subtler and more indirect way, reflecting a different understanding of
citizenship within a contrasting social environment. Recent developments
in Britain, however, point to a possible merging of the two approaches. A
concerted push is under way to place the teaching of politics in secondary
schools on more formal lines. At the same time the meaning of citizenship
is under constant surveillance, as is seen in the malaise with the class
structure of our society as well as the problems created by large-scale
coloured immigration. While this is taking place a protracted battle is
being fought around the structure of the educational system. The way these
various threads relate to one another is an important political, as well as
academic, issue, for it has widespread repercussions.

Underlying these cross-currents is the central problem of legitimating
role socialization in two societies that have universal values. In broad
terms I have sketched how British and American schools have assisted this
task. It is a process fraught with danger, for formal education itself has
certain inbuilt inconsistencies that work against the perpetration of simple
messages of social control. In an interesting, speculative article Hess
comments,

The process of political socialization is related to social class and intelligence, with the result that the children with less understanding of the phrases or the underlying concepts are working class and of low or moderate educational attainment. This means that. given the relatively lower level of education of minority and poor segments of the population, there is less understanding of the basic principles of operation of the system among those groups that tend to be excluded from the resources and rights of the society. Were this not true, there would have been in all likelihood much more protest sooner. It is no accident that a primary source of protest has been the student groups and that the leaders of the civil rights 'revolution' have been persons of considerable formal training and experience with ideas and the relevance of ideas to action.[48]

What Hess is saying is that one cannot rely upon the highly educated to support the status quo, and that they are capable of making a more effective critique because of the kinds of skills they have acquired while receiving an education. I would add that the critique would be more effective still if those who have received less education had not been successfully socialized into accepting some of the implications of this, in other words if inequality had not been legitimated. Education, therefore, is a potentially subversive force, for besides implanting values it can transmit the skills that enable individuals to question them or, failing that, to monitor their implementation. In both countries the schools attempt to implant a sense of patriotism alongside a rather bland and simple-minded notion of democracy. In neither case are these universal values likely to be anywhere near sufficient to placate the evident inequalities that are associated with role socialization.

I have argued that to appreciate the political impact of formal education it has to be understood in terms that relate it to its societal context. For example, schools cannot be considered independently of their social class composition for it is educational values and structures that partially determine that composition. Such an approach makes it impossible to ascertain the influence of formal education upon political behaviour independently of other variables. This may appear to be an all-or-nothing viewpoint, but it stems from a model of political socialization in which influences are integrated with one another rather than their acting as discrete entities. Political education is not simply civics education but is rather the attempt to implement a set of values through particular structures and associated curricula. Although schools may be no worse than the societies in which they are located it is hard for them to be much better.

Notes

1. As illustrated by the 1974 riots in the city of Boston.
2. See pp. 226–229.
3. This is one of the themes in the Black Papers on British education. See for example, R. Lynn, 'Comprehensives and equality: The quest for the unattainable', *Black Paper No. 2*, Critical Quarterly Society, London, 1969, pp. 26–33.

56

4. op. cit., p. 50.
5. T. H. Marshall, 'Social selection in the Welfare State', in A. H. Halsey *et al.* (eds.), *Education, Economy and Society,* Free Press, New York, 1961, p. 151.
6. op. cit., p. 116. Much the same point has been made with regard to formal politics instruction in British schools. See G. Mercer, 'Political education and socialization to democratic norms', University of Strathclyde, Survey Research Centre, Occasional Paper No. 11, pp. 27–30.
7. For a summary of this point of view see C. Jencks *et al., Inequality: A Reassessment of the Effect of Family and Schooling in America,* Basic Books, New York, 1972, pp. 253–256.
8. For an excellent discussion of the major trends in the history of American education see E. A. Krug, *The Shaping of the American High School,* Harper and Row, New York, 1964.
9. For some of the comments of the Taunton Report of 1868 see J. Stuart Maclure, *Educational Documents: England and Wales, 1816–1963,* Chapman and Hall, London, 1965, pp. 95–96.
10. ibid., p. 75.
11. ibid., p. 87.
12. The sceptic was Robert Lowe who was later to become President of the Board of Education. See R. Williams, *The Long Revolution,* Chatto and Windus, London, 1961, p. 141.
13. ibid., pp. 104–105.
14. So far I have construed the reasons for the state expansion of education in strictly one-sided utilitarian terms. Obviously they could be interpreted in different terms, i.e. how they benefited the individual, including members of the lower classes, besides the state and established elites. It should become clear as the chapter proceeds that I am acutely interested in illustrating the contradictions within and between education theory and practice. Perhaps Bentham pointed the way to a limited reconciliation of these contradictions by showing a calculating elite how to manipulate structures that aided societal stability while assisting the limited self-improvement of the people.
15. For a discussion of the debates on the position of the classics in the high schools see Krug, op. cit., ch. 3, 4.
16. ibid., p. 12. Care should be taken not to misinterpret this information. At this time the number of high-school graduates was very small indeed and their eventual careers (mainly the teaching profession) were not that prestigious. The point I am making is that American education is traditionally less of an instrument of social class control than the British schools. As I later note, it became a more potent instrument of social control as time passed, but again this has not been organized along class lines in the same way as it has in Britain.
17. On this see Tapper, op. cit., ch. 1, 10.
18. R. H. Tawney, *Secondary Education For All,* Allen and Unwin, London, 1922, p. 33.
19. For a discussion of this see Tapper, op. cit, ch. 5.
20. *ibid.,* pp. 18–25.
21. C. Lacey, 'Some sociological concomitants of academic streaming in a grammar school', *British Journal of Sociology,* **17** (1966), 245–262, and C. Lacey, *Hightown Grammar,* Manchester University Press, Manchester, 1970, pp. 57–62.
22. B. Jackson and D. Marsden, *Education and the Working Class,* Routledge and Kegan Paul, London, 1962, pp. 152–153, 158–159, 192–193.
23. Tapper, op. cit., pp. 18–25, 60–66.
24. This is true in spite of the broader American definition of higher education, and the fact that in most cases the cost falls on the individual and his family.
25. J. Floud and A. H. Halsey, 'Introduction', in A. H. Halsey *et al.,* op. cit., pp. 1–12.

26. See C. Jencks and D. Riesman, *The Academic Revolution,* Doubleday, New York, 1968, pp. 99–100.

27. For an interesting article on the 'cooling out function' of the junior colleges see B. R. Clark, 'The cooling-out function in higher education', in A. H. Halsey *et al.,* op. cit., pp. 513–523.

28. J. Coleman, 'Style and substance in American high schools', in P. Ehrensaft and A. Etzioni (eds.), *Anatomies of America,* Macmillan, London, 1969, p. 323.

29. Of course Jencks does not see education as totally irrelevant but that it should be justified in its own terms rather than what it can do to promote individual economic and social advancement. See C. Jencks, *et al.,* op. cit., p. 256.

30. op. cit., pp. 4–5.

31. A point made by R. Wilkinson, but as he notes the following verse is rarely sung by today's schoolchildren:

> The rich man in his castle,
> The poor man at his gate,
> God made them, high or lowly,
> And ordered their estate.

R. Wilkinson, *The Prefects: British Leadership and the Public School Tradition,* Oxford University Press, London, 1964, p. 25.

32. J. Gaus, *Great Britain,* Chicago University Press, Chicago, 1931, p. 157.

33. ibid., p. 162. For wider perspectives still see the various contributions to M. Ballard (ed.), *New Movements in the Study and Teaching of History,* Temple Smith, London, 1970.

34. See M. Weddeel, 'The teaching of citizenship through domestic subjects', in *Education for Citizenship in Secondary Schools* (a publication of the Association for Education in Citizenship), Oxford University Press, London, 1936, pp. 323–328.

35. Consider this quote by Oliver F. G. Stanley in one of their publications: 'The decay of democracy abroad has led many people to the conclusion that, if those democratic institutions, which we in this country agree are essential for the full development of the individual, are to be preserved, some systematic training in the duties of citizenship is necessary'. ibid., Foreword.

36. It is difficult to tie down the objectives of a journal, but I think this comment fairly reflects the content of editorial opinion as well as many articles appearing in the journal *Teaching Politics.*

37. 'A programme for political education: An explanatory paper', sponsored by the Hansard Society, associated with the Politics Association, and funded by the Nuffield Foundation. This is Document No. 1, July 1974, produced by B. Crick and I. Lister. Reg Prentice, the former Secretary of State for Education and Science, has provided the official encouragement. See R. Prentice, 'Civic education', *Teaching Politics,* 4 (1975), 5–7.

38. P. Abrams, 'Notes on the use of ignorance', *Twentieth Century* (Autumn 1963), pp. 67–77. Abrams is castigating the British Constitution course rather than civics programmes but his comments have this wider applicability.

39. For a discussion of the activities of some of the professional associations in this area see Krug, op. cit., ch. 14.

40. Quoted in M. Krug, *History and the Social Sciences: New Approaches to the Teaching of Social Studies,* Blaisdell, Waltham, Massachusetts, 1967, p. 198.

41. C. Merriam, *The Making of Citizens,* Teachers College Press, New York, 1966, p. 418. Note that this edition of Merriam's book has an introduction and notes by G. Z. F. Bereday.

42. G. Bereday and B. B. Stretch, 'Political education in the U.S.A. and U.S.S.R.', *Comparative Education Review,* 7 (1963), 9–16.

43. This review of American civics courses is based on the following material: L. H. Clark *et al., The American Secondary School Curriculum,* Macmillan, New York, 1965; E. A. Krug, *The Secondary School Curriculum,* Harper and Row, New

York, 1960; J. P. Lumstrum, 'The teaching of controversial issues in social studies instruction', in B. G. Massialas and F. R. Smith (eds.), *New Challenges in the Social Studies,* Wadsworth, Belmont, California, 1965, pp. 121–153; B. G. Massialas, *Education and the Political System,* Addison-Wesley, Reading, Massachusetts, 1969, ch. 3, and B. G. Massialas, 'We are the greatest', in C. B. Cox and B. G. Massialas (eds.), *Social Studies in the United States,* Harcourt, Brace and World, New York, 1967, pp. 167–195.

44. op. cit., p. 229.

45. The work of Mark Krug and B. G. Massialas falls into this category. See also this quote from Dewey: 'When the school introduces and trains each child of society into membership within such a little community, saturating him with the spirit of service, and providing him with the instruments of effective self-direction, we shall have the deepest and best guaranty of a larger society which is worthy, lovely and harmonious'. J. Dewey, *The School and Society,* University of Chicago Press, Chicago, 1915 (2nd edition), p. 29.

46. E. Litt, 'Civic education, community norms, and political indoctrination', *American Sociological Review,* **28** (1963), 74.

47. For the role of the teacher in the political socialization process see D. Jaros, 'Transmitting the civic culture: The teacher and political socialization', *Social Science Quarterly,* **49** (1968), 284–295.

48. R. D. Hess, 'Discussion: Political socialization in the schools', *Harvard Educational Review,* **38** (1968), 532–533.

Chapter 4

Political Socialization and Political Participation

Participation and socialization theory

Empirical political science has devoted a great deal of its time and energy to the study of political participation. Following in the footsteps of the pioneers, whole research centres have sacrificed themselves to the cause.[1] If one fact stands out from all the others, it is that many citizens of the Anglo-American democracies are decidedly politically apathetic. So great are the levels of apathy that some have been led to reconsider the character of democratic theory, with the result that this body of literature is both theoretically and empirically innovative.[2] The existence of several strata of participation — from the most intense forms of involvement to total political apathy — is a clear indication of political role socialization. One of the main strands in normative democratic theory is that citizens should be involved in the political process. This may have been modified somewhat by social scientists but still the exhortation in favour of participation continues unabated.[3] On the surface, therefore, the contradiction between the participatory norm and the prevailing level of apathy is evident. The central task of this chapter is to examine to what extent the socialization research can explain this conflict. Whereas the later chapters analyse the implications of contemporary crises for socialization theory, this concentrates upon one of the continuing characteristics of the Anglo-American polities and so represents a traditional research field.

In the previous chapter I argued that inconsistent educational goals made it difficult to predict the impact of formal education upon behaviour. There is a parallel in this chapter in that democratic theory, which provides the legitimation for participation, may be concerned with either the welfare of the individual or the character of the system, and the two are not necessarily complementary. When examining the contribution that socialization research has to make to our understanding of the contradictions between norms and behaviour, this theoretical context cannot be ignored. Although this may involve a limited number of short excursions into the realm of democratic theory, this will be in keeping with the general objective of trying to place the study of socialization within a wider framework.

Understanding participation

If political participation can be described as a democratic norm then it would be logical to expect the state to encourage socialization patterns that maximize participation. But in a representative democracy, and in all other political systems for that matter, there has to be a division of political labour.[4] The problem is not so much that some participate more than others but rather the presence of almost total political apathy amongst a sector of the population. The participatory norm does not mean that all forms of political activity will be accorded approval, for, as Kornhauser writes,

It is one thing for a population to participate at specified times and in institutional ways for defined interests, through trade associations and trade unions, or in elections. It is quite another to create *ad hoc* methods of direct pressure on critical centres of society, such as 'the invasion' of a state legislature, street political gangs etc.[5]

So some forms of participation are more acceptable than others. Whether an act can be accorded political status is of some significance, and considerable controversy surrounded the labelling of the protest movements of the 1960s.[6]

In order to aid stability socialization has to assist in the creation of certain forms, as well as a particular pattern, of political behaviour. But what happens if the end result for the individual, or his group, is one of powerlessness? Can he be expected to go on acting in the same old way as if this was irrelevant? It is widely believed that one of the defining characteristics of a democracy is that the rules governing political activity encourage all the varying shades of public opinion to be expressed. In other words, in a democracy all points of view are permissible but not all the possible forms of expressing those views.[7] If, as many believe, the rules result in certain biases in the distribution of power then socialization processes may be structured to promote powerlessness in the cause of stability.

In fact political scientists have taken the argument one stage further by explicitly praising the virtues of apathy. This has taken two somewhat different forms: a commendation of the virtues of the apathetic and a warning against too much participation. Lipset has argued that high levels of political activity may be as much a measure of internal conflict as of stability.[8] German data show that Hitler's Nazi party grew in strength as electoral participation increased. But, as Lipset himself points out, this was the reflection of growing societal tensions and not the cause of them.[9] Berelson has made the most elaborate advocacy of the functional need for apathy by claiming that it provides the American political system with both stability and flexibility.[10] A more neutral position stresses the need for a political apprenticeship before active involvement in the political process takes place. Intense participation is perfectly acceptable as long as it has been preceded by a slow induction into the mores of the system. If the aim is to maintain stability this makes sense because new participants are likely to be less attached to established parties and their sudden influx could upset delicate political balances. In Britain the franchise was expanded over a long period of time, gradually bringing new groups into the political process. This elite sponsorship of mass electoral activity could be viewed as a sophisticated attempt to control a potentially revolutionary working-class movement, especially as the Conservative party was active in recruiting working-class members.[11] The extension of the franchise to women and young people, as well as the removal of restrictions against Negro voting rights, has been followed by a steady increase in electoral participation on the part of these groups, rather than any dramatic influx of new voters.

Some of the socialization studies have added an additional refinement to the question of political participation. The ideal citizen is one who combines subject (deferential) and citizen (participatory) roles. The individual cannot be expected to be actively involved in each and every issue but he must feel he has a potential influence that can be exercised effectively if the occasion should arise. So the good citizen is not so much the active participant but rather the potential activist. This requires the individual to believe that he can have an impact upon the course of political events, so the democratic citizen is measured not so much in terms of his behaviour but more according to his attitudinal predispositions. Those who conform to this ideal type are said to be high in political efficacy. This view of participation is part of a general theme in the socialization literature that the good citizen is one who manages to reconcile a number of contradictions.[12]

It is far from clear, therefore, whether or not socialization patterns should maximize participation for doubts prevail as to both the desirable form and intensity of participation. This ambivalence follows from the general concern with system stability, and what may be good for the individual is not necessarily good for the political order. The socialization theorists have been criticized for too readily establishing a link between individual behaviour and system characteristics, but in fairness it must be said that some have been more inclined to make the connection dependent upon the characteristics of the citizenry than upon individual behaviour.[13] Some confusion exists in the work of Almond and Verba, for at times they imply that the range of characteristics found in the general population is also present within each individual.[14] It is possible to defend the democratic norm in favour of maximizing participation on the grounds that political activity improves the wellbeing of the individual and that this is more important than maintaining a certain type of polity, or that only by improving individual welfare can polities hope to maintain themselves, thus drawing a relationship between each and every individual and the nature of the political order. Contemporary political scientists saw this is a weakness in traditional democratic theory and so they set out to remedy it. The remedy was dependent upon the belief that democracies already existed (for example, the United States) and that they flourished in spite of the presence of considerable political apathy. Righteous indignation has been expressed at this apparent condoning of political apathy, but in reality the conflict is about the overall character of the Anglo-American democracies and whether this is worth preserving or not.[15] If it is worth preserving them presumably it is because the positive aspects are thought to outweigh the negative. The problem is, some political scientists implied, that the positive aspects were dependent upon the negative, and this meant the perpetuation of the latter (e.g. political apathy) to maintain the former.[16]

If the first problem in relating political socialization and participation is essentially a theoretical one (i.e. whether or not socialization patterns should maximize participation), the second is very much an empirical problem — how the relationship is to be measured. Most of the empirical work has centred around the essentially adult act of participation, that of voting, while most of the socialization studies have been based upon samples of children. At best political socialization can describe the prerequisites of participation. To some extent this is true of all the childhood studies, but the problems are more acute in relation to participation simply because there is a legally defined threshold at which one can vote, and this is the most widespread participatory act. Support, in all its various shapes and forms, can develop long before active political participation and even in adulthood may flourish independently of actual political activity. Of course plenty of surveys have been made of adult political participation and it is possible to draw out from these many implications as to the way socialization pressures shape participation, but this places the interpretations on a tentative basis.

A related reason for the lack of research into the foundations of political participation has been the overwhelming attention devoted to subject roles. This is partly because it is an easier research focus and partly because of a theory according to which subject roles developed before citizen roles. Furthermore, if the most important stage of the political learning process was the early years then participation would naturally flow out of what was learnt then, and it is not a separate problem that requires a separate explanation. So both the allocation of resources and the guiding assumptions have mitigated against a detailed consideration of participatory roles.

Unless adult political apathy is surrounded with positive connotations an evident clash emerges between the tenor of the childhood socialization studies and the realities of adult political behaviour. It is difficult to match the image of an emerging supportive democratic citizenry so prevalent in the socialization research with that of adult levels of ignorance, indifference, cynicism and outright anti-democratic attitudes. The task of matching the two bodies of evidence is made even more difficult by the tendency of the socialization theorists to work with models that prescribed an integrated process of political learning. So even if the empirical research failed to examine the development of participatory roles, the learning models suggested that this would complement the acquisition of the subject role and the end result would be the well-rounded democratic citizen.

If political participation is defined in ways that ensure it falls within established mores (e.g. voting or assisting in a party campaign) then there are clear relationships between that activity and numerous social variables. If, however, the definition is broadened to include what Kornhauser refers to as 'ad hoc methods of direct pressure on critical centres of society' then a new set of relationships will emerge. Numerous studies have found that political activity correlates highly with socio-economic status (measured by some combination of occupational status, income and education), sex, ethnic identity, age, marital status, group membership, place and stability of residence, and so on.[17] Although the bulk of the socialization evidence does not provide much information as to why these particular correlations should emerge, a limited amount of data at least suggests that the behaviour is partly a result of socialization experiences. The fact that the behavioural differences relate to social characteristics suggests distinctive life-style influences. Easton and Dennis found that under 50 per cent of the eighth-graders with low socio-economic status could be classified as high in political efficacy.[18] Greenstein found no class differences in political efficacy; none the less he comments, 'But wherever consistent class differences appeared they showed that upper-status children exceed lower-status children in capacity and motivation for political participation'.[19] In their studies of the Appalachian Mountain children Hirsch and Jaros have documented the pervasiveness of subcultural influences upon political behaviour. Jaros points to the consistency of this influence, for levels of political cynicism remained constant across the entire age range of approximately 11 to 17 years. Indeed, he is led to conclude, 'The nonvariant affect suggests the operation of a pervasive socialization agent early in the lives of these children'.[20]

These scattered pieces of evidence point to the continuous impact of socialization forces that are first felt in the early years and that continue to exercise their hold as the child grows older. However, the Easton and Dennis study also showed that the differences between groups widened as the children matured. In their sample, aged 7 to 13, both efficacy and inefficacy increased with age as the 'don't know' respondents declined amongst the older children. The adolescents who recorded the largest increase in high political efficacy came from the most-privileged families, while those who recorded the largest increase in low political efficacy came from the least-privileged families. This may be simply a consequence of greater familiarity with the meaning of the questions, or it could reflect the fact that social pressures are exerting an increasing grip, pushing the adolescents more and more towards their social class norm.[21]

Edward Greenberg has written, 'The primary question is whether orientations supportive of the present American political order are homogeneously distributed in the population, or whether subcultures of discontent and nonsupport are evident. The contention of this book is that the latter situation is closer to empirical reality.[22] In spite of this massive generalization Greenberg's own survey revealed that the younger black children showed 'great affection for the national political community', and it was only as they grew older that this affection was eroded. This erosion, he felt, was a result of having to face more directly the realities of what it meant to be a black man living in America. It seems reasonable to assume that if affection declines and alienation increases this will not encourage the more acceptable forms of participation. The outcome could be either political apathy or perhaps involvement in protest politics.[23]

What these studies suggest is that an important stage in the socialization process is the period in which the individual starts to assume his adult, including his participatory role. It is not that he may encounter new socialization experiences in the sense that he has previously, but rather what has already been learnt is now going to be put to the test in situations over which he has little control. Of course in the initial years of the life cycle the individual has few controls over his environment, but at least the socializing agents are personal figures, and the supposition — generally borne out — is that they are working in his interests. But now he has to encounter institutions rather than people and the extent to which they are prepared to accommodate him is likely to depend upon what help he can be to them, as much as anything else. The individual may be politically unaware at this stage for there are the more pressing problems of finding a job and making a living, but these concerns will influence the development of political perspectives.

Because political socialization was initially interpreted as induction into the norms of the political community, it has been interested in the prerequisites of participation than in participation *per se,* Several models of the way political behaviour is formed place attitudinal dimensions between socio-economic forces and the act of participation.[24] Foremost of these is political efficacy, and we have already seen how Easton and Dennis documented the existence of class differences in the formation of political efficacy amongst children. Not surprisingly the social and psychological variables tend to correlate, but most studies indicate that they have an effect that is independent of one another. In fact the attitudinal variables may be used to explain why a particular individual fails to follow his group norm. More interesting, and less easily understood, is the question of why individuals exposed to the same set of social forces have different psychological predispositions.

Although they have been widely employed, considerable controversy surrounds the various attitudinal concepts. It is very difficult to present mutually exclusive definitions of efficacy, cynicism, misanthropy, alienation etc., and even more difficult to formulate mutually exclusive measures. Even if the measures are discrete, what states of mind are they ascertaining? Is inefficacy simply an indication of individual powerlessness (and by implication an indictment of the individual)? Or is it a realistic response to the remoteness of the political system (and thus an indictment of the system)? This is important because it is bound to influence views of political apathy, whether to describe it in negative or positive terms. Confusions abound as to the precise relationship between participation and the psychological predispositions. It is far from clear whether the determinant of political behaviour is a specifically political attitude (e.g. political alienation) or whether the political attitude is in turn a reflection of a more general psychological predisposition (e.g. a state of anomie or distrust).[25] The explanatory strategy is both regressing and expanding!

One of the problems common to both the social and psychological explanations of political participation is that they invariably fail to clarify why a particular set of variables should have one kind of impact rather than another. The potential correlations are enormous, and the discipline has not been slow in presenting them, but it is of greater significance to know why one correlation should prevail over another. If the patterns are interpreted in the light of socialization theory then it is possible to arrive at some tentative conclusions. In his general text on political participation Lester Milbrath has argued that socio-psychological forces place some individuals closer to the political mainstream than others.[26] Over a long period of time a harmonious set of social and psychological forces have combined to tie the individual into a particular political lifestyle. At either end of the continuum are two ideal types — the activists and the apathetic — and in between are the moderately involved spectators.[27]

This conception of participation is dependent upon the notion that in order to be politically active the individual requires various kinds of skills, and that these are more likely to be learnt in one sort of environment than in another. What kind of skills are required depends upon the form of participation. To stand for office or to be actively involved in running a campaign requires organizational and/or public relations talents and, although these are by no means simply class-based, middle-class children are more likely than their working-class peers to have the opportunity to develop them. This follows from what is known about class differences in raising children, the way the educational system reinforces these familial patterns and the fact that different occupations provide unequal opportunities to develop and exercise the politically relevant talents.

It may require class-related skills to be active in politics but it scarcely takes anything other than a short time to vote, yet the evidence is that the variables that correlate significantly with high political involvement also correlate positively with voting behaviour. The individual needs a certain amount of motivation, rather than skill, to vote and he is more likely to acquire this if the act has some relevance to him. Of course this relevance can assume different forms, ranging from purely psychic satisfaction to a belief that the franchise has some impact upon the shape of public policy. Again, a socialization explanation is dependent upon the assumption that certain types of experiences will induce perceptions of relevance, while other life-styles will work against this. Presumably those who, in Milbrath's phrase, are in the centre of the political mainstream are more likely to accept the formal myths surrounding the act of voting because they can perceive tangible consequences to their behaviour. When voting is a supplement to other forms of political activity then these perceptions could be highly realistic and not simply the reaffirmation of a mythology.

A mechanistic interpretation of socialized participation would see political activity as a consequence of one set of experiences, apathy as resulting from the opposite influences, with a combination of forces producing a middle stratum containing the cross-pressured individuals. Cross-pressuring assumes that social and psychological forces exert influences that either harmonize with one another or are in conflict. The greater the degree of conflict the less likely the individual will be active politically, for he is exposed to different messages and a convenient way of resolving the dilemma is to do nothing. In a complex industrial society it is unlikely that many of us will be totally isolated from cross-pressures of one sort or another. In fact numerous examples exist where such conflict has been reconciled at least to the point where the individual is not politically immobilized. If resolution is possible in some cases then why not in others?

The socialization interpretation of participation can, therefore, easily degenerate to a simple-minded exercise in calculating the pressure and counter-pressure of various psychological and social dimensions. Ideal types exist at each of the continuum with the chances of permanent immobilization increasing towards the centre. This assumes that a particular social or psychological dimension will affect each individual very much the same way. So, except when there is cross-pressuring, it should be possible to predict behavioural outcomes. This is a very deterministic approach to understanding participation and one which implies a certain view of the socialization process, i.e. an essentially harmonious set of learning experiences that impart consistent messages to produce the involved or the apathetic citizen. Even in cases of cross-pressuring it is feasible to predict behavioural outcomes if one has a clear idea of the direction and strength of any one influence. If a democratic norm favours participation then the non-participants are those whose socialization experiences make it impossible for them to fulfil the norm. This is because to participate requires skills and predispositions that are more likely to be acquired in one environment than another. If a high value is placed upon the necessity of participation, then it could be argued that socialization experiences that fail to provide the essential skills are inadequate. This leads on to the notion of an ideal socialization pattern, and the politically apathetic can then be viewed as inadequate citizens who have suffered unfortunate experiences.

A more tentative socialization interpretation of participation would stress some of the complexities of relating learning experiences and behaviour. It is not simply a question of cross-pressuring but also the fact that the same variables can have a differential impact from person to person. Furthermore a model of the learning process in which stages interact, rather than accumulate, adds greater uncertainty to the eventual outcome. It is self-evident that political participation, especially beyond the level of voting, requires motivation and skills that are more likely to be acquired in some learning situations than others, and that strong class elements impinge upon participatory patterns. But the democratic norm in favour of an active citizenry also suggests that involvement is an effective way of controlling political elites and influencing the policy-making process. If the individual has come to the conclusion that the democratic norm in reality leads to few effective pay-offs, he may fail to act as if he were in the political mainstream, and this in spite of socialization experiences indicating that is where he belongs. The outcome could be either political apathy or intense involvement in the field of protest politics. This points to the presence of alternative continua to that of varying degrees of immersion in the political mainstream. It means that contrasting labels could be applied to the same political act, so that apathy, for example, becomes a positive gesture rather than a measure of political unawareness.

This reinterpretation of the participatory scale depends upon what meaning is attached to the democratic norm that individuals should be involved in the political process. To arrive at the conclusion that participation carries some connotations beyond the mere exhortation that citizens should be politically involved requires a certain level of sophistication. The persons most likely to acquire this are the very individuals who will have many of the skills needed to be active in the political mainstream. The evidence on student unrest suggests that the leading figures came from families in which democratic norms were used as guidelines for the family's daily routines, and Litt has shown that the subtlest and most complex interpretations of what it means to be a democratic citizen has been advanced in those schools with the highest middle-class intake.[28] This is no problem as long as the consequence is mainstream political activity but it raises a number of questions when the opposite occurs. Besides complicating the socialization explanation of participation it also confuses responses to behaviour that many may think to be reprehensible, e.g. riots. It is obviously in the interest of governments to label riots as non-political acts, and the rioters as criminals, but it is difficult to do this if it is widely felt that the riotous behaviour is a response to failings within the political system, especially the ineffectiveness of regular participatory channels.

The notion that the character of the political system is determined by a balanced pattern of citizens' behaviour necessitates making certain judgements as to what the particular acts mean within themselves. If political apathy is a counterweight to participation (i.e. they are functionally inter-related) then what is required are socialization experiences that will perpetuate that balance rather than maximize participation. This can be defended on moral grounds if the apathetic are perfectly happy with their lot, and along practical lines if they assist the functioning of the system. But what happens if the apathetic are in fact positive abstainers? Or, alternatively, if apathy is socialized (in the sense that the apathetic lack the requisite skills and attitudes) and this leads not only to political powerlessness but also to social and economic deprivation? In both cases apathy is a potential threat to system stability. When it is difficult to ascertain the precise meaning of apathy then stability is on safer grounds if everyone is participating in the political mainstream. This is especially so if it can be contained within the established boundaries but, as before, this is only likely if such activity has some meaningful consequences. However, once it starts to have such consequences (e.g. affecting the shape of public policy) this could lead to greater political instability as the pay-offs for participation are that much more tangible, and visible. So if the goal is stability it is far from clear what the best attitude towards participation should be.

If the idea of participation in the political mainstream rests upon a socialization process in which various experiences harmonize to produce an active citizen, then the concept of the potentially active citizen requires a similar blending of somewhat different ingredients. In the latter case there are presumably contradictory pressures that have to amalgamate in a complementary fashion to produce the split personality of the potential activist. As a maximization of participation requires a universal socialization process so does this alternative model of the democratic citizen, for the greater the numbers conforming to the model the more the likelihood of stability. The socialization literature has argued that the ideal citizen is a subtle combination of subject and participatory roles, and fortunately the learning process is such as to ensure that the two ingredients evolve, in sequence, within most individuals. Where this fails to take place, again it is possible to talk of inadequate or malfunctioning socialization processes. This view runs up against a reality in which a few Anglo-American citizens over-participate and a somewhat greater minority fail to participate at all. Either we are a long way from the perfect world or this is an inaccurate perception of the relationship between socialization and participation. The notion of potential activity is a particular interpretation of the democratic participatory norm. It provides no guidelines as to when it is appropriate to participate and when it is not. Perhaps even more important is the individual's ability to mobilize himself politically. Even if the citizen believes he can affect the political process it does not automatically follow that he actually has the ability to do this. Unless these skills are also transmitted in this universal socialization process, it may make very little difference that a common attitude towards participation exists, for power will accrue in the hands of those who are capable of putting the issue to the test. Generally speaking these will be the very same individuals who now participate successfully in the political mainstream.

There are, therefore, two interpretations of the relationship between socialization processes and political participation. The first sees participation as a consequence of long-term socialization pressures and the latter as the interaction of learning experiences and wider societal constraints, with differences between groups increasing as time passes. Both perspectives require some kind of understanding as to the meaning of participation. Participatory behaviour requires certain skills and predispositions, and socialization processes are influential in shaping its course because the prerequisites are more likely to be acquired in one setting than another. Because political participation is adult behaviour, its links to socialization theory are based on retrospective arguments. This has invariably started with the assumption that the act of participation has a particular meaning, and on the basis of that meaning it is possible to relate the act itself to its preconditions. Therefore, if voting is the acceptable way of exercising one's democratic rights, then it is both normal and desirable that socialization experiences should encourage the individual to vote. If certain correlations appear between a participatory act and social and psychological forces then it is not surprising that explanations should be sought as to why this is so. If the activity is designed as placing the citizen in the political mainstream, favourable individual characteristics will be deemed to emanate from the variables that correlate highly with that participatory act. Thus voting is desirable and it is significantly related to social and psychological variables that enable the individual to perceive its relevance. Perceptions of relevance — or for more intense forms of activity, the necessary skills — are desirable traits. In another example it is possible to see how apathy relates to a malfunctioning in the socialization process and the lack of skills. In each case the starting-point is the value placed upon the participatory act itself, and we have seen how if that value is changed then the links start to break down. It is thus impossible to avoid a normative theory of participation.

Socialized participation in its context

From an explanation of participation that depends upon making assumptions about socialized behaviour it is possible to travel in one of two directions — into its psychological or social context. To a limited extent I have already followed this course by trying to show that interpretations of socialized participation are heavily dependent upon evaluating the meaning of participation, including some of the normative themes that surround it. However, by placing participation in this still wider context socialization theory can be by-passed altogether. If participation, indeed all political behaviour, flows out of individual personality structures, as appears to be the theme of Robert Lane's work, this allows little room for the notion that behaviour is learnt.[29] Once the personality has been formed, and Lane places considerable stress upon early family-based experiences, then what follows is essentially a manifestation of this guiding master-plan. Of course how one behaves in the specific circumstances has to be learnt but what one learns is preordained.

As Lane has turned to the inner man so Nie and his associates have placed their faith in the deterministic powers of a general structural model. The central links in this model are as follows: [30]

Economic development	$\rightarrow$	Changes in the social structure	$\rightarrow$	Changes in the distribution of certain political attitudes	$\rightarrow$	Increased political participation

Economic development not only increases the size of the white-collar stratum but also stimulates group activities. It is within the group that the individual acquires the attitudes that predispose him to participate. They conclude that governments should sponsor organized group life, without waiting for the requisite level of economic development to occur naturally, in order to advance the cause of pluralistic democracy.[31] Besides being an absurdly simple-minded view of the relationship between complex forces this tells us nothing about the way in which the attitudinal prerequisites are acquired within the groups. What is it about group life that induces these attitudes, and is this true of all groups regardless of their aims and structures? What I am suggesting is that once you remove participation from its socialization context then the temptation to make dangerous generalizations arises.

It is obvious, however, that participation — regardless of the form it may take — is not simply socialized behaviour. Participation will vary in shape and size according to the characteristics of the political culture, the level of economic development, the nature of the social structure and the individual's personality.[32] Just as the system implications of political socialization and the assumptions about the process of political learning have been expanded in various directions, so it is possible to stretch the notion that participation is socialized behaviour. But as with the prior expansions the danger is that socialization becomes so all-embracing in its scope that nothing can be excluded. In relation to participation and socialization what is required is a more precise understanding of how the socialized behaviour interacts with its structural context.

If some of the main socialization assumptions are accepted, e.g. that important attitudes and behaviour are acquired early within the family and that these have a lifelong influence, what is required is more detailed knowledge as to how this interacts with a structural context to either reaffirm or reshape it. It is important to recognize that rather than looking at the socialization process *per se* attention has shifted to the interaction of socialized behaviour with wider societal constraints. The evidence that differences between social groups widen over time suggests that the societal constraints exercise an increasing influence as the child grows older. These may be partly political (for example, barriers against voting or the failure of parties to appeal to specific class interests), partly social (for example, a weak infrastructure of groups) or partly economic (for example, the inability to escape poverty). More than likely, pressures will interrelate to form a powerful barrier against participation. Individual responses to this situation will vary; what course they follow (and why) then needs to be charted.

The relationship, therefore, between the norm of participation and actual levels of participation is more complex than first impressions may suggest. The presence of considerable political apathy in the Anglo-American democracies is a fact. Explanations of why this is so invariably stress the importance of learning experiences, so political participation is another aspect of the political socialization process. Although I have not denied this, I have attempted to show how both interpretations of the participatory norm. as well as societal constraints, have a real bearing upon socialized behaviour. This can influence both interpretations of the behaviour, that is what meaning it has for the individual, as well as its probable consequences, that is what implications it holds for the political system. Any interpretation of the participatory norm other than that participation should be maximized severely complicates the relationship between socialization processes and political activity. A simple directive to maximize participation gives way to a tangled web intertwining certain forms of action, at certain times, in some ways rather than others, and by some individuals in preference to others. This may be sufficient to explain the gap between the democratic norm and actual behaviour but whether it legitimates it or not is another question. If behavioural differences between groups widen over time, in response to the increasing awareness of societal constraints, then what follows from these differences may be even harder to legitimate. The constraints may slowly force behavioural change but this does not necessarily obliterate the promise of what it supposedly means to be a democratic citizen.

72

Notes

1. This is best exemplified by the Survey Research Centre of the University of Michigan.
2. Whatever strictures may be levelled at this body of literature this is a strong point in its favour.
3. Even those who are sceptical of the meaningfulness of voting still favour political action. For example, 'Don't Vote, Organize' was the slogan of the Communist Party of Great Britain (Marxist-Leninist) in the 1974 General Elections.
4. Perhaps in someone's ideal world this may not be so but past and present realities are weighted against them.
5. W. Kornhauser, *The Politics of Mass Society,* Routledge and Kegan Paul, London, 1960, p. 38.
6. On this see pp. 170–173.
7. This is an extension of Schumpeter's notion that democracy is a set of rules governing elite competition for power.
8. S. M. Lipset, *Political Man,* Heinemann, London, 1960, p. 32.
9. ibid.
10. op. cit., ch. 14.
11. S. Rokkan, 'The comparative study of political participation: Notes toward a perspective on current research', in A. Ranney (ed.), *Essays on the Behavioral Study of Politics,* University of Illinois Press, Urbana, 1963, p. 73.
12. For a discussion of the importance of balancing contradictions within both the civic culture and the democratic citizen see Almond and Verba, op. cit., ch. 15.
13. D. Marsh has argued that the political socialization literature has constructed a too facile relationship between attitudes and behaviour. What I am saying is that behavioural dimensions (perhaps other than voting) have been rarely considered at all, for the assumption is that most democratic citizens are transfixed by a deferential immobilism. See D. Marsh, op. cit.
14. op. cit., pp. 474–476.
15. A good example of the righteous indignation is to be found in G. Duncan and S. Lukes, 'The new democracy', *Political Studies,* **11** (1963), 156–177.
16. This implies that change is a risky adventure for it could undermine a delicate (and beneficial) balance of social forces, which would result in more harm than good.
17. For a thorough, if somewhat dated, review of the varying influences that correlate with political participation see L. W. Milbrath, *Political Participation: How and Why do People Get Involved in Politics?,* Rand McNally and Co., Chicago, 1965. For a more recent survey of political participation in the U.S. see S. Verba and N. H. Nie, *Participation in America Political Democracy and Social Equality,* Harper and Row, New York, 1972.
18. See pp. 6–7.
19. *Children in Politics,* p. 94.
20. 'The malevolent leader: Political socialization in an American subculture', p. 570.
21. There is another example of the pressure of the job market making the individual more aware of his class position.
22. op. cit., p. IX.
23. Such a consequence is explicit in much of the work in this field. Note the title of the following reader: E. S. Greenberg *et al., Black Politics: The Inevitability of Conflict,* Holt, Rinehart and Winston, New York, 1971.
24. For a sophisticated model of this type see N. H. Nie *et al.,* 'Social structure and political participation: Developmental relationships, Parts 1 and 2', *American Political Science Review,* **63** (1969), 361–378, 808–832.
25. For the best and most detailed attempt to tie political behaviour into the general personality structure see Robert Lane's *Political Ideology.*

26. op. cit., pp. 110–114.
27. This assumes that a particular stimulus has the same impact upon all individuals. Note the voting studies have argued that *non-participation* is also a response to social and psychological cross pressuring. So some confusion exists as to what precisely is the structure of the continuum.
28. See p. 53.
29. This may be taking too deterministic a view of the personality structure, and presumably different environments can shape the same personality structure in contrasting ways. But these are difficulties that perhaps can be resolved only through the testing of specific hypotheses in contrived laboratory experiments.
30. op. cit., p. 372.
31. ibid., p. 826.
32. And of course participation will vary according to the relationship between political parties and the class structure. See S. Rokkan and A. Campbell, 'Norway and the U.S.A.', *International Social Science Journal,* **12** (1960), 72–74, 98.

Chapter 5

The Making of Political Elites

Political recruitment and elite socialization

Gabriel Almond linked political socialization to elite recruitment by making them two complementary input functions in his model of the political system.[1] General socialization processes build a common citizenship identity while elite recruitment provides another layer of socializing experiences, for, 'It recruits members of the society out of particular subcultures . . . and inducts them into the specialized roles of the political system, trains them in the appropriate skills, provides them with political cognitive maps, values, expectations, and affects'.[2] This is an explicit recognition of forms of political role socialization that go beyond subcultural differentiation, for elites are part of the established political process. This contrasts vividly with the indirect manner in which the relationship between socialization and participation has been explored. It is difficult to admit that socialization processes build behavioural patterns that contradict the democratic norm of participation, but as leadership is seen to be a normal part of the political system the same constraints do not exist.

In this chapter I intend to explore the pattern of political recruitment in Britain and the United States with a view to establishing the most important dimensions of this particular form of role socialization. Part of the process is the structure and content of elite socialization, for it is this that either confirms or waters down the parameters of political recruitment. As with the previous chapter the aim is to see how socialization *per se* relates to wider structural variables to produce patterns of behaviour. From here the analysis can follow two different directions: the wider consequences of this for the character of the political system and what new interpretations, if any, can be made of the socialization process.

Although there is a widespread recognition of the importance of elite recruitment and socialization, the empirical work is not extensive and rarely has it been given any theoretical significance. This is partly because of the way the socialization theorists have related the various problems to the more general socialization processes. Almond posited three socialization tiers — universal socialization patterns, subcultural differentiation, and elite political recruitment which set a sequence that the empirical work has followed. Almond also placed political recruitment at the end of the individual socialization process, i.e. it is something that happens after the basic political learning has already occurred.[3] In a formal sense this is true, for political positions are confined to adults and for some of the more elevated posts age barriers prevent premature promotion. But early socialization experience will influence who is, and who is not, recruited and certainly the recruitment structure will have a bearing upon subsequent behavioural constraints. So an analytical separation of these various stages should not disguise their actual integration, and the shape this takes will constitute another objective of this chapter.

For obvious technical reasons more research has been conducted into political recruitment than elite socialization. All kinds of information, much of it of very dubious quality, is available on who is recruited into politics. At the same time it is information that can readily be quantified, so satisfying the discipline's penchant for order. Elite socialization suffers from the same research disadvantages of all socialization studies in that it necessitates the examination of a process, and this requires the use of many resources. The aim is to examine the impact of the political career upon the politician's behaviour and this involved making a long-term commitment to detailed data collection and observation.

The fact that Almond made elite recruitment and socialization one of the input functions of his model of the political system meant that he saw it as a central ingredient in understanding political stability. Elite recruitment and socialization complement more general socialization processes in the system's search for stability. The pattern of recruitment and socialization will, therefore, tell us much about the wider assumptions associated with political stability. Elite recruitment may or may not reflect prevailing societal divisions, and the way in which it does or does not is likely to influence the style of institutional socialization. It is difficult to make generalizations because apparently similar societal cleavages do not have the same significance from country to country, and even if they have the same meaning they may have to be reconciled within radically different institutional settings. The political emergence of a dormant social group, leading to its institutional representation, will be handled in different ways, depending upon the established character of the institution, with the nature of the accommodation varying from one situation to the next.

The first element, then, in political recruitment is the extent to which the membership of political institutions is representative of the population. Robert Dowse has argued that because individuals can belong to numerous, perhaps conflicting groups it is absurd to base an assembly upon the principle of representation.[4] It would be impossible to agree upon the units of representation and even if agreement were possible the solution would be ridiculously complex. This implies that for a theory to be credible it must be possible to put it into effect. It may not be feasible to implement a theory in all its detail, and it may even be foolish to try, but it can act as a standard against which to measure contemporary realities. So the theory is not so much a blueprint for action but rather a measuring-rod for prevailing standards. This is especially important in the Anglo-American democracies, where one of the legitimations of the political system is its ability to represent all interests. The assumption is that representation results in allegiance and, although this may be hard to prove, the reverse is a highly tenable proposition, i.e. non-representation cements alienation. Before the abolition of Stormont there were many hallmarks of Catholic oppression but none as blatant or effective as the exclusion of the Catholic minority from executive power, and much the same has been true of the Negro American.

If political recruitment follows well-established procedures that lead to the selection of individuals from a defined social group, the likelihood of harmonious elite socialization patterns is greater. After all they have similar social experiences and have emerged via the same procedures. Few societies, however, are likely to have such harmonious patterns of recruitment, and when they do they can invariably be challenged for their unrepresentative character. In the Anglo-American democracies many ideological and social divisions have been reflected in the composition of national political institutions. Certainly they could be more representative institutions but they are not dominated by one social group. At the more local level this domination may occur, with the result that there are no apparent internal institutional cleavages, but what is likely to take place is that divisions will emerge within the dominant group to undermine its homogeneity. For example, one-party domination may result in internal religious, ethnic or class cleavages. Except, therefore, in polities that are highly centralized, dominated by one party and with well-defined ideological goals, it is difficult to think of complete elite harmony. What elite socialization may prevent is the opposite: groups with a different social and political basis being unable to cooperate with one another.

An analysis of the characteristics of those recruited into the political elite could suggest that it is highly fragmented. If the political parties were ideologically and socially self-contained entities then this initial impression would be strongly reinforced. The purpose of elite socialization is either to blur these differences or to enable compromises to be made in spite of their presence. John Dearlove has argued that stringent recruitment rules make it possible to keep the controls upon institutional behaviour both short and concise, for in such circumstances the institutional rules will be contained with in the recruitment procedures.[5] This is more likely to arise if, as in Dearlove's case study, the political institution is dominated by one political party. Where party representation is more even, institutional rules may be both explicit and elaborate in spite of all the parties enforcing stringent recruitment procedures. In certain one party districts it is conceivable that there are no formal rules for either recruitment or institutional behaviour, and control is maintained through a web of informal contacts and implicit norms.[6] In each case recruitment and institutional rules reflect social and ideological cleavages and they do not exist, or exert an influence, independently of this.

Patterns of elite recruitment and socialization take place within a specific context and, although this does not act as a straitjacket, it will influence the pattern of selection and the subsequent accommodation. The elite socialization processes may act as a mechanism for mitigating societal conflicts. This is not so much because elites will inevitably form an integrated elite stratum but rather because of the need to arrive at some conclusions about the distribution of scarce resources. So the elites may retain their identity as representatives of particular interests but still be prepared to arrive at accommodations with rival elite groups.[7] In such cases the institutional rules governing elite behaviour are likely to be intricate and could include informal agreements as to the boundaries that compromises should follow.[8] This means that elites must be in a position to bargain on behalf of those whom they represent and that institutions both facilitate interaction and make compromise worthwhile.

Where radically contrasting elites — in a social, ideological and perhaps even psychological sense — are in conflict with one another, the ability of institutional socialization processes to produce meaningful interaction is limited. By and large harmony has reigned in Anglo-American political institutions but they have existed within a societal context that has saved them from prolonged and extreme internal factionalism. In the latter part of the nineteenth century the House of Commons contained a significant minority of Irish Members of Parliament who were held together by their intense desire for Home Rule. This was their overriding goal and it meant that the compromises they were prepared to make with other parties depended upon the furtherance of this ultimate objective.[9] To see such compromises as just another example of elite accommodation is to stretch the understanding of that concept beyond the bounds of credibility, for the intent was to reshape the political system's size, form and even its mode of operation. To claim success for elite socialization processes means that the various parties involved in the game accept its essential character and want to perpetuate it rather than form alliances that they hope will eventually destroy its meaning.

Formally, the constraints upon the pattern of political recruitment in the Anglo-American democracies are limited. It is one of the rules of the game that all adult citizens have a right to seek office. This formal openness exists alongside the fact that it is almost impossible to be elected without wearing a major party label and receiving some backing from the party machine. This considerably restricts the kinds of persons who are likely to be recruited. After all it takes someone with a martyr complex to lose election after election, and even the nomination of one of the major parties may be only a stepping-stone to greater things.[10] So to enter politics it is essential to have a foothold in one of the established parties. Although this may severely limit the distribution of political power, the constraints are much greater within the institutions themselves. In fact institutional socialization processes exist primarily to perpetuate the prevailing distribution of power. Controls arise out of certain natural dimensions; for example new members will inevitably take some time to find their feet, and these are comparatively small bodies of men who have to interact at close quarters in a confined space over prolonged periods of time. This can be reinforced by both formal rules and informal norms that can be used to sanction erring members, and it is feasible for institutional socialization processes to wash out most of the more extreme differences arising out of an open pattern of political recruitment. In Britain, and to a lesser extent in the United States, the parties have considerable power for not only do they control the channels of political recruitment but also the prominent party members hold the institutional levers of persuasion.

The British referendum on continued membership of the European Economic Community saw a temporary erosion of the influence of institutional socialization processes. Conflict that was normally contained within institutions — especially the Cabinet and Parliament — came out into the open. Some went as far as to claim that the appeal to the people was being manipulated by some of the participants to further their own political careers, i.e. as a leverage to gain them more institutional power. In much the same way Congress is nowhere near the same closed institution that it was a few years ago. In the first place a Congressional career is now more of a stepping-stone in a career hierarchy rather than an end in itself. Secondly, the odium attaching itself to the Presidency following the Watergate scandal has forced a re-evaluation of Congress's role within the overall system of checks and balances. And finally the institutional equilibrium has received a severe shock from the influx of a greater proportion of new members, many of whom are simply not prepared to sit around for many years and wait patiently for power to accrue in their hands. In neither country is it clear what will be the outcome of these new forces, but that they represent a severe challenge to the power of traditional institutional socialization processes cannot be doubted.

In spite, therefore, of the claim that Britain and the United States are representative democracies, the structure of elite recruitment and socialization within itself works against this principle. This will be so for as long as political power is a scarce resource that helps to determine the distribution of other scarce resources. If, as Almond says, the aim is to perpetuate the stability of the polity, this is not a problem as long as it works. But the procedures governing elite recruitment and socialization invariably bolster the power of some interests over other interests. With the passage of time this can be conveniently disguised so that the rules are sanctified by the wisdom of the ages, or even by the grace of the deity.

The recruitment and socialization of political elites has considerable influence upon their relationship to both other elites and citizens in general. The more confined the recruits are to a particular stratum of society, the narrower the channels of entry, and the more esoteric the institutional socialization patterns the greater is the danger of elite isolation. If there are various elite groups who emerge through similar processes, the likelihood of their holding different perspectives of the world is very high, not to mention the potential for conflict between elites and citizens. Even those theorists who believe in the existence of a power elite, at either the national or local levels, usually see power as being channelled through the formal political institutions and offices.[11] Although the political recruitment and socialization patterns are highly specialized the politicians are still controlled by the power elite, which invariably means a combination of military and corporate influence. This could be interpreted simply in terms of who has the most power, and politicians toe the line drawn by their more powerful masters. Alternatively all the branches of the power elite work harmoniously with one another because they have similar societal perspectives. These similarities exist either because the elites have identical social backgrounds (for example they have the same social class origins or have attended public schools), or because career lines overlap (for example ex-military men join the corporations or corporate leaders are key political advisers).[12]

These reasons for the successful operation of the power elite make assumptions about both elite recruitment and socialization processes. If the perspectives are similar because of the kinds of persons recruited then this is a deterministic view of the socialization process, in which parallel experiences lead to parallel attitudes. At the same time it implies that early learning is of paramount importance and influences like social origins and education will exert a lifetime hold. This is also part of the notion that a smooth career line links the various branches of the power elite, for the individual never leaves the early socialization womb. As he moves from one elite sphere to the next he meets those who have been exposed to the same experiences as himself and who have reacted to them in much the same fashion.

A power elite thesis based upon the characteristics of its personnel ends up stressing the importance of recruitment patterns over socialization processes. Either no distinguishing learning experiences occur within political, corporate and military institutions or they have a common set of interests and procedures in spite of their own individual identities. Both interpretations are tenuous, for even particular institutions (for example, the United States Senate) are said to have a unique character and the central theme of socialization theory is that different experiences lead to contrasting behaviour. Of course what may unite the elites is so general as to contain all their behaviour, no matter how great the con- flicts appear to be. The power elite thesis, therefore, is dependent upon a conservative and deterministic interpretation of socialization theory and is saved only by retreating into untestable generalizations. What seems more tenable is that all elite groups are isolated from the public by their restricted recruitment paths and their internal socialization rituals. If this is so, the end result could be well-regulated elite recruitment and socialization procedures, but also considerable public discontent, because this very success leads to inaccessible elites.

If the first reason for analysing elite recruitment and socialization is that it sheds light upon the distribution of power, the second reason is its impact upon policy-making. Is it possible to predict policy outcomes on the basis of knowing something about the social backgrounds of those who have the responsibility for making it? Matthews writes, 'The convic- tion that the political decision-maker's behaviour and decisions are influenced by his personal life experiences not only has a long and honourable history but also is substantiated by modern psychological and sociological research'.[13] As one who has done more research than most into the social background of decision-makers, Matthews none the less willingly admits that it has not greatly enhanced our understanding of the policy-making process.[14] More recently Searing has argued that this is a fruitless approach to adopt:

The policy oriented attitudinal forecasting goal within the social background approach therefore appears unattainable. Where attitudinal data are available there is no need to forecast them. And where they are unavailable, the back- ground data necessary to forecast them will be unavailable as well. In short, the attitudinal forecasting goal of the social background approach may repre- sent a serendipitous step in the right direction. The research it stimulates, with a perhaps unattainable goal, turns our attention from policy science to more theoretically oriented social science problems of elite socialization.[15]

As the power elite theorists placed overwhelming reliance upon political recruitment, so Searing abandons this in favour of elite socialization and in the process narrows his focus to exclude policy outcomes. This is not just poor social science due to the failure of posit links between recruit- ment and socialization but also it implies an inward-turning discipline, one that shirks the task of the explaining probably the most important feature of the political process, i.e. its policy outcomes.

The bridge between elite social backgrounds and policy-making can be constructed with varying degrees of certainty. Few would be so naive as to predict policy outcomes simply on the basis of information about the social backgrounds of policy-makers. As Matthews' quote indicated, a decision-maker may be *influenced* by his personal life experiences but they do not automatically determine his behaviour. The Marxist concept of false consciousness is relevant here, for life experiences are changing over time and the extent to which perspectives implanted by social class origins remain 'uncorrupted' is an empirical question. Elite recruitment, whether it be into politics, the trade unions, civil service or what have you, is a long-term process and very rarely do individuals arrive at elite positions without serving lengthy apprenticeships. So, like elite socialization, elite recruitment is a gradual affair and the two are closely entwined. Moving up the career hierarchy means exposure to different pressures and experiences, with the result that the socialization milieu changes as the recruitment pattern unfolds. The extent to which social background will continue to exert an influence in spite of these forces will vary from person to person. But if we are victims of our environments then it is to be expected that working-class leaders will suffer from the sins of economism.[16]

Edinger and Searing have shown that within various national political elites adult socialization experiences were more important than childhood experiences in shaping attitudes. The two strongest determinants of elite attitudes were present or principal occupation and party affiliations.[17] All this really suggests is that when analysing policy perspectives it is necessary to consider the impact of long-term personal life experiences, to use Matthews' phrase. It is not that social background is irrelevant but it has to be looked at in relation to both recruitment procedures and elite socialization patterns. For some, active entry into political life will mean setting out on a long, possibly new and different, career line and in such circumstances radical attitudinal changes can be expected. In other cases politics may simply represent an honourable form of retirement and, as they make few demands of the institution or office, so they expect it to make few demands of them. In these cases the individual's attitudes may have been formed by adult socialization experiences but his formal entry into politics is unlikely to have much of an impact upon them. The character of adult, especially political, experiences will vary from case to case. For example, recruitment into an institution dominated by one social group that espouses a well-defined ideology is unlikely to result in many attitudinal changes because the chances of anyone but like-minded persons being recruited is slim.[18] The greater the social and ideological spread, regardless of the number of parties, the more likely is attitudinal change. What is then interesting is to see how institutional socialization processes work to both channel and contain those changes.[19]

Certain methodological problems arise when trying to relate social background characteristics to elite attitudes. It is true that individual variables — e.g. social class, education and age — may discriminate both between elites in a particular nation state and cross-nationally, but this kind of data does not tell us how individuals change their attitudes over time. The adult experiences may be more influential than those that occur in childhood but what is required is some idea of how early and later pressures interact within the individual. Agglomerating social variables does not create a social background any more than personality characteristics make an individual personality. What is required is some idea of how the discrete entities fuse to make the individual whole. Again this involves the very difficult task of following changes within individuals over time.

Although an analysis of individual career lines may be the most meaningful strategy to employ in considering the relationship between social background and elite attitudes, it does not guarantee that this within itself will provide the key to understanding why some policy positions are arrived at rather than others. Policy is made not only within an institutional context but also within a wider socio-economic and political framework. The social background characteristics and the structure of political institutions may reflect some of the wider context but they can be slow to adapt to the changing constraints. It is part of the background of US Senators that they act on behalf of certain regional interests (those affecting their states) and within the Senate they will attempt to occupy positions of power that can best serve those interests. Policies are therefore very much a response to local pressures and the interaction of those pressures with wider considerations. All that social background, elite recruitment and socialization may be doing is providing the context within which this political struggle takes place. However, these are still relevant to the policy-making process for they can influence the way policy demands are made, the kinds of compromises that are reached and in certain circumstances even the content of the demands. An example of the latter would be the reluctance to push a policy because of the realization of an unfavourable institutional response, for the structure of power within the political institutions can certainly delay effective action on many issues. So, although policy is made within a socio-economic and political environment that exerts great pressures, the elite recruitment and socialization patterns have a significant mediating influence and they are not merely a reflection of general societal forces.

Patterns of political recruitment and elite socialization in Britain and the United States

Basing his assessment upon British data, Jean Blondel has written, 'Whether one likes it or not, politics is a middle-class job and training appropriate for middle-class jobs is also training for politics.[20] And Matthews has reached much the same conclusion about American politicians:

All of the facts presented so far in this section suggest that the log-cabin-to-White House myth is rather far from the truth. For the most part political decision-makers are far from common men in either their origins or their achievements. This conclusion is greatly strengthened by the facts about their occupational backgrounds.[21]

This middle-class dominance depends very much upon the stratum of political offices under observation, for a decline in the occupational status of the incumbent follows the diminishing political importance of the office. So it is more accurate to state that at its higher reaches politics is essentially a middle-class occupation.

But even at the most elevated political echelons you will find some individuals with working-class origins. The extent of their presence depends upon the relationship between class and political structures; Matthews writes, 'Paradoxically, the more rigid and inegalitarian British society seems to have a larger proportion of the working class in positions of political authority than the more mobile and open society of the United States'.[22] The reason for this is perfectly straightforward, for the British Labour party owes its strength to the trade unions and while the party has acted as the unions' political spokesman so they have continued to provide it with organizational, financial and ideological support. Given these circumstances it was natural for the party to act as a channel of political mobility for some of its trade union members. As Guttsman has shown, the Labour party today has fewer Members of Parliament with working-class origins than it did in the past but still a considerable number of safe seats are union pocket boroughs.[23]

Whether trade union representation is the same thing as working-class representation is another issue. Trade unions usually select their parliamentary candidates on the grounds of loyalty to the union, which means long-time service as a union official. By the time the union official reaches the point of eligibility for selection as a parliamentary candidate he could be some way removed from being a member of the working class, but this is somewhat different from saying he cannot be an effective spokesman for working-class interests.[24] It is true that the union official is likely to perform duties similar to equivalent personnel in parallel bureaucracies, but to take a further step by arguing that he will consequently adopt identical political perspectives suggests a degree of occupational determinism that is hard to accept.

From the point of view of socialization theory a pertinent question is why legislatures should assume one particular class pattern rather than another. Blondel has argued that the kind of training received in a middle-class job equips one for politics so there is a direct transference of skills. But what skills and talents are required to be a successful politician? By Blondel's own reckoning they are formidable:

They are Jacks-of-all trades, knowing a little of everything, but really nothing in particular . . . They must be able to grasp quickly the main points of a question with which they are not familiar . . . they must be able to speak reasonably fluently in public, they must be able to argue a case in a debate with some cogency, they must be able to retort quickly and see the flaw in the other man's argument . . . They must also have a strong will-power and a rather thick skin. They must be able to sustain public criticism without being plunged into defeatism, or anger or both.[25]

It is difficult to imagine what occupations, middle-class or otherwise, will implant the skills that measure up to this eulogy. For forms of political activity that are non-demanding, and voting is the classic example, it is realistic to relate them to the basic prerequisites of skill and motivation. But formal entry into the political arena is structured along certain lines, and having the necessary talents may be a vital prerequisite for entry but it is by no means sufficient. Otherwise all that would be required would be to maximize the agreed skills and the processes of recruitment would be essentially irrelevant.[26]

Political sociologists from Max Weber onwards have commented upon the strong presence of lawyers in legislatures.[27] This specialist analysis provides several clues as to what it takes to establish a political career. In the first place the individual needs the personal skills that are part of the politician's repertoire — the ability to mediate, conciliate and advise.[28] These are roughly parallel to the kinds of characteristics stressed by Blondel. Secondly, the structure of the legal profession lends itself to a political career. Matthews argues that amongst the high-prestige professionals it is the lawyer who can most safely forsake his practice for a stint in politics.[29] Apparently the law changes so slowly that it is possible to keep abreast of developments and meantime pursue a political career! A law firm is prepared to dispense with one of its partners, as a political career could provide it with new contacts and business, and for the individual it opens up the possibility of a judicial appointment. So the skill requirements and the structure of the profession interact almost to promote entry into politics.

There is little evidence that other middle-class professionals are in the same apparently privileged position as the lawyer. Comparisons between the trade union official and the lawyer suggest the need for very specialized prerequisites rather than general social class traits. Both have common skills in the proffering of advice and the reconciliation of conflicting interests. They are also backed by the resources that enable them to enter politics. The lawyer will be supported by his partners and the union candidate can expect his campaign expenses to be paid. Before Members of Parliament received a salary the trade unions paid their sponsored members some living expenses. In both cases this is done for concrete reasons: the law firm is interested in establishing contacts and enhancing its prestige and the trade union wants to monitor legislation and have its spokesmen move into action when the need arises. This suggests that the prerequisites are a combination of skills and motivation backed by resources from groups that have specific interests to foster.

In Britain politics has traditionally been the career of the aristocracy and not the middle classes. The landed aristocracy exercised paramount political power some considerable time after the extension of the franchise to the urban proletariat and its power has slowly been eroded.[30] Even ✓ today important vestiges of aristocratic influence remain within the Tory party at both local and national levels.[31] This retention of aristocratic power throws some light upon the political recruitment process. One of the traditional myths was that aristocrats participated in politics because it was expected of them and out of a sense of *noblesse oblige* they dedicated themselves to public service.[32] This was not a consequence of family pressure but more a question of class rights and duties. Part of the myth is that not only did a particular class expect to govern but also others (i.e. the governed) expected it of them. Whether the mythology was a widely accepted societal norm we will investigate in another chapter, but its continuing popularity as an explanation of aristocratic power cannot be doubted.[33] If it was a class-based norm that politics was the business of aristocrats, it has also to be remembered that their societal position generated a real interest in their holding the reins of political power and that they were the largest class with both the leisure and skills necessary to follow a political career. These immense advantages were cemented by their institutional power-base, for the House of Lords provided the titled aristocrat with an automatic entrée into politics.

An analysis of the social origins of the members of the pre-1832 Reform Bill Parliament would probably lead to the conclusion that an upper-class background was highly conducive to a political career. This was simply because the criteria it took to establish such a career were the prerogative of that class, but when similar advantages accrue to other groups — whether they be American lawyers or Welsh coalminers — they are just as capable of taking advantage of them. Only a very small percentage of almost any group will pursue a political career, and this is as true of the British aristocracy who have a guaranteed right of entry into politics as of American lawyers who apparently have all the necessary qualifications. What distinguishes one social group from another is the overall pattern of their control of elite positions. Thus most coalminers remain manual workers throughout their lives, with perhaps a few becoming politicians or leading trade union officials. Members of the aristocracy, however, will have access to the elite stratum of the army, Church, civil service, industry and finance, to the legal profession as well as politics. These are positions from which they can exercise considerable indirect political influence, unlike coalminers who remain coalminers. What then becomes interesting is why, given a variety of possible elite careers, one of them should be chosen rather than the other. This undoubtedly means looking beyond skills and advantages to more personal characteristics such as motivations and interests, family patterns of socialization, personality traits and even chance.

Although Edinger's and Searing's data show that elite attitudes are not internally differentiated by prior educational experiences, it still remains true that political elites have a much higher educational level than the general population.[34] Matthews notes, 'Moreover although the long range trend has been toward more highly educated decision-makers they appear always to have been greatly superior in education to the citizens at large'.[35] Again the question is why this should be so. Formal education leads to the acquisition of certain skills, and if these skills are of help in establishing a political career, then this provides the link between education and politics. Alternatively, education could have a more indirect impact by opening up occupational opportunities that are especially appropriate for the politically ambitious. This would seem to be the case in the United States, where it is easier to correlate occupational types and political careers than formal education and entry into politics. Beyond the fact that in America politicians are better-educated than the general public, no special trends emerge. This is in direct contrast to Britain, where a strong relationship between a prestigious public school education and a political career still flourishes.

Unlike the American law school which imparts specific occupation skills, the British public schools aim to create 'the well-rounded' gentleman or, in Wilkinson's more cynical phrase, 'the synthetic gentleman'.[36] This is a throw-back to traditionally aristocratic values; the nineteenth-century public schools aimed to inculcate this tradition in the children of the bourgeoisie, Again, this kind of educational experience may be peculiarly appropriate for the budding political activist, but several facts suggest that we must look beyond the content of formal education. It is possible to mitigate the cost of private education, but without a substantial middle-class income it is almost impossible to send a child to one of the public schools. This is especially true of a school like Eton, which stands out even amongst the public schools for its political connections.[37] Given this type of pupil intake, a public school education will inevitably lead to the making of contacts which could prove decisive in establishing an elite career, political or otherwise. All the pressures pushing the individual towards a political career may arise from personal motivation or the family, but it is the public school where the rich and the potentially powerful can establish their mutually reinforcing contacts.[38] It is a central ingredient in the old-boy network.

A public school education isolates the individual pupil from aspects of the wider society. He receives his education at a private preparatory school, fellow pupils are of a similar class status to himself, the schools are single-sex establishments, inter-school contacts are with schools of the same type and status, and contact with the immediate neighbourhood is severely curtailed. In other words the school is his life for it is where he sleeps, eats, studies and plays. The formal content of the curriculum, as well as the informal rituals, are traditionally quite distinctive so adding a special aura to this isolated existence.[39] It is these experiences that have led some to refer to the public schools as closed societies and others to describe public-school pupils as a cloistered elite.[40] The end product of such a peculiar educational experience cannot help but stand out from the mass of the citizens. Besides the actual educational attainments constant reference is made to the public-schoolboy's dress, accent and even his mannerisms.

In what ways does this kind of educational experience help to promote a political career? It cements the links between members of various elite strata and in the process distinguishes them from other citizens. This helps to control entry into elite positions. The higher civil service is still dominated by ex-public-schoolboys and this is in spite of the fact that entry is, in theory, according to merit. The implication is that non-members of the magic circle do not even bother to apply; they simply perceive this sphere of the political elite is outside their frame of reference.[41] Institutional socialization will be smooth if most of the entrants have common class reference-points. This is another example of the incorporation of the socialization process within the pattern of recruitment, and if this bias is public knowledge it give the insiders, those who are most likely to fit in, considerable psychological advantages in their pursuit of an elite career.

The traditional public school ethos propagated the blessings of government service and part of its educational experience was to explicitly encourage pupils to enter its ranks.[42] As the relative economic advantages of a public as opposed to a private career have shifted steadily in favour of the latter, this ethos has declined, but one of the past hallmarks of a gentleman was his devotion to public service coupled with his refusal to dabble in 'mere trade'. In the latter half of the nineteenth century the state faced the problem of administering an increasingly complex industrial society at home as well as an enormous empire overseas. What better way was there for the public-schoolboy to show his devotion to the state than to bring the benefits of white civilization to some remote and hostile corner of the world?

The public school influence upon politics has surfaced in several areas. Although in the mid-nineteenth century the Northcote-Trevelyan reforms placed entry into the civil service on an open and competitive basis, terms still conveniently favoured those who had received a public school education.[43] The ideal recruit was the well-rounded scholar, one who had received a general, classics-based education. (Whether the classics were used by the public schools to provide a broad educational experience or became a routinized exercise in learning dead languages is a matter of controversy[44]). Since the Second World War the number of public-school entrants into the higher civil service has declined steadily, but their entry is still disproportionately high and this is especially so in the more prestigious Foreign Service. It is doubtful if even these small shifts can be interpreted to infer that the administrative class is less educationally exclusive, for the Oxbridge stranglehold on recruitment persists. Certainly more suburban grammar-schoolboys are finding their way into its ranks, but before entering they have spent three years in one of the twin ivory towers.[45] Graduates from other universities simply do not apply in anywhere near the same numbers, with the result that these highest echelons of the civil service are an Oxbridge, rather than a public school, preserve. What is particularly interesting is why graduates from other universities should accept this state of affairs. It is as if their perceptions of what is required to enter lead them to rule themselves out. A career image helps to maintain that image by controlling the pattern of recruitment.

The Conservative party has been a refuge for ex-public-schoolboys for quite some time and their numbers in the parliamentary party are as high today as at any time this century. What is as significant is the steady increase the number of ex-public-schoolboys within the ranks of the parliamentary Labour party. This trend could be interpreted as evidence that the public schools have a peculiar talent for training politicians to the point that they infiltrate the ranks of a party that has shown varying degrees of hostility towards private education. But this could be a consequence of more general political developments. As the Labour party has grown in size so its social base has widened, and as it has grappled with the problems of government so its ideological position has blurred and become more moderate.[46] The outcome is a major intrusion of middleclass personnel into the party both within and outside Parliament, to the point where Hindess can talk of 'the decline of working class politics'.[47] Labour prime ministers have even shown the same tendency as Conservative prime ministers to appoint Cabinet members who 'wear the same old school tie' as themselves.[48]

As with the recruitment of class or occupational strata into politics, it can be pointed out that the actual percentage of ex-public-school pupils who follow a political career is very limited. Given that the size of the national political elite — no matter how defined — is small, this would be true of the political recruitment level of any large social group, and so it makes much more sense to consider the composititon of the political elite itself and perhaps the comparative chances of different social groups gaining entry into it. From this perspective it is reasonable to stress the important contribution that American lawyers make to American politics and the public schools to British politics. The additional point is that, although only a small percentage of public-schoolboys enter politics, most of them becomes members of one elite group or another, which gives them considerable indirect, as well as direct, political power. Thus the fact that under 1 per cent of a group may pursue a political career is no indication of the way the political recruitment process is tilted for or against that group, and certainly no measure of the amount of political power it wields. In circumstances in which all groups contribute under 1 per cent to the political elite, other comparisons must be made to discern the patterns of recruitment and power.

The social background of political elites could be extended *ad infinitum* to include such factors as age, past political experience, sex, ethnic origins, membership, in voluntary associations, religious affiliations, etc. Besides being a tedious task the returns from such an examination would diminish with each additional item. So rather than pursue this line of enquiry I will turn directly to the question of elite socialization.

Prewitt assesses the impact of recruitment experiences upon the behaviour of politicians as follows:

Intervening between initial socialization and incumbent behaviour are political experiences that condition subsequent behaviour irrespective of factors associated with initial socialization . . . Recruitment and induction experiences may be of this kind; such experiences are closer in kind to those of the incumbent office-holder. They serve as guidelines for the incumbent's present behaviour.[49]

The recruitment and induction experiences are supplemented by another layer of socialization, the politician as office-holder. Prewitt continues,

In addition, institutional considerations and pressures undoubtedly provide direction as the officeholder relates to his constituency, his party, or his interest groups; and his interactions within the legislative or council setting may be the primary factor accounting for how he evaluates his own performance.[50]

Both local and national political elites in Britain and the United States work within an institutional context and it is the learning experience of this environment that constitutes elite socialization.[51] That this is a closed, even esoteric, learning experience is reflected in the literature. Anthony Sampson, making a commonplace observation, notes, 'It is the sense of a club which is the most obvious feature of the Commons'.[52] William White refers to the Senate as 'the Citadel' and Donald Matthews writes of 'US senators and *their* world'.[53] This conveys the impression that these institutions are hallowed, and only the initiated can hope to understand the rituals and participate in the magic ceremonies.

A norm that appears to be common to all institutions is that new entrants should serve a reasonably lengthy apprenticeshhip. The new recruits are required to be deferential and by and large they appear to accept their menial role. Dearlove quotes the senior councillors of the Royal Borough of Kensington and Chelsea as giving the following advice to newcomers: to keep quiet and learn the ropes, attend regularly and make sure they have done their homework, specialize their interests, show loyalty to their party, and curtail their outside interests.[54] In their study of freshmen Californian state legislators Price and Bell suggest that such norms are learnt quickly, and that the degree to which they are internalized exercises considerable influence upon who will subsequently hold positions of power.[55] It is fascinating to see this norm under pressure in the House of Representatives with so many new entrants of late.

A natural complement of the apprenticeship rule is that the most powerful positions accrue to those who have seniority. This is partly a consequence of institutional rules, as in the US Senate, and partly a result of the accumulation of experience that accompanies long-serving membership.[56] Polsby argues that the seniority rule is part of the institutionalization of legislatures.[57] As the size and work-load of legislatures has increased so the organization of business has been placed on a more rational footing. This is seen in the adoption of standard procedures that help to mitigate conflict by providing clear behavioural guidelines for the interested parties. But at the same time this can consistently place power in certain hands and just as consistently exclude others. The seniority rule is of this nature and, although it may seem a rational way to conduct business, these wider political implications cannot be ignored.

By dint of their profession politicians are engaged in political controversy, but much of the conflict is ritualized and nowhere is this better exemplified than in their legislative behaviour. The debating style determines who can speak, what can — and more importantly cannot — be said, and the acceptable form of response. These arrangements embody practical considerations, given the intensity of the interaction and what is at stake, but they also help to mitigate political as well as personal conflict. It is not that party policy will be modified by the debating style but that it will help to contain some of the more extreme mavericks. Even mavericks will want certain things from the institution and the price they have to pay is working within the rules. If the legislature contains a maverick group, rather than an individual, then the group's power may depend more on its size and tactical alliance than on conformity to the rules, but even in these cases a deliberate sabotaging of institutional procedures is unlikely for it may upset allies as well as enemies. The style of interaction helps to isolate the political elite by providing them with a common socialization experience that is not shared by other citizens. For example, just as the British civil service has its own internal language, so it responds to citizens' complaints in an equally stylistic, perhaps incomprehensible, manner.[58]

Central to the elite socialization experience is the notion of institutional loyalty. It is expected that members will make periodic noises to the effect that the chamber is an august body that should be accorded respect and dignity.[59] This can help to cement institutional ties in the face of a cynical world; and it enables the more conservative members to cast a benevolent eye upon the most wayward of their colleagues so long as they profess loyalty to the group. What particularly upset many of the fellow Senators of Huey Long and Joe McCarthy was that their rabble-rousing would bring disrepute upon that most elevated of bodies, the US Senate. As Huitt has commented, they continually committed the unpardonable sin of flouting the dignity of the Senate.[60]

These formal rules and informal norms are not a narrow straitjacket, but will bear differently upon individuals according to the goals they set themselves and the position they occupy within the institution. Old hands appear to be able to do things that are not permitted newcomers but their ability to manoeuvre is sanctioned by the rules and so confirms their legitimacy.[61] What is more pertinent is the scope that leadership gives to the incumbent. Lyndon Johnson was an extremely adroit Senate leader and he exercised more power than previous holders of the post.[62] As such he was able to reinterpret the rules in ways that magnified his own power. So, although universal institutional rules and norms may exist, there is also an internal division of labour that requires some to act differently from others. Furthermore each particular role can be reshaped somewhat according to the individual's and group's power and inclinations.

This flexibility depends upon differentiation in the pattern of rules and their interpretation, but occasionally external factors can intrude to upset the balance. A well-entrenched member of the California State Legislature complained about the cockiness of the 1966 freshmen legislators. Their nerve had been bolstered by an especially large intake of new members in that year and this provided them with a base from which to attack the rules.[63] As the US Senate becomes more of a springboard for the Presidency, rather than a career goal within itself, so it must become more difficult to keep the ambitious junior members in line. They have a name to make and they are not going to make it by keeping quiet and waiting patiently to be accepted as members of the inner sanctum.

The unequal mutual need within political institutions means that rules can usually be maintained without the application of overt sanctions. The speaker or chairman has powers to ensure the orderly conduct of debates. If it is deemed necessary a member can be called upon to retract his remarks and in more extreme cases can be suspended or even expelled. Persistent misbehaviour may result in a member being ostracized by his peers; Harold Wilson once called upon the Commons to treat a Member of Parliament as a 'parliamentary leper' almost before the man had taken his seat.[64] Wilson felt this man's presence brought the Commons into disrepute and he should be treated accordingly. These are cases of friction that surround the edges of every smooth-running institution. Members are kept in line by the fact that regardless of the goals they set themselves, these can rarely be accomplished without the co-operation of fellow members. They have a common interest, therefore in making the system work and this transcends most boundaries. If real power is in the hands of those who formally control the institutions then it is obvious that they will command the most deference. It is the large number of freshmen legislators in the present US House of Representatives that has helped to balance the mutual needs of new and old members.

The first and obvious function of institutional rules and norms is to enable the incumbents to achieve their designative goals, but the rules ensure that they will be achieved in one way rather than others. If power accumulates in the hands of those who abide by the rules then the best-socialized member will also become the most powerful member. It is central to both White's and Matthews' views of the Senate that the institution is run by a powerful insider clique who uphold the sanctity of the rules. Although Huitt is correct to point out that perhaps not every Senator wants to become a member of this ruling oligarchy, it is difficult to imagine any objective being achieved without some accommodation to institutional norms, even today's troubled times.

The boundaries that contain elite behaviour are not inflexible, and within them the individual works out the role he is going to play. Generally speaking, the more he wishes to maximize his power within the institution the more closely he will follow the path set by those who hold the reins of power. While it can be expected that certain rules will be accepted by everyone — for example institutional loyalty and ritualized interaction — the extent of obedience will depend upon what goals the representative has set himself. But few goals can fail to include the successful promotion of desired legislation and this means courting the goodwill of those who exercise most control over the legislative process. It is this dependence on others, a dependence that is rarely mutually balanced, that bolsters support for the rules. There may be 'outsiders' and even 'mavericks' but precious few 'loners'.

Differences in the structure of British and American politics have a bearing upon recruitment and elite socialization. First and foremost is the fact that the British system is unitary while the American is based upon the separation of powers. This means that political career lines are inevitably more fragmented in America than in Britain. In the United States there is movement between the local and national branches of government, as well as between the executive and legislature, but these represent significant shifts in a career pattern rather smooth transitions. This separation of powers means that effective political power is more diffuse in the United States than in Britain, with the consequence that in America more meaningful careers can be established either within legislatures or at the local rather than the federal level. The expansion of the Presidency has undermined this, but the Senate is still a long way from being on a par with the House of Commons or a state legislature with a borough council. This confines career aspirations, for what would be a promotion in Britain represents a demotion in America. Lyndon Johnson is a classic case, for until that eventful day in Dallas he was as ineffectual as the nation's formal second-in-command as he had been powerful in the Senate.

The centralized character of British politics is reinforced by the political parties. They select the overwhelming majority of candidates, they control the behaviour of their members within the political institutions, and their strength determines who will form the government of the day. In the selection of the Labour and Conservative parliamentary candidates a delicate balance prevails between the power of the local constituency's selection committee and Transport House or the Central Office of the Conservative party. In theory, the latter have the final say in the choice of a parliamentary candidate, but in reality it is unwise of them to intervene directly in the selection procedures.[65] To do so would antagonize the local party stalwarts and most likely ensure the rejection of any candidate they favoured. Local parties have no clear guidelines as to why they choose one candidate rather than another, but in the case of the Labour party strong constituency links can bind them to a trade union or the Co-operative Society, while in the Conservative party the occasional seat has a family tie. One member of a selection committee in a safe Tory seat has written, 'We need to know, before we start on the procedure of interviewing and so on, that the person concerned is a sound, decent person who has some knowledge of politics and public life, and who is, above all else, a good Conservative'.[66] If it is such an open race then we may well ask why the selection process is so biased against women, Jews and Catholics, the under-30s and over-60s, immigrants, and, in the case of the Conservative party, trade unionists.[67]

The power of the local party activists is indirectly curtailed by the fact that candidates do not have to fulfil a residency requirement. Candidates may deem it politically wise to maintain a residence in their constituency as well as London but it is not obligatory. It makes sense for a constituency to opt for a man with some experience of campaigning, and what better experience could he have than the prior contesting of an election elsewhere? The politically ambitious can search for a safe seat on which to base their political futures. The selection committee may be very parochial but it is not always easy to resist the claims of the talented, and perhaps well-known outsider against the local nonentity, especially as the procedures will highlight the differences. The local party could be flattered by a prominent member representing it at Westminster, especially if he can marry his fame with what is known as being 'a good constituency MP'.[68] Regardless of how the prospective Member of Parliament is selected, it is the fact that the candidate wears a particular party label that will determine his or her electoral prospects. Personal characteristics — both positive and negative — have only a marginal influence so it is difficult for the individual to survive in British political life outside the party system.

In the United States centralized party control of recruitment runs up against the obstacle of residency qualifications and party primaries. Residency requirements make it absolutely vital for the ambitious politician to secure his local base for if he loses that he cannot find a safe haven elsewhere as can happen in British politics. Primaries make it possible for outsiders to challenge the power of the party machine and, although it may be hazardous to do so, no one can be absolutely sure of the outcome until after the primary. The influence of the parties upon recruitment will vary from state to state depending upon the degree of party competitiveness, the strength of the party organizations and the legal requirements on primaries and voting qualifications.[69] The distinction between the influence of parties in British and American politics is nicely reflected in the reasons American politicians put forward to explain their involvement. The emphasis is upon personal, often non-political, motivations that have been stimulated by friends or business considerations.[70] Naturally the same kind of motivations must also influence British politicians but, given the power of the parties, one would expect more explicitly political reasons.

In Britain a political career is at the same time a party career and as such the parties have an immense control over the pattern of elite socialization. Those who will eventually be Cabinet ministers have entered Parliament at the comparatively early age of mid-30s to early 40s, and have been re-elected without prolonged interruptions a number of times. After a respectable apprenticeship as a backbench promotion up the political ladder, following an elaborate hierarchical route, commences. The initial step is to serve some time as a Parliamentary Private Secretary, followed by a post as a Minister of State or Under-Secretary, and before finally reaching their pinnacle of power (the Cabinet) it is usual to serve as a minister of non-Cabinet rank.[71] In recent years governmental and quasi-governmental posts have swollen in numbers, so increasing official control of the Commons. At the same time this has structured more clearly the political career hierarchy, so that the ambitious politician can be on the ladder within a short time of entering the House. This early apprenticeships makes it more difficult and more dangerous to be a political maverick. So the way to high office is through a formalized and controlled socialization process, but whether this will make for adept Cabinet ministers is another question. Richard Rose has argued that the skills it takes to succeed in the Commons are different from those necessary to run a department, so the long socialization process may be entirely inappropriate for the end goal.[72] But if the individual is wedded to the governmental machine at the start of his Commons career this may increase his departmental potential, but the price that has to be paid is high — more control over MPs and a consequent diminution in the already diluted powers of Parliament.

Government in Britain is party government and this gives the party leadership control over the institutional socialization processes. The separation of powers in the United States weakens this party control. The executive and legislature may be controlled by different parties and even when they are not there is no guarantee that the patronage available to the former can keep the latter in line. They are independent power bases within their own right and, given their opposing constitutent interests, they are just as likely to clash as harmonize. So what control the parties within the legislatures may wish to exercise over their nominal members depends partly upon their own institutional resources. This cannot be as great as the control that an executive exercises, for it has at its disposal that most powerful of temptations, the fruits of government office.

In spite of this fundamental difference many similarities exist. Within the legislatures of both countries power accrues in the hands of the long-serving members. Although the parties may be less powerful in the United States, the leaders can be very persuasive and this has been put to good effect on many occasions.[73] The individual member is likely to be dependent upon his party to push through his legislation and he may even need assistance to secure his re-election. In return for such favours he must reciprocate in kind and this can only mesh him into the party network. But when all is said and done this is not quite the same as tempting someone with a government post, and the looser party control is reflected in the greater degree of independence American politicians periodically exhibit.

Politics as a career

If a career is a full-time and life-long pursuit then there are few career politicians in either Britain or the United States.[74] However, many features associated with political recruitment and socialization patterns suggest that the reference to politics as a career is not entirely inappropriate. The political recruits are distinguished from other citizens in several ways: their class origins, their occupations, their education, age, ethnic background and religious affiliations. The party differences in political career patterns are on the wane; for example public-school men are infiltrating the ranks of the parliamentary Labour party in increasing numbers, while in the United States politicians from the two major parties are formally better educated than ever before. Besides recruiting individuals with particular social backgrounds, elite socialization processes then expose the new politician to special learning experiences. Institutional norms may be flexible but power accumulates in the hands of those who play the game. The fact that there are internal socialization experiences establishes a parallel between other professions and politics as a career. These experiences help to create a group identity that distinguishes politicians from other professional groups as well as from citizens in general .

Late entry into political life and the threat of premature exit separates the political career from most others, but the evidence suggests that power goes to those who are recruited early and who have the greatest security of tenure. The problem is that such politicians are the exception and not the rule; can we allow them to determine our understanding of a political career? These are the professional politicians who are at the core of the institutions, whilst their satellites gravitate around them. But all professions have an internal power hierarchy and those at the top have served long apprenticeships, accumulating in the process the resources necessary to rise. Of course the ambitious politician has to build a safeguard against electoral vagaries but a number of safe and peaceful havens do exist.

In certain respects politics is now more professionalized than ever before. Party control over the recruitment is all-powerful and the kind of candidate selected increasingly conforms to a well-educated, middle-class norm. In Britain the ossification of the political career structure has been intensified by the elaboration of the governmental machine, and in the United States by what Polsby has termed the institutionalization of legislature. In both cases this means the political career line is clearly marked out and, in all but the most exceptional circumstances, the individual who reaches the power centre is going to have to follow it over a long period of time. Polsby's analysis of the US House of Representatives shows 'a distinct decline in the rate at which new members are introduced into the house'.[75] So in this case even the number of recruits, that is those who intend to establish a political career, is on the decline, thus confining the scope of the political elite within narrower boundaries.

Matthews has written reassuringly about the biases in political recruitment patterns:

. . . both the Marxists and the elitists overlook the fact that a group or class need not be literally represented among decision-makers, at least under democratic conditions, in order to have political power or to have it exercised in their behalf. As long as sympathetic agents of a group or class can achieve high public office, actual members of the group need not.[76]

This smacks of the old argument against giving women the vote — they had no need of the franchise because their husbands would take their views into consideration. Technically speaking, the white liberal politician can represent the interests of the urban ghetto black but whether this will satisfy the latter is no longer a matter of conjecture — it won't! In the United States politics has been channel of mobility for the ethnic groups, especially if you look beyond the national elite located in Washington. But if politics is becoming more of a professional career, the extent to which increasing the spectrum of political recruitment will satisfy previously excluded groups is open to doubt. The elite socialization pressures can make it difficult for the new member to act as an effective representative and if he is ineffectual then it may not be long before he is also irrelevant. This affects the meaning of political representation for specific social groups, but it can be extended by arguing that a highly professionalized and inbred political career structure could result in a general estrangement of citizens from politicians or even politics.

In an era when it is common to talk of pressure-group politics, power elites and military–industrial complexes it may seem absurd to talk of isolated politicians. But the professionalization of politics may assist the control of politicians by particular interests. If the career structure frees the individual from external constraints, in particular the vagaries of electoral fortune, then those who are best in a position to exert their influence could have considerable power. In this respect it is not at all surprising that most politicians view the lobbyist as an integral part of the political process and as a necessary aid to the better performance of their jobs.[77] This does not mean that the politician is a pawn serving a well-defined combination of malevolent interests, but rather that some are much better placed than others to make themselves heard, and the fact that politics is increasingly a career aids the process.

The implication is that elite socialization processes have a much greater impact upon policy-making than recruitment patterns. But policy is not simply a consequence of individual recruitment and socialization experiences for it is also an *institutional* output. In fact socialization experiences are more influential because they are the product of the institutional structure and as such have an impact upon all incumbents, regardless of their origins. But socialization processes cannot resist for all time the entry of new personnel with different policy perspectives. If these new forces are sufficiently strong then eventually they will assume a position of institutional power. By this time the policy goals might have been modified but that they will be achieved, in one form or another, cannot be doubted. Even the rules and mores of that august body, the Senate, could not hold back forever the force of black protest and the persistent pressure of white liberals, both within and outside the political institutions. Now we are witnessing the influx of a new generation of representatives, and what their impact upon elite socialization, and even more significantly, on policy, will be remains to be seen, but that they will help to structure another elite socialization matrix cannot be doubted.

Notes

1. G. A. Almond, 'A functional approach to comparative politics', pp. 26–33.
2. ibid., p. 31. Note the allowance that Almond makes for subcultural peculiarities in the general socialization processes.
3. ibid.
4. R. Dowse, 'Representation, general elections and democracy', *Parliamentary Affairs,* **15** (1961–1962), 331–346.
5. J. N. Dearlove, *The Politics of Policy in Local Government,* Cambridge University Press, Cambridge, 1973, pp. 140–142.
6. This is probably true of those districts once controlled by a powerful local family which occurrence has undoubtedly declined in importance in this century.

7. A. Lijphart, *The Politics of Accommodation: Pluralism and Democracy in the Netherlands,* University of California Press, Berkeley, 1968; R. Presthus, *Elite Accommodation in Canadian Politics,* Cambridge University Press, Cambridge, 1973.

8. This was what the British government was hoping for in Northern Ireland after the formation of the power-sharing executive.

9. R. C. K. Ensor, *England, 1870–1914,* Oxford University Press, Oxford, 1936, p. 57.

10. Reasons other than the desire for victory may motivate the candidate and this picture of major party control varies according to the type of election being fought and where the contest is taking place.

11. For example, C. Wright Mills makes the Presidency one of the three branches of his power elite, but he is very disparaging with regard to Congressional power. See C. Wright Mills, *The Power Elite,* Oxford University Press, New York, 1956, ch. 10.

12. Smooth links may exist between the various branches of the elite because of the work of lobbyists. But this assumes that perhaps different interests have to be reconciled or that politicians have to be made aware of corporate or even military perspectives. Although the lobbyist may very well end up controlling the politicians, they do so on a very different basis from that contained in the power elite thesis.

13. D. R. Matthews, *The Social Background of Political Decision-Makers,* Random House, New York, 1954, p. 2.

14. ibid., p. 59.

15. D. D. Searing, 'The comparative study of elite socialization', *Comparative Political Studies,* **1** (1969), 495.

16. V. Lenin, *What Is To Be Done, Collected Works,* Vol. 5, Lawrence and Wishart, London, 1961, pp. 397–408. In much the same way it is possible to point to even greater constraints on individual thought and action within Lenin's model of party organization.

17. It could be disputed, at least in the Anglo-American context, that party affiliations are an adult socialization experience.

18. It is hard to think of empirical examples that fit these precise conditions. The representative bodies of very specialized interests are likely to come closest to fitting the bill. This could be a trade union or professional association representing a small group of men with precise skills, or the representatives of small family firms that make or trade in only one product.

19. Certainly any institution would find it difficult to function smoothly if there was considerable fluctuation in individual behaviour.

20. J. Blondel, *Voters, Parties and Leaders,* Penguin Books, Harmondsworth, 1963, p. 133.

21. op. cit., p. 28.

22. ibid., p. 47.

23. W. L. Guttsman, *The British Political Elite.* MacGibbon and Kee, London, 1968, ch. 9.

24. Those Labour MPs who were sponsored by the trade unions worked very effectively against the Labour government's attempts in the late 1960s to regulate prices and incomes, and industrial relations. As such, it could be argued, they were effective working-class spokesmen.

25. op. cit., pp. 131–132.

26. As with Plato's guardians, for they had the intrinsic qualities necessary to rule and no others were capable of performing the task.

27. M. Weber, 'Politics as a vocation', in H. H. Gerth and C. Wright Mills, *From Max Weber: Essays in Sociology,* Oxford University Press, New York, 1958, pp. 77–128.

28. Matthews, *op. cit.,* p. 30.

29. op. cit., p. 31. As the tone of my following remarks indicates, I am very suspicious of Matthews' reasons, How many law firms can readily spare a partner and how necessary it is to keep abreast of legal changes are contentious points.

30. On this see Guttsman, op. cit., ch. 5.

31. ibid., ch. 10. Blondel in his study of the Reading Conservative Constituency party writes, 'Something undoubtedly remains of the old idea that certain Conservatives have a sort of family right to shape the Association's destiny, while new members, as it were, should be content with having been admitted as members'. J. Blondel, 'The Conservative Association and the Labour Party in Reading', *Political Studies,* 6 (1958), 108. To what extent this is still true is uncertain but that Blondel could write this in 1958 shows considerable retention of power by these families.

32. W. Bagehot, *The English Constitution,* Oxford University Press, London, 1958 printing (World's Classic Edition), p. 85.

33. See pp. 107–113.

34. L. J. Edinger and D. D. Searing, 'Social background in elite analysis: A methodological enquiry', *American Political Science Review,* 61 (1967), 434.

35. op. cit., p. 28.

36. op. cit., p. 4.

37. A. Sampson, *Anatomy of Britain,* Hodder and Stoughton, London, 1962, p. 175.

38. For an interesting study of the network of elite relations see T. Lupton and C. S. Wilson, 'The social background and connections of "top decision makers"', *Manchester School of Economiics and Social Studies,* 27 (1959), 30–52.

39. For example see J. Wakeford, *The Cloistered Elite,* Macmillan, London, 1969.

40. See ibid., I. Weinberg, *The English Public Schools: The Sociology of Elite Education,* Atherton Press, London, 1967, ch. 5.

41. Sampson has argued that the top civil servants form an Oxbridge rather than a public school preserve. Op. cit., p. 224.

42. Wilkinson, op. cit., pp. VIII and X.

43. For the Northcote-Trevelyan Report see *Public Administration,* 32 (1954), 1–16

44. Wilkinson, op. cit., p. 68.

45. Technically speaking there is now an integrated career line so this should be taken to mean those who perform the tasks of the civil servants who were in the administrative class. On the substantive point see Sampson, op. cit., p. 224; R. K. Kelsall, *Higher Civil Servants in Britain,* Routledge and Kegan Paul, London, 1955, pp. 135–145; C. D. Dodd, 'Recruitment to the administrative class, 1960–1964', *Public Administration,* 45 (1967), 80.

46. This has changed somewhat dramatically in the 1970s and the left-wing of the party is much stronger at all levels. This is perhaps reflected in more radical policies (e.g. the extension of state nationalization of industry), but in terms of controlling the nation's prevailing economic crisis the Labour government is following a path laid down by the Tories.

47. B. Hindess, *The Decline of Working Class Politics,* MacGibbon, London, 1971.

48. The difference is that there have been fewer Labour prime ministers, but Clement Attlee was inclined to favour 'the old school tie', although not to the same extent as Stanley Baldwin before him and Harold Macmillan subsequently.

49. K. Prewitt *et al.*, 'Political socialization and political roles', *Public Opinion Quarterly*, **30** (1966–67), 582.

50. ibid.

51. In the following section I discuss legislative political elites. At the executive level the picture is more concealed and perhaps allows greater individual initiative in shaping the dimensions of the office.

52. op. cit., p. 51.

53. W. White, *The Citadel: The Story of the U.S. Senate*, Houghton Mifflin, Boston, 1968; D. R. Matthews, *U.S. Senators and Their World*, Vintage Books, New York, 1960.

54. op. cit., pp. 123–130.

55. C. M. Price and C. G. Bell, 'The rules of the game: political fact or academic fancy?', *Journal of Politics*, **32** (1970), 839–855.

56. For a case study of the latter see Dearlove, op. cit., ch. 7.

57. N. Polsby, 'The institutionalization of the U.S. House of Representatives', *American Political Science Review*, **62** (1968), 144–168.

58. For a beautiful illustration of the coded language of the British civil servant, and an even more beautiful translation of it by W. J. M. Mackenzie see R. Rose, *Politics in England*, Faber and Faber, London, 1965, p. 167.

59. Thus the frequent reference to Parliament as 'the mother of Parliaments', and for the adulation of the Senate by Senators see Matthews, *U.S. Senators and Their World*, pp. 101–102.

60. R. K. Huitt, 'The outsider in the Senate', *American Political Science Review*, **55** (1961), 570.

61. Matthews, *U.S. Senators and Their World*, p. 94.

62. ibid., p. 128.

63. C. M. Price and C. G. Bell, 'Socializing California freshmen assemblymen: The role of individuals and legislative sub-groups', *Western Political Quarterly*, **23** (1970), 174. The same pattern has appeared in recent years in the U.S. House of Representatives.

64. The man being Peter Griffiths, former Conservative MP for Smethwick.

65. A. Ranney, *Pathways to Parliament: Candidate Selection in Britain*, University of Wisconsin Press, Madison, 1965, pp. 270–273. But note how the Central Office list of official candidates was pruned, when Mr Heath was leader of the party, with the intention of preventing potential supporters of Mr. Enoch Powell from becoming MPs.

66. Quoted in A. King and A. Sloman, *Westminster and Beyond*, Macmillan, London, 1973, p. 42.

67. Ranney, *Pathways to Parliament*, pp. 272–280.

68. A rather exceptional example, at least until he resigned his Wolverhampton seat, has been Mr Enoch Powell, who combines prominence, rebelliousness and 'a good constituency MP' record.

69. For a discussion of the impact of these influences see H. Eulau *et al.*, 'Career perspectives of American state legislators' in D. Marvick (ed.), *Political Decision-Makers: Recruitment and Performance*, Free Press, Glencoe, 1961, pp. 218–263.

70. ibid., pp. 228–229.

71. For a discussion of various aspects of this mobility pattern see D. J. Heasman, 'Parliamentary paths to high office', *Parliamentary Affairs*, **16** (1962–63), 315–330; F. M. G. Willson, 'The routes of entry of new members of the British Cabinet, 1868–1958', *Political Studies*, **7** (1959), 222–232 and 'Entry to the Cabinet, 1959–

1968', *Political Studies*, **18** (1970), 236–238; P. W. Buck, *Amateurs and Professionals in British Politics, 1918–1959*, University of Chicago Press, Chicago, 1963; R. Rose, 'The making of Cabinet ministers', *British Journal of Political Science*, **1** (1971), 393–414.

72. ibid., p. 404.

73. For Lyndon Johnson's brilliant exploitation of his power as Senate majority leader see R. Evans and R. Novak, *Lyndon B. Johnson: The Exercise of Power*, New American Library, New York, 1966, ch. 6–8.

74. For an elaboration of the thesis that politics is *not* a career see Blondel, *Voters, Parties and Leaders*, pp. 153–154.

75. op. cit., p. 148.

76. *The Social Background of Political Decision-Makers*, p. 56.

77. J. C. Wahlke *et al.*, *The Legislative System: Explorations in Legislative Behavior*, Wiley, New York, 1962, p. 341. For a somewhat different view of the role of interest groups see B. H. Zisk *et al.*, 'City councilmen and the group struggle: A typology of role orientations, *Journal of Politics*, **27** (1965), 618–646.

Chapter 6

The Working Class Tories:
Perspectives on False Consciousness

The class basis of British politics

One of the best-documented facts about British political life is its class basis, and in comparison with similar political systems social class is still a significant dividing-line.[1] Electoral support for the major parties neatly illustrates the point for, in spite of Conservative party claims that they are a truly national party and the appeals of several Labour party leaders for middle-class backing, they continue to draw the bulk of their voters from their traditional class bases.[2] The more equal spread of class support enjoyed by the Liberal party confirms rather than contradicts this, for the party leaders have portrayed themselves as men of the moderate centre in pawn to neither big business nor the trade unions. In the process of trying to bridge the class divide they are tacitly recognizing its potency.[3]

This relationship between class and politics results in an interesting problem in comparative analysis. By comparing British political behaviour with that of citizens in many other countries we find that social class is a more potent influence in Britain than elsewhere. But it is evident that British political life would be very different if class exerted a *more* powerful hold on electoral behaviour. If the two major parties experienced a simple and complete division in their class support, for the foreseeable future the Labour party would hold the reins of power and the Conservative party would be doomed to permanent opposition. The British class structure may be changing but it will be some time before manual workers become a minority of the work force.[4] Likewise if all the middle-class voters deserted the Labour party, and the Tories retained their working-class support, the shift in political power would be almost as dramatic.

In view of this, what sense does it make to maintain that the class basis of British politics is of particular importance? This raises the question of what standards are to be employed in comparative analysis for although, in comparative terms, a variable has more influence in one country than another, can any significance be attached to this when it is equally clear that the non-effectiveness of the same variable within that nation state is almost as important as its effectiveness?[5]

Barry Hindess has talked of 'the decline of working-class politics', implying that there was once such a thing as 'working-class politics', and that this is now on the decline and presumably will disappear.[6] An examination of national electoral trends suggests that this is a gross, premature judgement. The fluidity in party allegiances is probably on the increase but class differences in party support are perpetuated when it comes to the concrete act of voting.[7] This rapid fluctuation in the popularity of parties, although of great significance, makes it all too easy to predict the demise of a party on the findings of an opinion poll or two.[8] Electoral data show that even in Britain it is a too-simple-minded generalization to talk of straightforward working-class politics. Many ambiguities surround the concept of working-class Tories, as later analysis will show, but no one could deny the continuous part they have played in helping the Conservative party to secure office. An historical perspective of the Labour party's leadership would throw similar doubts on Hindess' thesis. In its early days the members of the parliamentary Labour party were overwhelmingly working-class in their social origins, but this ignores the considerable element of middle-class leadership (for example from intellectuals like the Fabians) in the party at large.[9] Once the parliamentary party grew in numbers so its middle-class element inevitably expanded; none the less it is still a channel of mobility for a few working-class citizens and comparative terms Parliament has more MPs with working-class origin than many legislatures.[10]

As manual workers make up approximately two-thirds of the work force, all political parties have to attract at least a sizeable minority of the working-class vote if they are at all serious about winning political office. Due to the Conservative party's historical links with the aristocracy, and by the end of the nineteenth century the plutocracy, this poses special problems for that party's leadership. It is ironic that it was the founder of the modern Conservative party, Disraeli, who was responsible for extending the franchise to the urban proletariat.[11] The party's history of electoral success since that date suggests that his 'leap in the dark' has paid off handsomely. However, if the focus is narrowed to the post-Second World War period the judgement would have to be more tentative, and some would even conclude that the chickens are finally coming home to roost.[12]

Disraeli's understanding of working-class political behaviour convinced him that it would not harm the fortunes of the Tory party to extend the franchise. If he had reached the opposite conclusion it would have been interesting to have seen his course of action. In his penetrating introduction to Bagehot's *The English Constitution* Richard Crossman has pointed out that not all his contemporaries shared Disraeli's view of the British working class.[13] John Stuart Mill proposed a variety of electoral manipulations to dilute the political influence of the masses until they had been sufficiently civilized by education.[14] The constitution had a built-in conservative bias, in the sense that the House of Lords exerted considerable political power and it remained free from electoral pressures. In spite of this the defence of Toryism rested more upon perceptions of working-class behaviour, coupled with an appreciation of the context within which that behaviour was formed, than upon straightforward subversion of formal democratic principles.

Obviously the way the Labour party relates to its supporters influences both the extent of working-class Toryism and explanations of that allegiance. The contemporary Labour party contains within its ranks a wide spectrum of the British political left but on achieving power it has adopted reformist programmes of an essentially moderate nature.[15] It is by no means a revolutionary party committed to pursuing the interests of just the working class. Some would argue that the party has always been this amalgam of forces and its original goal was not to promote distinctive policies, but rather to increase working-class political representation.[16] Alternatively, others would claim that this reformist nature, especially the willingness to accept a modified version of the capitalist economy, has become more pronounced since the Second World War. The intra-party battles of the post-war period have not resulted in a clear victory for any of the factions, but the options selected and followed while in office show where the heart, if not the soul, of the party now lies.[17]

If the Labour party is not, and has never been, simply a class party then it can hardly appeal to the electorate in terms of furthering particular class interests. As the party has grown in size its class image has faded. To obtain power through the electoral process, therefore, a non-class programme is essential, and on gaining office the party has preferred to compromise with those who hold economic power rather than to pursue radical policies that would bring about a confrontation. Thus the Labour party has encompassed 'moderate reformism', 'revisionism' or even 'meritocratic socialism' in its bid to win electoral support.[18] Hindess also argues that the party has adopted a peculiarly middle-class style in its approach to problem-solving, and as the policy-making echelons of the party are now dominated by the middle class so this style pervades the party. This is epitomized by the professional technocrat who sees problem-solving as the proper allocation of resources to achieve desired goals, and yet the technocrat is personally unaffected by the problem itself or the proposed solution.[19]

If the Labour party is not, and has never been, a working-class party then it cannot expect the allegiance of this social class on the grounds of the party's class appeal. But surely it is even more incongruous for the working-class citizen to vote for the Tory party? None the less, during the 1950s the Labour party lost three consecutive General Elections and its representation in the House of Commons correspondingly dwindled.[20] Many felt that the traditional class basis of British politics was on the wane for the Conservative party was attracting the vote of the newly affluent workers. True or not, it is sufficient at this point to note that elements within the leadership of the Labour party felt this was so, and accordingly suggested new policy perspectives that would fit current realities rather than suggest a perpetual tilting at obsolete windmills.[21] But if this was *not* true, and yet the party became even less the champion of working-class interests, then the party itself was encouraging the erosion of its traditional basis of support — in a sense digging its own grave.

Given the existence of a mass electorate, and two parties which, in an endeavour to gain sole control of the governmental apparatus, appeal to various broad socio-economic groupings, it can surely be expected that class overlap as well as class differentiation will occur in most facets of political life, including party support. The reasons why the class overlap is considered to be such an anomaly is that well-developed assumptions have been made as to how the working class should behave politically. Britain is a highly urbanized nation with a large, well-established proletariat and, if the Marxist interpretation of society is accepted, these are the minimum conditions for the development of a class-conscious proletariat. In fact Marx himself argued that it was conceivable that Britain could avoid the proletarian revolution in the inevitable march towards socialism.[22] This shows that perhaps Disraeli had a more acute understanding of the nineteenth century British working class than did Marx. In fairness to Marxists, although they may have misinterpreted the class consciousness of the British working class they have not been slow to castigate its designated leaders — the trade union officials — for the sin of economism.[23]

If the assumption is accepted that social classes have a natural content and form to their political behaviour, it still remains to be explained why class should be a more potent force in Britain than elsewhere. Richard Rose maintains that class protrudes so strongly in Britain because of the absence of other potentially divisive influences.[24] As the United Kingdom is a comparatively homogeneous social unit the one discriminating variable cannot help but appear as overwhelming in importance. Where the social unity breaks down conflict is associated with other forces; for example in Northern Ireland religion provides the main boundaries of political life.[25] Rose argues that regional conflicts would loom more threateningly if the minority nationalities formed a higher percentage of the population. (From the standpoint of 1975, even without a large percentage of the total population of the United Kingdom the threat they pose to the perpetuation of the political community seems real enough!).

Although class may be the most evident dividing-line in British politics for the reason Rose states, many social scientists do not see this a threat to political stability. Not only do the vast majority of citizens — regardless of their class backgrounds — vote for parties that work within the political mainstream, but also they provide many positive indications that they accept the legitimacy of the political status quo. In the terms of Almond and Verba the civic culture pervades all social classes. What class differences exist do not prevent agreement on such fundamental questions as the legitimacy of established political authority, the regime norms or the boundaries of the community.[26] This view has been summarized by Stanley Rothman, who claims that the class and ideological conflicts that occur in Britain do so within the framework of a more inclusive attachment to the community.[27] So even if there is a class basis to British politics what this means is open to different interpretations.

The meaning of working-class conservatism

Working-class Conservatism is a facet of the more general relationship between political behaviour and social class. It is important because the Conservative party can only win elections if a section of the working class manifest what some Marxists would call false consciousness. At the same time, when it was believed that class defection was on the increase the Labour party modified its image to counteract the apparent trend. Besides these reasons that are of particular interest to the parties, the working-class Tories symbolize the cross-cutting cleavages that form the basis of British political life. They are evidence that political divisions do not simply follow social boundaries and, thanks to their allegiance, the Tory leadership can claim that theirs is a national party that transcends class boundaries.[28] Many social scientists stress that the stability of a democratic polity depends partly upon the relationship between political life and its social base. Where there are cross-cutting ties, of the sort that the working-class Tories represent, the chances of political stability are enhanced. This could be very significant in Britain where, as Richard Rose has argued, class is the largest single social cleavage.[29]

For the working-class Conservative to be a true measure of cross-cutting ties he or she must ideally have internalized a set of values that coincide with those of the party, for if not the allegiance may be little more than a fleeting romance, to be broken whenever the going gets rough. The fact that the Conservative party, in spite of its famed pragmatism, stands for an evolutionary approach to political change does not mean that all of its supporters have embraced the same ideology. Although this may be true, it is difficult to conceive of the reverse circumstances, i.e. a conservative party supported by revolutionaries, or even potential revolutionaries! Trying to understand why some working-class citizens vote for the Conservative party can, therefore, tell us something about the relationship of social variables to political values. I have made the point that, given the attempt of the major parties to appeal to a broad range of interests, a certain amount of cross-cutting cleavage can be expected. But that is not the end of the matter, for only by arriving at an understanding of why the individual holds his allegiances can wider significance be attributed to them. Within itself the pattern of allegiances may be used as a symbol that all is well with the political system, but without this further information this can only be a tentative conclusion.[30]

The false consciousness thesis implies that working-class Tories have been socialized into accepting the legitimacy of a society in which they are inferior in the distribution of the scarce resources of income, status and power. If the working-class Conservative vote cannot be interpreted in this fashion then precisely what does it mean? Explanations have been posited at two different levels: individual motivations and the structure of British society. These two levels of explanation are mutually reinforcing, for in every case the individual motivations can be linked to a special structural context. So from the point of view of political socialization theory an analysis of working-class Conservatism has a lot to offer. It means working in an area that has practical pay-offs in terms of deciding the distribution of political power. At the same time this stems directly from a traditional socialization problem, i.e. why do some individuals behave in a way that appears to legitimize their own inequality? Finally it is that richest of socialization fields for within it individual behaviour can be related to a socio-economic context, and a changing one at that.

The traditional society and the deferential working class

Historically the most prevalent explanation of working-class Toryism is that this represents a deferential state of mind. Walter Bagehot is usually credited as the originator of the thesis; it is true that in about the middle of the last century he wrote, 'The mass of the English people are politically contented as well as politically deferential'.[31] Approximately one hundred years after Bagehot wrote those words the deepest empirical study of British political culture summarized it as a 'deferential civic culture'.[32] Although Bagehot was concerned that the proletariat should be seduced by the ceremonial aspects of government, he — like Almond and Verba — was convinced that deference extended beyond the boundaries of the working classes. For Bagehot deference had to be encouraged to secure certain political objectives, above all the perpetuation of Cabinet government in which a propertied and educated elite was to govern the country without feeling constrained by a propertyless and illiterate mass. This meant that ' . . . the low mentality and deplorable living standards of the mass of the English people' necessitated the promotion of deference.[33] But Cabinet government could be perpetuated without deference if ' . . . the business community is dominant and the mass of the people are literate and comfortable enough to use their vote in order to give their betters authority'.[34] Unfortunately such conditions did not exist in nineteenth-century England and so arose the need to sponsor deference.

Unlike Disraeli, Bagehot was far from happy about the 1867 extension of the franchise for he felt that the new working-class voters posed a threat to political stability. At the same time he recognized in the proletariat an ingrained hostility to some of the symbols of established authority, and in this respect he made specific reference to the police.[35] In spite of this he believed that deference was part of the English mentality which incorporated the deference of the working classes to the monarchy, of the middle classes to the upper classes, and even of the plutocracy to the aristocracy. So there is this ambivalence in his work with deference forming part of the English way of life, but a parallel fear that Cabinet government was under siege and only the skilful manipulation of traditional symbols and ceremonies could preserve it.

The content of deference can be interpreted in varying ways. Central to Bagehot's understanding was the notion of showing deference to those of superior social status, and at the pinnacle of the hierarchy rested the hereditary nobility and the monarchy. Given the political realities of his time, deferring to this class was not simply social deference for these were people who still exercised considerable political power. So what appeared to be straightforward social deference may in fact have been socio-political deference. Bagehot tended to underestimate the political power of what he called the ceremonial aspects of government; but it does not follow that the nineteenth-century working class were similarly duped.[36]

The idea that deference is shown to a social elite is another continuing theme in the literature, and quite recently Nordlinger could write,

It is this *social* deference — the preference for leaders with high social rank and conformity to their hierarchical expectations, justified by the assumption that there is a close correspondence between social rank and leadership — which is a marked characteristic of English political culture.[37]

Although few social scientists would completely rule out deference as an ingredient in the shaping of English political behaviour, it is rarely viewed in Nordlinger's simple terms. Nowadays greater reference is made to the educational background of elites. Richard Rose has argued that this represents a shift towards meritocratic deference because the educated person is assumed to have the competence to make the decisions that have to be faced in politics.[38] He or she has acquired this competence thanks to a lengthy period of formal education. This may be so but it assumes that the acquisition of formal education is based on meritocratic

principles, or, if it is not, it is none the less perceived in purely meritocratic terms by those who are evaluating its meaning. But given the
elitist and class-based character of the British educational system it is
difficult to accept that education has only this meaning and no other.
This is especially so as the most exclusive schools have such a close
association with the Tory party. In other words, educational deference
could be merely a disguised form of social deference.

British politicians have to spend the greater part of their time and
energy worrying about the management of the economy. Due to this
predominance of economic affairs it makes sense for voters to support
politicians on the grounds of their assumed competence at running the
economy. This provides another example of the subtle mix of elements
contained in the concept of deference. The working-class Tory may vote
for the party because amongst both its leadership and supporters it
contains many wealthy men and he is deferential towards wealth. But
this deference could contain the belief that wealthy men are better at
managing the economy because men who have made money know about
these things. This may also include a great deal of personal instrumentality, i.e. without economically competent political leaders his living
standards may decline or he could even lose his job. Thus instrumentality
and deference go hand in hand to the point where it is difficult to tell
where one starts and the other leaves off.

Jessop, in the most detailed dissection of deference, has formulated
four categories: [39]

1. The individual defers to all political authority regardless of its
   social composition. This is political deference.
2. The individual believes in the presence of a social elite that is
   uniquely fitted to hold office. This is the ascriptive socio-political
   deference Bagehot wanted to promote and Nordlinger felt certain
   sectors of the English working class actually believe in.
3. The individual defers to a social elite without necessarily ascribing
   it with any special political competence. This is ascriptive social
   deference.
4. The individual defers to a traditional moral order. This is socio-
   cultural deference.

Jessop's empirical evidence revealed that the most widely implied
definition of deference — ascriptive socio-political deference — was not
very prevalent amongst his sample, and it exerted as strong an influence
upon the middle class, in the direction of voting Tory, as upon the
working class. Where ascriptive socio-political deference was present it
rarely had any impact independent of socio-cultural deference, so it eked
out its remaining life in the midst of that small band of citizens who
continue to swear by traditional values and a vanishing way of life.
Jessop concludes,

It would thus seem that there is far less constraint on the relations between social values and political behaviour in the working class than is assumed by the deference theorists: it may well be that political loyalties are simply inherited without overmuch attention to possible contradictions with wider social values and that calculation of self-interest often outweigh the constraints of attachment to, or alienation from, the dominant value system.[40]

If these definitions of deference fail to produce any significant differences between the values of working-class Tories and other socio-political groups, the question arises as to why this should be so. Jessop suggests two opposite explanations: the individual inherits party loyalties (socialized within the family) or he votes according to his own perception of his self-interests. If the latter hypothesis is valid then party preferences are stable because perceptions of self-interest are also stable. Frank Parkin has attempted to rise above such *ad hoc* explanations through an analysis of British social values. He maintains that in Britain 'dominant' or 'core' values pervade the society.[41] These values flow out of the society's power centres — especially 'the institutional complex of private property and capitalist enterprise which dominates the economic sector' — and they are incorporated within the Conservative party's ideology. When and where workers are exposed to these values, they are likely to vote for the Tory party. Conversely when the various institutions perpetuating these values are weak then an alternative value system can take root, with the consequence that working-class Conservatism will find it more difficult to flourish.

Parkin's theory suggests that, as the values of Conservative party permeate British society, it is those working-class citizens who vote for the Labour party, and presumably parties further to the left, who are the true political deviants. The thesis is partially verified by the fact that support for the Labour party is much higher in traditional working-class communities, especially where they are isolated from the main cross-currents of the wider society and are heavily dependent upon a single industry.

This could explain the political militancy associated with the mining, fishing and lumbering industries throughout western industrial society.[42] If these traditional industrial centres decline, resistance to the dominant culture may come to depend more and more upon the structure of the work place. Again the evidence shows that where factories are large, and the trade unions well organized, the barriers against voting Tory are strong. The thesis is bolstered as much by those who vote for the Conservative party as by those who do not. Runciman has described the ideal working-class Tory voter as

. . . a woman in her seventies living in a country district in the Midlands whose father was in a non-manual occupation, who stayed on at school beyond the minimum age, who thinks of herself as 'middle class' and who would like to attend regularly at an Anglican church but is prevented by age or illness from doing so.[43]

The various social ingredients of this ideal type — sex, age, residence, class origins, home-centredness and religious affiliations — make her an easy prey for the dominant culture and certainly isolate her from the institutions associated with traditional working-class mores.

Besides being an explanation which depends upon placing the working-class Conservatives in their structural position, Parkin's thesis fits in neatly with some of the assumptions implicit in the over-socialized conception of man. Men are the victims (or beneficiaries) of the cultural context in which they happen to be located for their attitudes and behaviour are patterned as this culture dictates. If one escape the clutches of the dominant culture it is because one is surrounded by a more powerful subculture. Parkin writes,

. . . manual workers do not vote Conservative *because* they are deferential, or *because* they conceive of themselves as middle class; rather they have a deferential *and* a middle class *and* a Conservative outlook when they are isolated from structural positions which provide an alternative normative system from that of the dominant institutional orders of society.[44]

This begs the question of both the form and intensity of cultural interaction. Few persons are likely to fit either Runciman's ideal type of the working-class Tory or its opposite, so how is the process of cultural conflict decided? The meaning that individuals attach to cultural pressures has to be taken into consideration for it is not simply a question of the messages one receives, or even their intensity, but also how they are interpreted. The interpretations may well depend upon factors that are independent of the immediate, or even the past cultural environment — for example, 'deference' or perceptions of oneself as a 'middle-class' citizen! To deny the individual a self-identity with which he can interpret for himself his cultural environment is to succumb to the naive transmission model of socialization.

The fact that certain working-class communities in Britain are much more likely to vote Labour than Conservative is no proof that they are culturally distinctive from other working-class communities, or even middle-class suburbs if one believes there are some universal features to the political culture. Jessop's study showed a diffusion of cultural values amongst the working classes with few distinctions between Labour or Conservative voters.[45] This could mean that the Labour party is associated with the dominant ideology so that giving the party electoral support is no more deviant than voting Tory. Alternatively the dominant ideology may be much less coherent and inclusive than Parkin would have us believe. After all, the institutions from which the dominant values supposedly flow — the monarchy, the Anglican Church, the public schools, the ancient universities and even capitalism — have been the subject of controversy for decades now and some of this would have rubbed off on to working-class Tories as well as miners, dockers and trawlermen. In much the same way, not all traditional workers are immune from the seductions of Toryism, but this does not make them any less a coalminer, docker or what have you. It is as if the working-class Tory is not really a member of the proletariat; therefore his class credentials have to be devalued, for this is the only way his aberrant behaviour can be explained. The component parts of Runciman's ideal type make this quite clear. It is a short step, therefore, from making generalizations about values to the creation of cultural stereotypes, and in the process it is hard to avoid being both patronizing and unrealistic.

The dominant value theory not only insults the intelligence of the working classes but it also greatly underestimates the potency of political manipulation. If there are dominant values that are incorporated in the Tory party it is clearly in the interest of the party to perpetuate them and the processes that preserve them. This implies that the ideal strategy for the Tory party is to propagate a static ideology within a traditional society for a deferential citizenry. But in the past hundred years or so, although rapid social, economic and political changes have occurred in Britain, the Conservative party has continued to more than survive. This is partly thanks to its pragmatism, for the Tory leadership has had the ability to adjust to changing circumstances while still clinging, or pretending to cling, to much of the old order. So the party has been associated with changing values and the emerging institutions that promote them. After all the party existed before capitalism, and, who knows, it may well survive its demise![46]

The deference and dominant value theories are similar in the sense that voting Tory merely represents a manifestation of a wider cultural background. In both cases voting Tory is simply another expression of socialized experiences for the individual has an implicit *weltanschauung* from which his behaviour flows. The extreme alternative is to deny that any consistency exists between values and voting behaviour, which begs the question of what then determines how people vote. This does not square with what is known about the relationship between cultural mores and social variables, or even social variables and political behaviour. I have attempted to steer a middle course by arguing that cultural constraints are interpreted by individuals and it is the interpretations that are made that will determine voting behaviour. To think otherwise implies a degree of cultural determinism that devalues the act of voting Tory, casts doubts upon the individual's working-class credentials and allows no room for party flexibility.

As an explanation of working-class Conservatism the deference thesis has suffered a loss of popularity. This is partly a consequence of the empirical evidence that deference as traditionally understood (i.e. ascriptive sociol-political deference) is not widely distributed in the population, and partly because the social group where it is located (women over seventy who are members of the Anglican church, etc.) is on the decline. In a sense, however, representative democracy encourages deference for the voter is asked to exercise his franchise on behalf of someone else, and it is the someone else who then conducts the business of politics. If one feels the elected representatives are incompetent one is free to enter the game, but it is not a game without its biases, as the previous chapter should have shown. So the real alternative for many people may be between political deference or political alienation. So deference may mean not so much that you feel others are superior to you but rather that you have come to terms with inequality. Working-class Conservatism is likely to be an extreme manifestation of this for it encompasses social and economic as well as political variables.

The affluent society and the embourgeoisement of the working class

In the 1950s Britain experienced a significant growth in living standards, to the point where some were prepared to talk of the emergence of the affluent society. This economic change was accompanied by three consecutive Tory victories, by increasing margins, in the General Elections of 1951, 1955 and 1959. It was tempting to link the political and economic events, especially for those who felt this signified the erosion of class politics and a major step in the growth of a non-revolutionary, working-class consciousness.[47] In fact few of the social scientists who have been classified as proponents of this embourgeoisement thesis foresaw a complete breakdown in class differences. In their 1959 election study David Butler and Richard Rose viewed some workers as class hybrids, '. . . working class in terms of occupation, education, speech, and cultural norms, while becoming middle class in terms of income and material benefits'.[48] In his *The Worker in an Affluent Society* Zweig made very much the same distinction 'The cleavage between classes in economic terms is fast breaking down, but new cleavages are being erected, stronger and more powerful than ever, namely cleavages of education and culture'.[49]

In between the economic developments and the act of voting is the emergence of a new social context for the affluent worker and he is now part of what Mark Abrams called the home-centred society.[50] As community activities decline and the factory becomes just a place to make money so the worker spends more time in the home with his family.[51] In the process his working-class consciousness is transformed, so ' . . . the personal elements of class consciousness seem to be gaining the upper hand over the collective elements'.[52] Once the worker becomes home-centred this makes him more amenable to dominant values (assuming that such things exist) than someone who is strongly integrated into the work situation. So a number of well-defined assumptions bridge the state of affluence and voting Tory, and it is not simply a theory of economic determinism. The point at issue is whether the social processes associated with increased affluence do in fact take place and whether the political consequence of those social processes is voting Tory.

Goldthorpe and Lockwood have been the most persistent critics of the notion that affluence produces Tories. They have written,

The main objective of this study was to test empirically the widely accepted thesis of working class embourgeoisement: that is, the thesis that as manual workers and their families achieve relatively high incomes and living standards, they assume a way of life which is more characteristically 'middle class' and become in fact progressively assimilated into middle class society.[53]

Their attack has various dimensions: the economic security of affluent workers is in fact less certain than that of most middle-class occupations, there is no evidence to show that affluence leads to either a more middle-class pattern of friendships or changes in 'values, attitudes and aspirations, in behavioural patterns', and, to cap it all, their workers — drawn from affluent Luton — retained a high degree of loyalty for the Labour party. What they do question is the basis of working-class support for the Labour party. In traditional working-class communities the workers show 'solidaristic collectivism' which flows out of their 'communal sociability', where as the Luton workers are 'instrumental' or 'pragmatic' in their approach to the world which matches their 'privatized' life-styles.[54] To put it more concisely, the affluent worker gives the Labour party conditional allegiance and he will continue to support it only as long as it holds out the prospect of improving his living standards.

The extent to which 'privatized' workers are different from 'home-centred' workers is a moot point, especially as neither life-style precludes an interest in the economic rewards of the job. It is this latter consideration that prevents any worker from escaping the constraints of his work place, for what ever life-style he wants to lead depends very much upon the weekly pay packet. The interest he has in his work can vary but he cannot escape its economic clutches, and in a period of high inflation this will naturally intensify. Goldthorpe's and Lockwood's test of embourgeoisement is rather stringent for what they are suggesting is that to be embourgeoisified the worker must 'become progressively assimilated into middle class society'. In fact embourgeoisement could be interpreted as being *like* the middle classes without either actually having contact with them or being on the verge of joining them. Goldthorpe and Lockwood accept this alternative but see it as a stage on the way to complete embourgeoisement, rather than as a distinctive lifestyle in its own right. The problem is how to ascertain what degree of similarity there has to be before the placement can be made — in other words, what are the precise ingredients that determine 'privatization', 'embourgeoisement' or straightforward 'middle-class' membership?

It could be argued that the privatized worker is on the way to becoming the embourgeoisified worker, for he has broken free from many of the traditional working-class cultural restraints and it is only a matter of time before he starts to acquire certain middle-class characteristics. Obviously class patterns and values change slowly over long periods of time, and most of the empirical studies — including Goldthorpe's — have taken static snapshots. Even their data showed that some affluent workers, noticeably those who owned their own homes, were more likely to vote Tory than others.[55] In the meantime, what is the nature of this privatized worker? He is interested in his personal standard of living above all else, and will adjust his behaviour, including his political perspectives, to preserve and improve this. This is what Goldthorpe and Lockwood term 'instrumentality' and it assumes a calculating individual who can match his behaviour to his goals. Robert McKenzie and Alan Silver have divided the working-class Tories on a deference — secularism continuum.[56] The allegiance of the seculars to the party is dependent upon its ability to deliver the economic goods and the threat is clear — if the goods are not delivered then support will be withdrawn. Working-class Labour party instrumentalists have a close affinity to working-class Conservative party seculars. The only difference is that for the time being they have contrasting evaluations as to which political party is most likely to satisfy their interests. Nordlinger has subdivided the working-class Tories on the basis of their perceptions of the Tory leadership. The deferentials credit it with power and wisdom while the pragmatists are prepared to put it to the test, and presumably could find it wanting.[57] So in each case there are large bodies of people who have no permanent party affiliations, and given the right circumstances they could shift their loyalties in a comparatively short space of time.

The socio-economic boundary between Tory deferentials and Tory pragmatists or seculars follows a similar line to that distinguishing working-class Tories in general and working-class Labour voters. The deferentials conform to Runciman's ideal type while the seculars/pragmatists are higher paid, younger and males. The message is clear: in the future the Tories cannot count upon an automatic base amongst the working class. The working-class loyalists are dying out and they are unlikely to be replaced by an equally committed cohort. Young working-class citizens have had very different experiences from those of their parents and grandparents. They have been the subject of new learning processes, and they have been brought up within a context that has different social, economic and political dimensions.[58] So the Conservative party will have to reinforce its pragmatic appeal and convince the electorate that it is the party most capable of governing the country. On the other hand, if the affluent workers of Luton are at all typical, the Labour party can draw little comfort from this for it likewise will be judged on its record, even amongst some of its most faithful past supporters.

Although the basis of support given to the two major British political parties may have shifted its ground, it is far from clear how the new pressures are translated into the act of voting by the individual worker. Is the thesis that affluence leads to embourgeoisement which results in Tory voting any more naive than one in which affluence leads to an instrumentality resulting in the switching of party preferences? In both cases the economic changes bring about a new working-class life-style and it is from this that the political consequence flow. Both theses make sense at the level of socio-political change but neither translates the process into individual behaviour. Do all traditional workers have an equal commitment to the same mores? How much erosion of this commitment has to occur before political behaviour changes? Is the pattern of change the same in each case, and if not, why not? What is required is an attempt to fill in the stages between the individual's structural context and his behaviour.

One of the difficulties with the thesis that workers have an instrumentality or pragmatism that determines their political behaviour is that it tells us little about the surrounding political context. If workers are going to change their preferences then they must have another viable horse to back. Will the parties place themselves in the market in such a way as to appeal to these potential working-class waverers? It is possible they can make certain steps in this direction but they have to consider their wider pattern of support as well as to counter the charge that they are making reckless promises. At the same time it requires considerable individual oscillation to believe in one election that the Labour party is your best bet and in the next the Conservative party, or vice versa. What happens if neither party has changed its policies? So, although Goldthorpe and Lockwood may be right about the emergence of a new working class, and this has been paralleled by a shift in the basis of working-class Conservatism, it is much more tenuous to take these trends one step further and talk of a different kind of political consciousness. The fluctuations and uncertainties in political allegiance may be simply that rather than a reflection of a new-found instrumentality.[59] It is not unexpected that the two major political parties should have caused periodic disillusionment amongst their supporters in the past decade or so, given their evident failure to grapple successfully with the country's economic problems. What is perhaps surprising is the extent to which the working class has remained loyal to the Labour party. As the Luton study shows, the affluent workers were not seduced by the prosperity of the 1950s, although the Tory party received a great deal of credit for this. If instrumentality was part of the affluent worker's make-up he should have deserted the Labour party sometime before Goldthorpe and Lockwood conducted their survey. Since the 1950s the Labour party's working-class vote has continued to hold up fairly well in spite of six years in office during which it suffered considerable setbacks and many of its supporters became further disillusioned. Finally it was the solidity of its working-class support that enabled the party to emerge from the 1974 General Elections as the largest parliamentary party.[60]

Instrumentality can assume non-political, notably industrial, forms. Certainly the links between industrial action and economic self-interest are more direct and concrete than voting and improving one's general standard of living. So rather than showing fluctuating support for political parties instrumentality may be manifested in industrial, as opposed to political, action. This has been complicated by direct government intervention in wage bargaining. Although this has involved both major parties, it was taken to greater lengths by the Tory government in the period leading up to the General Election of February 1974. At the same time the Industrial Relations Act brought further confrontations between that government and the trade unions. This gave the political left even greater incentive to bring down the Heath government and, clearly, to do this it had to mobilize working-class support. In these circumstances industrial and political action complemented one another, but what does the worker do if a Labour government should make the same 'mistakes?'[61] They are unlikely to flock to the Tory party in large numbers; a more probable outcome is a withdrawal of support from the Labour party accompanied by an increase in industrial action. The pragmatic working-class Tory voters must have been under considerable stress in the past few years, but whether it was a change in their behaviour or a higher turn-out by traditional working-class Labour voters that was responsible for the two electoral defeats of the Tory party in 1974 remains to be seen.[62]

The idea that voters may be instrumental in making their party choices is a return to Paul Lazarsfeld's early voting studies research.[63] In his *The People's Choice* the parties were seen as packages on the shelves of a supermarket and the voters as the shoppers. Purchases would be made on the basis of fulfilling needs established before entering the shop but the individual could be swayed by skilfully presented images. In fact Lazarsfeld felt that the individual arrived at his choice during the election campaign. Subsequent voting studies stressed the long-term influences that induced stability in voting behaviour. These varied from socio-economic forces and personal social interaction to socio-psychological variables. Obviously fluctuations in party preferences occurred but the emphasis was on stability rather than change.[64] Although we may not want to return to Lazarsfeld's model, the evidence suggests a new flexibility in party preference, at least as far as Britain is concerned.[65]

Central to socialization theory is the notion that learning experiences produce stable behavioural patterns. The evidence on instrumental working-class Labour voters and secular working-class Tory voters implies that this can no longer be taken for granted. These individuals are detached from the restraining influence of a cultural context as it is traditionally understood, and their behaviour is essentially a response to a calculating self-interest. It is not that these individuals fail to have learning experiences but that their learning experiences direct them to value one goal above all others — economic self-interest. This is in direct contrast to the deferential working-class Tories or the traditional working-class Labour voters. In these two cases the preferences arise out of a broad social context that ties the individual to the political party. They are interested in their economic well-being but this fits into a wider pattern of interests and values. If embourgeoisement means assimilation into the middle class then the attachment to the Tory party would have deeper roots than economic self-interest, i.e. the basis of party allegiance would become more like that of other solidly aligned groups by having socio-cultural as well as economic dimensions. I have already indicated this view of temporary party preferences presupposes that the individual can make viable alternative choices if he feels the need should arise. Given the structure of British political life this is unrealistic, and the only course is to opt out of politics or to take action in other fields.[66] Of equal importance is what meaning can be attached to instrumentality. If the workers of Luton were so instrumental then why had they failed to desert the Labour party by the late 1950s in spite of all the Tory-sponsored affluence? Perhaps instrumentality had always existed and the Luton workers were expressing traditional reasons for supporting the Labour party, in much the same way as some working-class Tory voters have always based their allegiance upon that party's record in delivering the goods. In this sense pragmatic allegiances are a rationalization for a deeper level of commitment. Even if this is not so then there is no reason why conditional support based on one plank cannot be turned into permanent support based on many reasons. So over time the political act has built into it a meaning that consists of social and cultural factors as well as economic self-interest.

The changing occupational structure and the new middle classes

A prevalent idea in contemporary educational sociology is that working-class children who pass the 11-plus examination are not really members of 'true' working-class families. They may be considered to belong to the 'submerged' middle class, or their family's socio-economic circumstances may be somewhat more advantageous than those of the average working-class family, or, if all else fails, they could be children whose parents have given them strong encouragement to succeed educationally — and we all know how alien that is to working-class culture![67] A parallel trend can be seen in one explanation of working-class Conservatism and likewise it takes various forms, each of which devalues somewhat the individual's membership of the working class.

Runciman has made the most thorough analysis of the hypothesis that working-class identification with the middle class induces Conservatism.[68] Class self-placement can mean different things to different people and this led Goldthorpe and Lockwood to make the observation that, 'It would seem virtually impossible to interpret such data in any way that would provide reliable indications of respondents' class awareness or class consciousness; the scope for arbitrary variations and ambiguity is far too great'.[69] Undeterred, Runciman probed the meaning of such self-placements in face-to-face interviews. He concluded that when middle-class self-placement was interpreted in one of the three following ways it was associated with voting Tory: a non-manual occupation, a life-style and purely personal criteria. When the probing revealed that the individual's idea of belonging to the middle classes meant someone in a manual occupation, he was just as likely to vote for the Labour party as a self-rated working-class citizen.[70]

Most individuals who self-rated themselves as middle-class did so on the grounds of 'some personal criteria or approval', which led Runciman to conclude that few of them were aspiring to become members of the middle class. Why then were they more prone to vote Tory than the self-rated working class? Runciman suggests it is because the middle class acts as a normative reference group for them but, as they are more fickle in their loyalties than the self-rated working-class Tory, it is either a tentative reference group or perhaps one in which voting Tory cannot be taken for granted. In any case their uncertainty gives them an affinity with McKenzie's and Silver's seculars and Nordlinger's pragmatists.

The middle class acts as a normative reference group for these working-class Tories because they are in direct contact with it, and so it provides a standard against which they can measure their behaviour. This is another form of deference, for not only do these working-class citizens recognize the presence of a superior external standard, but they also adopt it as a behavioural model, i.e. they attempt to follow its dictates, even if they have no wish to become part of it. This may be different from deferring to traditional forms of authority, as suggested by ascriptive socio-political deference but, none the less, behaviour is modified in response to a higher social class reference point. This reference point can be either personal acquaintances or a wider social context. Goldthorpe and Lockwood argue that it was not affluence that makes Tories out of the working class but rather middle-class contacts in the family environment. This can take various forms: parental socio-economic status, wife's present or past occupation, the social status of in-laws or a previous job. These contacts exercise an influence independent of all the affluent variables — income, home ownership and place of residence.[71] The precise ways in which these middle-class links induce Tory voting is never made clear by Goldthorpe and Lockwood. The social interaction could lead to direct exposure to Tory influences (e.g. a father-in-law who votes Conservative), or the middle-class influences exert pressure against those forces that help to keep the individual within the Labour party fold (e.g. the wife would prefer the husband not to spend his time on union activities) or, thirdly, no positive political inferences may be involved but the individual gradually develops a state of consciousness in which voting Tory becomes acceptable or, perhaps more neutrally, it is not unacceptable. In each case the assumption is that a natural class division exists in

British political life and these are individuals who are crossing, more or less unconsciously, that divide.

Runciman was thinking of a middle-class presence in less specific terms. He notes that working-class Conservatism is stronger in some industrial areas than others, depending upon the nature of the local industrial base as well as the prevalence of local working men's clubs affiliated to the Tory party.[72] Margaret Stacey's study of Banbury shows that the capitalist entrepeneur has continuing political influence where the smallness of the firm still permits some face-to-face interaction between the boss and his workers.[73] It is not so much that the boss acts as a normative reference group but rather that deeply entrenched local cultural traditions perpetuate the Tory allegiances. These local cultural traditions are being slowly undermined by industrial amalgamations, the spread of semi-skilled assembly-line processes, and the growth of new towns and large working-class council estates. It is important to keep these trends in perspective; although the affluent workers of Luton may provide the model for the future, millions of workers will continue to earn their living outside that kind of socio-industrial context.

Changes in the occupational structure provide a number of variants on the theme that working-class Tories are really disguised members of the middle class. Robert Alford writes, 'The shift of the occupational structure has undermined the objective basis of Labour support by reducing the actual size of the working class, and this change probably accounts for part of the loss of Labour votes. Labour's traditional electorate may be as solid as ever'.[74] Besides assuming a straightforward relationship between social class and party preference, as well as an inability on the part of the Labour party to change its 'objective basis', Alford provides no detailed analysis of how these individuals who were actually affected by changes in the socio-economic structure responded to this in political terms. It is possible that some workers moved from declining working-class occupation to expanding middle-class jobs. Given the need for new skills, and perhaps even formal qualifications, it is doubtful whether much of the change was quite as dramatic as this. Even in the cases where it occurred it is unlikely that it would have resulted in a change of allegiance, except perhaps in cases where party wavering was already well established. Some industries contracted by buying out part of their work forces or not by employing more personnel as the older workers retired. This would have led to only a limited amount of movement across class lines, and it is difficult to see how it would have resulted in changes in party loyalties.

Clearly the notion that the shifting balance of the occupational structure has an impact upon the changing pattern of party preferences is heavily dependent upon those experiencing inter-generational mobility. The educated sons and daughters of the working class are moving into the expanding white-collar stratum and in the process, so the thesis assumes, realigning their party preferences. The evidence indicates that what impact inter-generational social mobility has upon party preference depends upon how social mobility is defined. On the basis of a definition that included both objective and subjective information, Butler and Stokes concluded that it had very little influence. In a reinterpretation of their data, dependent mainly upon dropping the subjective elements from their definition, Paul Abramson has written, 'Upwardly mobile persons were more likely to vote Conservative than were persons of working class-origins who were not upwardly mobile . . . '[75] As inter-generational mobility takes place over time anticipatory socialization could occur.[76] The individual has plenty of time in which to adjust his behaviour to an emerging new life-style. This is especially so when mobility depends upon the gradual acquisition of formal educational qualifications, for this may well entail cutting oneself off from a working-class life-style. But neither the educational nor the occupational seductions should be over-stressed for strong left-wing allegiances may be sufficient to resist both.

All three variations — class self-placement, social contacts and social mobility — on the theme that the working-class Tories owe their political allegiances to middle-class connections reaffirm the potency of the class basis of British political life. But it is a reaffirmation that is fraught with danger. The fact that the Tory loyalties of the self-rated middle-class manual workers are more fragile than those of the self-rated working-class Tory indicates the instability and vagueness of this middle-class reference point. As politics in Britain is not simply class-based it is impossible for any social group to serve as a *clear* political guideline, as implied in Runciman's concept of a normative reference point. Secondly, it is a thesis that reintroduces, admittedly in a somewhat unique form, the notion of deference. It assumes that the middle-class contacts seduce the working-class citizen into betraying his true consciousness; that the worker is a ready prey to the middle-class temptations that cross his path. This devalues the manual worker's loyalty to the Conservative party, for the implication is that without the seductive voice of the middle class his political behaviour would be different. Finally, and more damagingly, it devalues the working-class Tory's membership of the proletariat, for not only does his party preference make him suspect but also his middle-class ties suggest a lack of true commitment to his class.[77]

The political socialization of working-class adolescents

The various explanations of working-class Conservatism have only limited affinity with some of the central socialization assumptions. Except for the deference explanation, the stress is more upon the impact of adult, especially work-centred, experiences rather than childhood learning patterns. Furthermore, these are experiences that are as likely to result in fluctuating political behaviour as in stable predispositions. This reflects a general weakness in the political socialization research in its coming to grips with actual behaviour as opposed to attitudes. In spite of these short-comings a certain amount of socialization literature has at least an indirect bearing upon some of the issues.

One body of evidence shows that British schoolchildren, very much in line with their American cousins, manifest a high degree of support for the political system.[78] In a statement not atypical of its genre Stradling writes, 'The political institutions and procedures have gradually adapted to changing circumstances; the society is homogeneous and integrated; and supportive attitudes have been successfully transmitted from generation to generation'.[79] So, if deference is defined as support for the established political system, the political socialization process appears to be successful in perpetuating deference, but this is a characteristic of the total samples under observation and not just of the working-class adolescents. Fred Greenstein is one of the few authors to refer to explicit class differences in the political attitudes of British schoolchildren. In his sample working-class children were more likely than their middle-class peers to think the Queen ruled as well as reigned, and, in spite of a greater political awareness amongst the older children, the class differences persisted.[80] In a speculative interpretation Greenstein suggested that this could help to explain adult working-class deference. This is another example of one of those amazing leaps from childhood attitudes to adult behaviour that have brought justified rebuke to political socialization research.[81]

Much firmer evidence that certain forms of political socialization encourage deference is found in some studies that show considerable adolescent discontent with the structure of our society.[82] This may sound something of a contradiction, but one of the firmest trends to emerge is in relation to those who refrain from adventuring opinions rather than those who are either satisfied or dissatisfied with the status quo. The evidence is incontrovertible: the politically passive are disproportionately working-class girls in the least prestigious schools.[83] This form of political passivity is complemented by a self-reported low interest in politics and a retardation in the formation of party preferences.[84] Although in these particular cases the passivity may not persist into adulthood, it does follow similar adult trends. At the same time these are adolescents who have very realistic future job expectations, i.e. they are destined for the unskilled working class, or, in the case of the girls, an early marriage. So various dimensions of an integrated passive role start to take shape during the years of formal education.

This creation of a passive role fits the notion that the educational system exists to perpetuate inequality, but this is not the same thing as legitimizing inequality. The politically passive may, to use Mann's phrase, accept their lot, but this is a long way from being happy with it.[85] A number of behavioural measures that rarely intrude into the political socialization research illustrate this: truancy, violence and vandalism within and outside school, petty delinquency and even the desire to leave school as soon as the law permits. My own study revealed a high degree of realism in working-class views of this society. Many of them were aware of the inegalitarianism of the class structure and more specifically how this was manifested in the distribution of educational and job opportunities.[86] Of course the lengths to which they are prepared to go to do anything about these grievances is another question, and Mann argues that as industrial workers grow older the fatalistic acceptance of their lot in life increases.[87]

Much of the research that points to a declining level of adolescent support for the political system has been undertaken by Americans, but British social scientists have not been slow to attack their interpretations.[88] This is a reversal of traditional roles, for in the past American social scientists have been prone to stress the merits of a deferential working class, while the critique has come from this side of the Atlantic.[89] The attack upon this adolescent data centres around the technical quality of the information and, more significantly, the extreme and tenuous interpretations that have been made of it. It may be unwise to take up the cry of a prophet of doom on the basis of such evidence, but it does make it more difficult to sustain the idea that British socialization processes are successfully training a deferential working class. Dominant values may emanate from a ruling class but they are of little avail unless the messages in which they are contained are received, internalized and acted upon. The working classes may not be abounding with true consciousness but it does not follow that they are readily lulled into a false consciousness.

Dominant values and the class basis of British politics

The explanations of working-class Conservatism contain two central themes: as social class is the dominating feature of British political life this peculiarity must be understood in class terms; alternatively the explanation can be rooted in the fact that British society is pervaded by dominant values. Parkin has linked the two variations by arguing that dominant values emerge from a particular class and are super-imposed upon other classes (in particular upon the working class).[90] This is in direct contrast to, for example, Almond and Verba, who make no reference to class differences in the British interpretation of the civic culture.[91] However, even the most ardent dominant value theorist acknowledges the existence of islands of resistance in which working-class culture withstands the seductions of the advanced capitalist society. It is hard to imagine that there are cultural enclaves in Britain that are completely cut off from dominant values, and if local and dominant cultural patterns clash what is of interest is the form this clash takes and how it is resolved. I have stressed the importance of individual resolution of these potential clashes (i.e. individuals interpret the conflicts) in order to avoid a simpleminded socialization explanation of behaviour.

The much maligned deference thesis could be reinterpreted as a variant of the dominant value theory. The deferential working-class citizens who vote Tory have been exposed to more dominant values, at a greater level of intensity, than their non-deferential class peers who vote for the Labour party. Even if this is so the evidence suggests such deference will decline in the future because the social categories most susceptible to its influence are on the wane. If dominant values still exist either their influence also declines or the behavioural alternatives (e.g. voting for the Labour party as opposed to the Conservative party) become meaningless gestures. That is, they present no challenge to the established order. If this is true then it is up to the proponents of the theory to tell us what constitutes a real escape from dominant values. Implicit in the dominant value theory is a static view of the world, for there has been little discussion of how values change in response to new circumstances. In fact some evidence points to a move away from values incorporating ascriptive socio-political deference towards a value pattern based on meritocratic deference; so education and alleged competence become the guiding lines for inequality rather than birth.

Although traditional forms of working-class Conservatism may be on the decline, it does not follow that working-class support for the Tory party has reached the end of the road. Deference appears to be making way for pragmatism and in the process the allegiance given to both the Labour and Conservative parties has become more tentative. This is in tune with contemporary political realities, more specifically the failure of both the major parties to deal successfully with economic problems. If at the same time economic self-interest weighs more heavily in deciding voting behaviour then the end result will be greater political pragmatism, especially when no one appears to have a viable solution to our economic ills. Rather than being guided by more economic self-interest, the pragmatic working-class Tory voters could be exhibiting meritocratic deference. They think the Tories, because of their links with finance and industry, are better at running the economy, and a fortunate by-product of this is their own economic wellbeing. This suggests the emergence of a value system in which the forms of property ownership are of secondary importance to the efficient management of the economy.

A crude statement of the affluent worker thesis is that prosperity is driving the proletariat into the ranks of the middle class and thus they come to realize that their interests are better served by voting Tory. In other words, voting Tory is merely a manifestation of their general embourgeoisement. More sophisticated variations of this thesis suggest that it is middle-class contacts, rather than affluence, that induce working-class Conservatism. But this devalues the working-class Tory's membership of his social class for it implies that he is in some way or other tainted by middle-class influences; complementing this is the devaluation of his Tory affiliation for the suggestion is that without the middle-class influences his political behaviour would be different.

Both the class and dominant value theories depend upon the over-socialized conception of man. Apparently the only way to escape the tentacles of dominant values is to be trapped by an equally powerful subculture. Similarly, the working-class citizen will not vote Tory unless he or she has been exposed to middle-class stimuli. It is as if no traditional workers vote Tory whereas all members of the middle class do. Regardless of what the statistical evidence may show, the social scientist has to face the problems of *why* certain cultural forces have one impact rather than another and *how* they shape behaviour. No matter how powerful the cultural context, invariably there will be a number of different responses to it. These responses point to individual interpretations of external stimuli rather than a mechanistic and predetermined course of action. The class and dominant value theories can be viewed in this more flexible manner and to do so raises interesting questions about their interaction with other forces in the making of behaviour. However, this has not taken place, with the result that not only has the whole field of learning theory been ignored but also simple-minded generalizations have been built into the dimensions of working-class membership and what it means to vote Tory.

Interest in working-class Tories has been stimulated by their apparent contradiction of the class basis of British political life, as well the related assumption that no member of the proletariat with true consciousness would be voting for the Tory party. I have shown some of the limitations involved in trying to defend both the class basis of British political life as well as the concept of false consciousness. In a society in which two broad-based political parties seek to gain total control of the governmental apparatus through the electoral process the probability of not having party preferences that cut across social groupings is very slim indeed. This is especially so when, in statistical terms, the only major divisive force is social class and the size of each particular social class is so large. All the theories have to face this simple fact of political life. Of probably greater interest is what the research has to say about more general political trends. In this respect I would like to stress the importance of work-related socialization experiences, and the increasing tentativeness surrounding political allegiances. Both point to a degree of flux, and indeed instability, that contradicts some of the central assumptions of the political socialization research as well as some of the more established views of the British political process. It is not that working-class Conservatism requires no explanation but that these explanations can mean all things to all men. They have served to promote ideological causes rather than social understanding.

Notes

1. R. Alford, *Party and Society: Anglo-American Democracies,* John Murray, London, 1964, ch. 6. This is reinforced by D. Butler and D. Stokes, op. cit., ch. 4, 5.

2. Although class may be declining in importance, it is still the most significant line dividing Tory and Labour party voters. Furthermore, it could be fairly argued that the Labour party won most parliamentary seats in the two General Elections of 1974 because of the solidity of its working-class support. Ironically, the Tories appear to have suffered a major erosion of their middle-class support as seen in their waning fortunes in Scotland (to the Scottish Nationalist party) and in southern England (to the Liberal party). For further discussion of the allegedly declining importance of class in relation to electoral behaviour see D. Butler and D. Kavanagh, *The General Election of February 1974*, Macmillan, London, 1974, pp. 6–7, 272–273.

3. Butler and Kavanagh suggest that the Liberals took votes from both the major parties in the February 1974 General Election, which affirms their median, if not moderate, position. However, with the exception of Rochdale, which has historical links with the Liberal party, they have been singularly unsuccessful in winning power in urban constituencies, although this is untrue of local elections. In terms of votes their major breakthrough in 1974 came in the more middle-class south.

4. At the moment manual workers outnumber non-manual workers by roughly two to one.

5. It could be disputed that the non-effectiveness of social class is *almost as important* as its effectiveness, for although approximately one-third of the working class votes Tory, two-thirds vote Labour, and the split within the middle class favours the Tories by a somewhat greater margin.

6. Hindess, op. cit.

7. See the comments in notes 1 and 2 above. The situation has been complicated by the rise of the nationalist parties and the resurgence of the Liberals; the permanence of these developments has a great bearing upon future trends.

8. See for example Hindess' reliance on a poll conducted by M. Abrams, *op. cit.*, p. 22.

9. For an excellent account of the amalgamation of forces leading to the emergence of the Labour party (the Labour Representation Committee in its early days) see H. Pelling, *The Origins of the Labour Party, 1880–1900*, Oxford University Press, Oxford, 1965.

10. See p. 83.

11. R. McKenzie and A. Silver, *Angels in Marble*, Heinemann, London, 1968, pp. 7–8.

12. ibid., pp. 36–71; D. Kavanagh, 'The deferential English: A comparative critique', *Government and Opposition*, 6 (1971), 347–350.

13. R. Crossman, 'Introduction' to W. Bagehot, *The English Constitution*, Collins, London, 1963, pp. 26–29. I do not intend to imply that Disraeli did not think of electoral manipulation to limit the political influence of the working classes but that he was more aware than most of the prevailing social constraints within which working-class consciousness would develop.

14. ibid., pp. 9–10.

15. This is still essentially correct in spite of the very recent increase in left-wing influence within the party.

16. H. Pelling, *A Short History of the Labour Party*, Macmillan, London, 1965, p. 4.

17. If a distinction were made between the Labour movement and the parliamentary Labour party perhaps this could be disputed, but I would argue that to posit such a sharp dichotomy is too simple a way of dealing with an inherent tension that the Labour party has to learn to live with and until now it has succeeded in doing so.

18. R. Miliband, *Parliamentary Socialism: A Study in the Politics of Labour*, Merlin Press, London, 1973; see especially ch. 10; Hindess, op. cit., ch. 8; F. Parkin, *Class, Inequality and Political Order*, MacGibbon and Kee, London, 1971, pp. 121–128.

19. op. cit., pp. 71–81.
20. But it is far from certain whether this was a direct result of the loss of working class support.
21. C. A. R. Crosland, *The Future of Socialism*, Macmillan, New York, 1957.
22. K. Marx, 'The Chartists', *New York Daily Tribune*, August 25, 1852. See T. Bottomore, *Classes in Modern Society*, Allen and Unwin, London, 1965, p. 62. Of course Marx did not live long enough to witness the seductive influence of parliamentary democracy.
23. Witness the tirade of Lenin; op. cit., pp. 397–408.
24. R. Rose, 'Class and party divisions: Britain as a test case', Occasional Paper No. 1, Survey Research Centre, Strathclyde, 1968.
25. A recurring theme in R. Rose, *Governing Without Consensus: An Irish Perspective*, Faber and Faber, London, 1971.
26. These are the three areas established by Easton and Dennis. See pp. 3–4.
27. S. Rothman, 'Modernity and tradition in Britain', in R. Rose (ed.), *Studies in British Politics*, Macmillan, London, 1966, pp. 4–20.
28. See p. 102.
29. If class is indeed declining in its political importance then this is less significant.
30. Otherwise the symbol may evaporate rapidly in a crisis situation.
31. op. cit. (World's Classic Edition), p. 250.
32. Almond and Verba, op. cit., pp. 455–469.
33. Crossman, op. cit., p. 26.
34. ibid.
35. For Bagehot's fears on the extension of the franchise see the 'Introduction to the Second Edition' of his *English Constitution* (1872), pp. 260–278. For his views on attitudes towards the police see ibid., pp. 254–255. But the police were not then an established authority symbol in quite the way they are today.
36. For evidence that the political power of the aristocracy continued way beyond the granting of universal male suffrage, see Guttsman, op. cit., ch. 5.
37. E. A. Nordlinger, *The Working-class Tories*, MacGibbon and Kee, London, 1967, pp. 34–35. Note that emphasis in original text.
38. *Politics in England*, p. 41.
39. R. D. Jessop, 'Civility and traditionalism in England political culture', *British Journal of Political Science*, **1** (1971), 1–24.
40. ibid., p. 14. For another dissection see Kavanagh, 'The deferential English: A comparative critique', pp. 336–342.
41. F. Parkin, 'Working-class Conservatives: A theory of political deviance', *British Journal of Sociology*, **18** (1967), 278–290.
42. See Lipset, op. cit., p. 112.
43. W. G. Runciman, *Relative Deprivation and Social Justice*, Routledge and Kegan Paul, London, 1966, pp. 175–176.
44. 'Working-class Conservatives: A theory of political deviance', p. 289.
45. op. cit., p. 14. For similarities in their political attitudes see McKenzie and Silver, op. cit., pp. 160–162.
46. The point I am trying to make is not confounded by the fact that it is difficult to pinpoint either the foundation of the Tory party or the stirrings of British capitalism.
47. Lipset made a statement to this effect in relation to political trends within Europe in general. S. M. Lipset, 'The changing class structure and contemporary European politics', *Daedalus (Winter* 1964), 271–303.
48. D. Butler and R. Rose, *The British General Election of 1959*, Macmillan, London, 1960, p. 15.
49. F. Zweig, *The Worker in an Affluent Society*, Heinemann, London, 1961, p. 211.
50. M. Abrams, 'Social trends and electoral behaviour', *British Journal of Sociology*, **13** (1962), 241–242.

51. For a review of this and other theories on contemporary developments in industrial society see M. Mann, *Consciousness and Action Among the Western Working Class*, Macmillan, London, ch. 3, 4.

52. Zweig, op. cit., p. 138.

53. J. H. Goldthorpe *et al.*, *The Affluent Worker: Political Attitudes and Behaviour*, Cambridge University Press, Cambridge, 1968, p. 1.

54. These are all terms used by Goldthorpe and his co-authors.

55. op. cit., pp. 40–42. See also I. Crewe, 'The politics of "affluent" and "traditional" workers in Britain: An aggregate data analysis', *British Journal of Political Science*, 3 (1973), 29–52.

56. op. cit., ch. 5.

57. op. cit., pp. 66–81.

58. For example, the Labour party has been an established national party all their lives which was certainly not true in the case of their grandparents and only partly true in the case of their parents.

59. For a claim that there is a pattern of social direction behind this change see Crewe, op. cit., pp. 41–44.

60. On this see note 2, above.

61. As happened in the 1966–1970 period when the Labour Government was forced by a combination of trade union and party pressure to abandon its attempt to regulate the process of free collective bargaining. At the time of writing another Labour Government is trying to follow the same course, with what consequences we will wait and see.

62. It is possible that even if the Tory working-class vote had remained solid the Conservative party would still have lost both the 1974 General Elections.

63. P. Lazarsfeld *et al.*, *The People's Choice*, Columbia University Press, New York, 1968 (3rd edition), pp. 3–8. See also P. Rossi, 'Four landmarks in voting research', in E. Burdick and A. J. Brodbeck (eds.), *American Voting Behaviour*, Free Press, Glencoe, Illinois, 1959, pp. 15–17.

64. The Campbell studies were somewhat different for they were meant to answer the question why, in spite of only small changes in the socio-economic structure, the outcomes of the 1948 and 1952 Presidential elections were so very different. See Rossi, op. cit., pp. 36–38.

65. Of course we may be witnessing the formation of new rigid patterns of party preferences rather than an oscillation in loyalties, but the rather dramatic shifts in the past few years make it hard to believe that the party preference pattern will now settle down into a new mould.

66. Some will turn to the fringe political parties of both the left and right; their resurgence is another feature of the current British political scene.

67. These are all explanations that have arisen in British educational sociology. Perhaps the best known is Jackson's and Marsden's submerged middle class thesis. B. Jackson and D. Marsden, op. cit.

68. One of the central problems analysed in his *Relative Deprivation and Social Justice;* see especially pp. 175–176.

69. J. H. Goldthorpe and D. Lockwood, 'Affluence and the British class structure', *The Sociological Review*, New Series, **11** (1963), 144.

70. op. cit., p. 177.

71. op. cit., pp. 54–60.

72. op. cit., pp. 54–60. Again this is an extraordinary generalization that completely fails to explain the pattern of community behaviour. Just as the socialization studies fail to fill in the links between childhood attitudes and adult behaviour so Runciman makes no attempt to explain how community norms work themselves out in terms of individual behaviour.

73. M. Stacey, *Tradition and Change: A Study of Banbury*, Oxford University Press, London, 1960, p. 169.

74. op. cit., p. 133.
75. P. Abramson, 'Intergenerational mobility and partisan choice', *American Political Science Review*, **66** (1972), 1292.
76. Jackson's and Marsden's book is an interesting study of children being prepared, and preparing themselves, for future middle-class roles.
77. In this respect Runciman with his emphasis on community cultural norms is less patronizing than Goldthorpe and Lockwood with their reference to specific middle-class reference points. At least Runciman has not personalized deference to quite the same extent.
78. See the concluding comments in R. E. Dowse and J. Hughes, op. cit. F. I. Greenstein *et al.*, 'Queen and Prime Minister: The child's eye view', *New Society*, **14** 369 (1969), 635–638. R. Stradling, 'Socialization of support for political authority in Britain: A long-term view', *British Journal of Political Science*, **1** (1971), 121–122.
79. ibid., p. 121.
80. 'Queen and Prime Minister: The child's eye view', p. 635.
81. A position which he scarcely modifies in an extended and more recent version. See F. Greenstein *et al.*, 'The child's conception of the Queen and Prime Minister', *British Journal of Political Science*, **4** (1974), 285–287.
82. What follows relies heavily on my *Young People and Society*, especially chs. 7, 8 and 9. For other British data see J. Dennis *et al.*, *op. cit.*, pp. 25–48; P. Abramson and T. Hennessey, 'Beliefs about democracy among British adolescents', *Political Studies*, **18** (1970), 239–242; P. Abramson and R. Inglehart, 'The development of systematic support in four Western democracies', *Comparative Political Studies*, **2** (1970), 419–442.
83. Tapper, op. cit., pp. 111–117.
84. ibid., pp. 103–106.
85. M. Mann, 'The social cohesion of liberal democracy', *American Sociological Review*, **35** (1970), 423–439.
86. Tapper, op. cit., pp. 136–138.
87. op. cit., ch. 3.
88. For the American attack see the references listed in note 82 above, and for the British defence see the reviews of Dennis' article: I. Budge, 'Support for nation and government among English children: A comment', *British Journal of Political Science*, **1** (1971), 389–392; A. H. Birch, 'Children's attitudes and British politics', *British Journal of Political Science*, **1** (1971), 519–520; D. Kavanagh, 'Allegiance among English children: A dissent', *British Journal of Political Science*, **1** (1972), 127–131.
89. Nordlinger, McKenzie, Silver and Rose — all North Americans — have placed considerable emphasis upon the importance of working-class deference for the stability of British political life. Parkin, Runciman, Kavanagh and Mann have all shown considerable scepticism as to both the reality of working-class deference and even more so as to its alleged consequences.
90. Of course in Parkin's thesis dominant values are essentially class values, i.e. a combination of middle-class values with some aristocratic appendages. This would make working-class values essentially subcultural values. I would argue that certain features of what Parkin calls dominant values are not simply class-based (e.g. nationalism certainly transcends class boundaries), and I am far from happy to relegate two-thirds of the population to the status of a subculture.
91. See Rothman, op. cit., for a similar interpretation of British political culture.

Chapter 7

Students in Conflict

Student conflict and political socialization

Between the summers of 1964 and 1970 radical student protest in Britain and America reached unprecedented heights.[1] The Berkeley Free Speech Movement that commenced in late 1964 marked the beginning of sustained political protest on many campuses in western industrialied society. Besides its prolongation another distinguishing feature of the conflict was its intensity, and some of the most sedate and illustrious of institutions witnessed scenes reminiscent of a Latin American or Asian university. Although so much of the protest centred around the American involvement in the Vietnam war, another unique facet was the emergence, in rapid succession, of a number of mutually reinforcing issues. At Berkeley aspects of the Free Speech Movement dragged on for two years, to overlap with such diverse matters as the course of American foreign policy and the university's attitude towards the People's Park.[2] At the London School of Economics disturbances arising out of British support for American policy in Vietnam entwined with attempts to prevent the new director, Walter Adams, from taking up his post because of alleged co-operation with the racist Smith regime in Rhodesia.[3] At both universities further waves of protest emanated from the disciplinary procedures which sanctioned those who had incurred the authorities' wrath in the initial confrontations. Another innovation was the tactics employed by the demonstrating students. Following the lead of the civil rights movement, to which many students belonged, civil disobedience came to the campus: marches, sit-ins and teach-ins were the tactics pursued by American students, and their influence soon spread.[4]

These developments contrasted starkly with the mood of American, and to a lesser extent British students in the 1950s, who were described as 'the silent generation'. Their previous passivity highlighted the radicalism of the subsequent generation, and it was not surprising that there was a general interest in the reason for it and what should be done about it. The purpose of this chapter is to examine the answers to these two questions within a political socialization framework. The explosion of radical student protest runs directly counter to some of the major tenets of socialization research. It was ironic that the expansion of empirical research into the political predispositions of children should parallel the growth of student militancy. On the one hand we were presented with a picture of highly supportive schoolchildren, while on the other hand many students were challenging the judgement and honesty of political authorities, the morality of public policy and the supposed virtues of the political structure and its underlying values. If the political socialization research had any viability, student protest should not have arisen. Although the initial confrontations did not occur at the most prestigious private universities, the students involved were none the less a privileged group of predominantly white middle-class citizens, receiving their higher education at good state universities, of which Berkeley was the epitome. It was these very individuals whom the socialization research had found to be supportive of the political system in childhood. The general acceptance of the proposition that the most important dimensions of political behaviour were acquired in childhood, and that what was learnt earliest stayed with the individual longest, were impossible to reconcile with the spectre of student militancy. Perhaps a limited amount of post-adolescent political disillusionment could be tolerated but not the kinds of attacks that actually took place.

So the student revolt threw into question some of the central assumptions surrounding the political learning process. Those with an interest in this field were forced to retrace some of their steps, and in particular to ponder upon the relationship of early learning experiences to the structural constraints that become more explicit as individuals mature into adults. Besides this, students are still receiving formal education so their training for adult roles is incomplete. In many respects higher education builds upon knowledge acquired within a prior educational context and so a certain degree of continuity in learning experiences can be assumed. However, the evidence of student militancy pointed to a dramatic break in the cycle, which raised the question of the uniqueness of learning processes in higher education. So the changes in behaviour may not be just a consequence of a growing awareness of the realities of life (i.e. structural constraints becoming more evident) but also learning experiences *per se* may change. This argument rests heavily upon the claim that the university occupies a special place in western society and as such it is able to structure experiences that differentiate its members from the wider society.

One explanation of student revolt argued that it arose out of a changing relationship between the wider society and the university. What precisely these changes were I will explore shortly, but this proposition raises the key issue of the link between socialization agents and their societal context, and how shifts in this context can influence the shape of the learning experience and ultimately behaviour. So the protest movement should enable us to examine some of the dynamics of the political socialization process. This is of some significance because the research has assumed that the ingredients of the socialization process are static entities which all reasonable men know to be influential. Rarely is there a discussion of why certain socialization agents are important, or how over time they can take different forms and exert their influences in different ways. Part of this problem is the traditional debate as to the relative importance of the socialization agents. In this case, however, it has more fascinating connotations than the usual sterile question of whether the family is more influential than the school or vice versa. This follows from the widespread condemnation of certain manifestations of the student movement and how blame was to be apportioned. In relation to the university it was possible to point to 'the alienating nature of a multiversity education', or the corrupting influence of 'soft' subjects like sociology, or even to direct an accusing finger at both sympathetic faculty and spineless administrators.[5] On the other hand many a beleagured academic or administrator was quick to note that students had been charges of the university for a comparatively short period of time and that recklessly permissive middle-class parents should own up to their share of the responsibility.[6] It is the intrusion of the political element into the debate — i.e. that blame has to be apportioned — that adds a certain amount of spice to this essentially theoretical question of the relationship of socialization agents to one another.

A major theme in the American political sociology of the 1950s and 1960s was that the stability of the Anglo-American democracies rested upon a consensus of attitudes and behaviour. The belief was that as time passed this consensus was growing stronger. In Britain affluence had persuaded many working-class citizens that it was sensible for them to vote for the Tory party, thus helping to increase cross-cutting cleavages. In the United States such factors as increasing urbanization and better educational opportunities were bringing previously excluded groups, like poor rural blacks, into the political mainstream. Accompanying this was the belief that the major ideological divisions within both societies were drawing to a close. In both Britain and the United States the main political parties had long accepted that the route to political power was through the electoral process, but now they also defended a socio-economic order based upon a mixed economy and a meritocratic social structure. Given the widespread acceptance of these fundamental political, social and economic principles, it was realistic to talk of 'the end of ideology'.[7] Political socialization processes were meant to function in ways that ensured the perpetration of this state of affairs, and in this sense they incorporated a set of ideological premises.[8] The student conflict challenged these assumptions, and although the New Left had no coherent ideological position it clearly questioned the realities, if not the theory, of Anglo-

American democracy. The fact that the critique of contemporary society was so campus-centred also suggested that political socialization processes were not a co-ordinated indoctrination programme at the disposal of the ruling class.

Along with other social movements in the 1960s student protest helped to undermine the view that the stability of the Anglo-American democracies depended upon a well-defined behavioural consensus. As we shall see, some commentators felt that the protest movements were just a temporary phase that would be followed by a more integrated and consensual society and, indeed, that the conflict was a necessary stage in the journey to the promised land. Be that as it may, the tremors of the 1960s undermined a societal image that had been painstakingly created by many social scientists over the past decades. Students were a special case study for their movement represented the revolt of an elite cadre rather than of the masses. This increased the interest in them for it raised the question of why the privileged and pampered should feel any necessity to revolt. Students are members of an institution that is apparently well integrated into the wider socio-economic and political structure. The modern university institutionalizes both its faculty and its students, so that it is much more realistic to talk of career academics and trainee professionals than of intellectuals and budding scholars. Lipset makes a distinction between institutionalized and freelance intellectuals and believes that challenges to the status quo are increasingly more likely to emerge only amongst the latter.[9] By the mid-1960s it was impossible to hold to this proposition as confrontation spread from one university to the next, engulfing students, administrators and faculty alike.

The student eruptions also posed a problem for some left-wing critics of Anglo-American society. It was difficult to portray socialization processes as blindly inducting future citizens into inegalitarian roles, as well as imparting bland societal norms, while students were attacking some of the prevailing inequalities and were demanding that the society should live up to its values. It was necessary to explain this apparent inconsistency, and the peculiarity of the student experience became very much the vogue amongst writers of different political persuasions. Socialization assumptions have been used by both consensus theorists as well as left-wing critics of the liberal democracies to bolster their respective cases; on occasions actual political events have undermined one or another of the supposed theoretical truths, and in the process exposed the limitations of the varying positions which were dependent upon them.

A final point of interest arising out of the relationship between political socialization and student conflict is the practical implications it held for the academics, especially those involved in teaching politics. Political socialization research was very much an academic interest which examined how this particular function of the political system aided stability by building citizen support. With its concentration upon childhood political attitudes its consequences were at the best long-term, and certainly had no direct impact upon the lives of the various researchers and teachers. The contrast with the analysis of student demonstrations could not have been greater: the conflict was occurring on the academic's own doorstep, and he was asked to pronounce on events in which he had a real stake. In certain cases academics had formal responsibility for handling alleged student indiscretions; they were forced to abandon their seemingly neutral role and had to embroil themselves in the ensuing conflict, which frequently led to bitter internal faculty splits. The policy implications, therefore, of the explanations of the student movement had for academics a much more tangible meaning than their pronouncements on other social issues.

Evaluating student conflict: The process of inflation and deflation

Even the most optimistic proponents of the view that political socialization builds citizen support for the established order would be reluctant to claim 100 per cent success. The most persuasive processes and institutions must have their inevitable failures. If only a minority of individuals fail to conform then they can be labelled as deviants who, for one reason or another, have opted out from the mainstream. This was a common view of student protest, especially when the movement was in its infancy. In 1965, in a comment on the Berkeley Free Speech Movement, William Petersen wrote,

That a tiny number, a few hundred out of a student body of more than 27,000, was able to disrupt the campus is the consequence of more than vigor and skill in agitation. This miniscule group could not have succeeded in getting so many students into motion without three other, at times unwitting sources of support: off-campus assistance of various kinds, the faculty, and the university administration.[10]

Taking a much harder line in 1966, Lipset and Altbach wrote that student opposition to the Vietnam war 'seemed to vanish into limbo' once 'a responsible opposition emerged within the political elite' and it was then that the press recognized the student radicals for what they were: as insignificant, attracting a small minority of students and opposed by the most.[11]

From the point of view of explaining socio-political movements a long wrangle about the numbers involved rarely serves much purpose. Much the same pattern of involvement can be expected in the activities of the established political parties as in student demonstrations. The instigation and running of a demonstration will be the work of a small minority of the total protestors and how large this latter group turns out to be will vary according to the issues at stake and the context within which the movement is taking place. As the 1960s unfolded it became increasingly difficult to view student protest as simply the consequence of the skilful manipulations of a few malcontents. The kinds of institutions caught up in the turmoil, its intensity and prolongation, and the numbers involved all undermined the credibility of such an explanation. In 1972 Lipset posited a much more moderate version of his previous perspective: 'The opinion surveys of American students indicated that the large majority are not sympathetic with radical doctrines and tactics; most of them seemingly are conventional with respect to appearance, use of drugs, and dedication to academic achievement and a "straight" career'.[12]

Throughout this decade a constant determinant of the numbers involved in a demonstration was, as Petersen indicates, the university's response to a confrontation. Some members of the political right believed that the authorities encouraged protest by failing to crack down firmly in the initial stages of a demonstration. But if there is one established reference point it is that attempts to impose penalties upon the alleged 'ringleaders' widened the arena of conflict, and nothing was more guaranteed to turn a minority into a majority. Such a course of action also changed the nature of the protest, for the university's disciplinary procedures became the centre of attention and the right to cross-examine witnesses sometimes replaced the morality of the American military involvement in Vietnam as a *cause célèbre*. Although the university authorities may not have welcomed this new focus of attention, at least it meant that the issues were now being raised within their sphere of influence. In all the subsequent protest movements we will see that the institutional response has important bearing upon the numbers involved and the issues under discussion.

Various forms of deviance have been ascribed to these supposedly limited numbers of student activists. In the early days it was noted that protest was confined to the large and prestigious state campuses such as Berkeley, Michigan (at Ann Arbor) and Wisconsin (at Madison). Some British commentators saw the key to the continuous troubles at the LSE in its similarities with its American counterparts. Regardless of where the movement in the 1960s originated, by the end of the decade it had spread far and wide. In Britain nearly all the universities experienced minor shock waves which filtered into various polytechnics, only to emerge as volcanic eruptions in the art colleges of Guildford and Hornsey.[13] In the United States protest travelled upwards to the prestigious private universities, both large and small, as well as downwards into the lesser-known state universities and colleges. Two of the bloodiest confrontations took place at Harvard and Kent State, not quite two ends of a prestige continuum but none the less poles apart. In spite of this proliferation of the conflict the centres of fiercest confrontation stood out from the general mêlée, but it became more difficult to neatly categorize them according to specific criteria. So, by 1970 the confrontation centres were certainly not deviant in educational terms.[14]

The deviance labels usually have a social or political content that carries more derogatory connotations than labelling certain educational institutions as protest centres. Various forms of political extremism and/or social deviance were used to describe many of the demonstrators. How widely these characterizations were meant to apply is not always clear, but the temptation to describe all participants as long-haired, pot-smoking anarcho-syndicalists at times has been barely resisted. In the United States the Students for a Democratic Society (SDS) was in the vanguard of many eruptions; until its fragmentation in 1969 it was a loose amalgam of several left-wing groups. It purposely failed to elaborate a coherent ideology and was more noted for its tactical ingenuity than for its ideological virtuosity.[15] Its apologists felt this was one of the sources of its strength, for it was claimed that the Old Left was rendered more ineffectual by petty doctrinal wranglings and it was essential that the New Left should not make the same mistake. The SDS was paralleled in Britain by the Radical Socialist Students' Federation (RSSF), which emerged in opposition to the more moderate leadership of the official students' negotiating body, the National Union of Students (NUS).

Although many of the radical student leaders came from within these broad left-wing alliances very specific political labels were applied to them. With reference to the Berkeley FSM Clark Kerr, then president of the University of California, claimed, 'I am sorry to say that some elements active in the demonstrations have been impressed with the tactics of Fidel Castro and Mao Tse-tung. There are very few of these, but there are some'.[16] And at a slightly later date he further commented, 'Experienced on-the-spot observers estimated that the hard core group of demonstrators . . . contained at times as much as 40 per cent off-campus elements. And, within that off-campus group, there were persons identified as being sympathetic with the Communist party and Communist causes'.[17] Such claims, with variations in the labelling and ferocity of utterance, are part and parcel of the history of the analysis of the student movement. Although one may wonder at the perception (and identity) of Kerr's 'experienced on-the-spot observer', these claims are probably close to being accurate factual statements, but it is naive to defend them simply on these grounds. These are political labels that have negative connotations and they are used to convey a certain image of what is taking place. It was inevitable that left-wing groups would be involved in the demonstrations, but given the broad ideological perspective of the New Left it was inappropriate to apply specific political tags, and especially one like 'communist', which was so outmoded in the context of student politics in the 1960s.[18]

In Britain the political labelling was somewhat different, and, in view of a less paranoid perception of communism, this was to be expected. Max Beloff was an important figure in the debate as to whether student radicalism could be termed 'fascism of the left' or just plain 'fascism', and in his characteristic style he arrived at another of his strong conclusions:

If then we look at the 'student revolt', with its consistent attribution of the injustices and wickedness it finds, or professes to find, in contemporary society or in universities themselves, to ill-defined scapegoats — 'the system', 'the power-structure', 'the elite', 'the bureaucracy', we see an exact parallel to the fascists' denunciation of 'the system', 'capitalism', 'communism', 'the world Jewish Conspiracy' and so forth. The student movement is not 'left-wing fascism', it is 'fascism', there is no other term that so aptly places it in its historical context. And that is why a liberal society cannot compromise with it and should not.[19]

Beloff's reference to 'the student revolt', and indeed to 'the student movement', implies that they were well-defined, ideologically coherent entities, but one of the prominent features of student revolt has been its fragmentation, inconsistency and lack of direction. Furthermore, although he attempted to legitimize his choice of a label, its derogatory connotations are beyond dispute, and could have scarcely escaped Beloff's notice.

The 'social deviance' descriptions are more numerous and harder to classify. A recurring claim is that the disturbances were neither caused nor led by students, and 'off-campus elements' (to use Kerr's phrase) were credited with much of the responsibility. Given the proximity of Berkeley to a cosmopolitan, metropolitan centre this is undoubtedly true. One of the better-known Berkeley confrontations has been termed 'the Battle of the People's Park' and not, you will note, 'the Battle of the Students' Park'. But, unlike Berkeley, most American campuses are not located in the large urban cities but rather in small towns which are much less likely to support the subcultures that abound in conurbations.[20] Defining the boundary between students and non-students is not as easy in the American context as it is in the British. One of the blessings of American university education is its flexibility in allowing students to opt in and out of a degree course without necessarily losing credit for past studies. Why not then take a year off from studies and work for the civil rights movement or one of the various Vietnam war protest groups? During this year the individual concerned is technically not a student but it is inappropriate to classify him or her as an 'off-campus element'. Incidentally, the drafting of temporary drop-outs made it a very hazardous step to interrupt one's studies.

Assuming that students were running and manning the demonstrations, to what extent were they representative of the total student population? One proposition is that they were drawn in disproportionate numbers from those who were not fully integrated into the university community. The list of possible candidates is extensive: the first-year undergraduates, graduates on a one-year programme, the recent transfers, the foreign students and those resident in flats or apartments as opposed to campus-based accommodation.[21] The implication is that these are students who have not been, or will not be around long enough to establish a meaningful relationship with the university. Presumably time and the right pattern of social and academic interaction help to build loyalty to the institution and promote the internalization of community norms. At the LSE constant references were made to the fact that foreign students, especially South Africans and Americans, were at the centre of the troubles and they were importing issues and tactics that had no place in this society. William Letwin was moved to write, 'The most important fact about the revolutionaries is that they are alien'.[22] I assume he was not simply alluding to their residential status.

If the student activists are few in number and deviant socially, academically and, above all, politically, presumably the central political socialization assumptions hold good for everyone else, i.e. the overwhelming majority. But if the majority have been deceived the defence of the status quo has to be made on other grounds. One significant counter-attack was to question the objectives of the movement, as opposed to the number and kind of persons involved. The theory was that the demands for change, and the accompanying demonstrations, disguised the movement's true meaning. It was not that the goals were illegitimate, or even unreasonable, but they were simply irrelevant to the needs of the contemporary society. This led Brzezinski to describe the student demonstrators as counter-revolutionaries rather than as revolutionaries.[23] Raymond Aron arrived at much the same conclusion in answering his own question, 'Student rebellion: Vision of the future or echo from the past?'[24] Why are students prone to advocate irrelevant societal models? The answer lies in their own identity and role anxieties and their desire for a society that will relieve these rather than solve more basic problems. Lewis Feuer and Bruno Bettelheim have suggested that the activism has other, hidden meanings. Bettelheim writes, 'I refer to their feeling that "youth has no future" because modern technology has made them *obsolete* — that they have become socially irrelevant and, as persons, insignificant'.[25] The consequence is a surfeit of restless nihilism that has to be channelled constructively before it provokes a reaction that ushers in Armageddon. In equally grandiose terms Feuer refers to student conflict as generational conflict in which children seek to debase their parents by destroying the old order and creating the new.[26]

These general socio-psychological explanations are sufficiently vague to incorporate all the available evidence and as such they cannot be either proven or, more importantly, disproven. More specifically, how is it to be decided whether a demonstration against the Vietnam war is indeed a protest against American involvement rather than a rebellion against one's father? Although all these authors recognize different kinds of student radicalism they are somewhat vague as to how the chaff can be distinguished from the wheat, so one is left with the impression that they wish to record blanket, rather than selective disapproval. Not everyone, for example, may be enamoured of Brzezinski's ideal of the future — the technetronic society — but is it automatically counter-revolutionary to make proposals that appear to run counter to its demands?

By placing the contemporary student movement in its historical context Feuer links two explanatory strategies. Besides claiming that the ostensible reasons for conflict merely disguise a deeper meaning, he also implies that such conflict has occurred before and will occur again. This second interpretation of student unrest views it as an inevitable and normal part of the socialization process. The student experience is seen as an extension of the adolescent years, which are typically a time of turmoil for the individual in which he or she is seeking an adult role and a permanent, meaningful identity.[27] Many students face a more intense identity crisis than adolescents for, although they may be adults emotionally, physically, intellectually and now even legally, they are still economic dependents and so much of the definition of the adult role is tied up in one's economic status. This perspective has been used to explain why students in vocationally oriented courses (e.g. law, medicine, education and business studies) have been more quiescent than those studying social sciences and humanities.[28] Following this line, the spread of student radicalism in the 1960s could be accounted for by the immense expansion in all the social sciences. In earlier decades students faced the same conflicts but they simply took different forms. Then it was possible to channel the trials and tribulations of extended adolescence into harmless social and athletic activities which led to occasional ritualized confrontations with the powers that be.

Even if adolescence is extended it is still only one phase in the life cycle, and as the individual matures so old problems are left behind and new responsibilities have to be shouldered. Students do eventually find jobs, marry and raise families and this gives them a similar relationship to the community as other adults. The assumption is that student political rebels increasingly become conformists as they grow older. Conservatism may increase with age but it must be remembered that these students commence from a much more radical starting-point and they will be replaced by a new cohort of students who could be even more politically militant.[29] It is also becoming easier to hold on to university life-styles after leaving the campus and some individuals stay close to the physical confines of their Alma Mater to better maintain their student identities — perhaps they have no wish to resolve their identity crises![30]

Another variation in the theme that the conflict of the 1960s was an expression of traditional forms of combat depended upon interpreting the movement as a response to specific issues. In the United States campus radicalism was triggered off by student involvement in the civil rights movement and it was the struggle to use the facilities of Berkeley as a base for civil rights demonstrations that constituted a central ingredient in the Free Speech Movement. As the decade proceeded so American involvement in the Vietnam war became the central rallying-cry, and the range and depth of the protest intensified with the inability of the government to extricate itself from that morass.[31] Lipset related these issues to other variables in the following manner:

The larger explanation for the rise of activism during the past half decade must be primarily in political events: the emergence of the civil rights and Vietnam issues in a particular post-Stalinist epoch. These gave to the more radically disposed students the issues; their social situation gave them the stimulus; and the campus situation furnished them with the means to build a movement.[32]

The milder pattern of British student protest could be explained by the absence of such morally divisive issues. The Vietnam war was a focal point for student radicalism, but it was difficult to stimulate the same fervour given the very indirect involvement of the British government. The war had little personal meaning for British students; they were not in danger of being drafted — a fate awaiting new American graduates. In Britain there was something of a desperate search for wider issues, with Rhodesia, and more recently Northern Ireland, providing mild stimulants. The consequence has been the focusing of conflict around specific campus grievances — for example, disciplinary procedures, course content, student participation in university life — which has given the university a greater control over events.

In the 1930s the campus conflict centred around the state of the American economy and foreign policy, i.e. isolationism versus interventionism, and the assumption is that just as protest waned when those issues were 'resolved' so in the 1960s the demonstrators would respond to positive action in the new issue areas. Certainly in relation to the Vietnam war a plausible case could be made out in defence of this position. Although protest may be alleviated by tackling the problems that supposedly give rise to it, at best this will be a temporary remedy unless one can imagine that a paradise, in which no problems arise, is coming to pass. In fact to see student conflict as a response to the great issues of the day implies that it is a recurring problem, for students are expected to react to societal problems more vociferously than most. While their educational experiences sensitize them to the contemporary problems, so their social circumstances provide the means for them to act. This is not necessarily a pessimistic view of Anglo-American society, for such conflict may be inevitable in a complex modern industrial state, and it is not a product of inherent weaknesses or internal contradictions.

While the first view of student protest saw it as irrelevant, and the second as constituting a normal part of the socialization process, the third accepts it as a product of a number of fundamental changes in learning experiences. At the root of these changes is the technological revolution and the influence it exerts over the structure of the economy and social relations. For various reasons the technological revolution has more impact upon students, and this is why they are at the centre of political and other forms of protest. Feuer claimed that this was a problem with real historical dimensions, for every generation of students recognized their parents' obsolescence; the emerging technology made them mere drones who were on the verge of being swept away by historical forces.[33] My thesis is more conservative: change in all its forms has a greater impact upon the lives of young people, particularly students, and the pressures that have shaped the socialization processes of the past decade or so have been especially intense. So this generation of students is rather special, in the sense that they represent a more intense break with the past.

In its early phase the leadership core of the student movement was confined to individuals from certain kinds of social backgrounds.[34] They were invariably the children of professionals and academics, from upper-middle-class families. These were families with a traditional allegiance to the political left; in the 1930s many would have looked forward to the emergence of a new socio-economic and political order and perhaps, as Lipset suggests may have belonged to the American Communist party.[35] Although the students themselves might be irreligious they would identify their families as either Jewish or Protestant. This kind of family is a special product of the modern technological society: nuclear, irreligious and comparatively prosperous. The interaction between parents and children is high, and parents are inclined to discuss issues with their offspring, listen to their opinions and try to justify their own inclinations.[36] This is the modern, democratic family in action, in which children are not rebelling against their parents but trying to fulfil values which the parents believe in but are too weak to act upon.[37]

This view of the modern family can be interpreted in different ways. Some have argued that it is too permissive an environment and that as all the earlier needs of the student have been gratified so he likewise expects the university, government, or what have you, also to succumb to his political demands. If the authorities fail to respond to his wishes then he immediately flies into a temper tantrum — in much the same way as when his parents thwarted him at home — but now instead of breaking toys he burns down a building or two! In Feuer's terms he is simply extending the de-authoritatization process: first his parents, next the university and tomorrow the government.[38] This line of argument has been neatly characterized by slogans of which 'the Spock babies' or 'the babies who were picked up when they cried' are two examples.[39] But not all explanations of this genre are automatically accorded negative connotations. The democratic family environment is perhaps a good model for parents to create. Kenneth Keniston, a highly sympathetic observer of contemporary students, has shown how student radicals originate from liberal family environments in which there is a tendency for mother dominance.[40] Keniston feels that within such a family context the individual is sensitized to social issues and that radical political behaviour is a response to his realization that such values are undermined by societal structures.[41] In this sense the student radical is over-socialized, for he finds it difficult to accept the non-fulfilment of values.[42]

Perhaps a more explicit manifestation of technological change is its impact upon the modern university. Somewhat ironically, the much-abused ex-President of the University of California, Clark Kerr, was one of the first to point out these developments.[43] Kerr argued that the 'multiversity' was the model of the future. It was distinguished by its size, its numbers and its agglomeration of interests. Even in Britain, where the universities are comparatively small, the Robbins Report ushered in an era of expansion which exceeded its own predictions.[44] As numbers grew so did specialization, which meant a big increase in vocationally oriented courses, as well as a lengthening of formal training. Specialization also led to greater emphasis upon research and, as a more or less integral part of the campus, various research institutions have mushroomed, covering practically every topic from the potty-training of infants to the study of nuclear physics. Inevitably these trends have been reflected within the university departments themselves, with the enrolment of graduate students proceeding at a faster pace than the increase in undergraduates. Since the promotion of faculty was so dependent upon publications, the graduate students took over some of the teaching duties, and many undergraduates had no direct contact with their professors.[45]

A mass system of higher education inevitably necessitates a bureaucratization of the educational experience. But this was intensified by the economy's growing demand for specialist skills, which pressurized the university into providing the requisite trained manpower. In the 1960s both government and industry poured vast sums into the universities, to the point where some feared that they would end up as pliable instruments at the disposal of external interests. So three different trends came together: the relationship of the university to the external society, and most importantly to other power centres, changed; the internal structure of the campus grew more diffused and complex; and educational processes were increasingly bureaucratized as witnessed by growing specialization, refined grading techniques and a longer training period. The university was now a microcosm of the advanced technological society with its own alienated proletariat, the students. Processed by the computer on entering the university, forced to take irrelevant courses taught by dissatisfied graduate students, and ending up with a narrow qualification which either fitted them for a slot in the technocratic society or was already redundant, is it any wonder that this was a decade of student protest?

Within these developments some individuals would hold particularly sensitive positions. The graduate students were a crucial power block for they were usually sophisticated enough to voice grievances and organize protests, and at the same time their grievances were frequently both real and specific, i.e. the exploitation of their labour. The position of many of them was very marginal for besides exposed to these potentially radicalizing influences they were also trainee professionals who were expected to show loyalty to the university and, more significantly, to the academic staff who could exercize a decisive say over their future careers. Younger members of faculty were in a somewhat similar position except that the professionalization ethnic would bear more heavily upon them. In both these cases it was conceivable that the individual could be walking a tightrope, worrying about tenure and promotion on the one hand and yet sympathizing with many of the radical demands on the other. In this respect the charge that protest was more likely to be instigated by those who were not fully integrated into the university was certainly justified. These were individuals who were not acting out a well-defined role within the bureaucratic edifice; they were either cross-pressured in different directions or were in a position to stand aside from the structure and perhaps see it a different perspective from the entrapped participants.[46] The likelihood of this occurring would depend partly upon the pressures of anticipatory socialization. Although one may not fully belong, it rarely takes much perception to ascertain what the rules of the game are and how full membership depends upon following them. Of course in this decade the rules themselves were under attack, which increased the possibility of nonconformity, thus making individual responses more complex and interesting.

The democratization, or more negatively the increasing permissiveness of family life points to changes in the primary socialization agent as a central stimulant of student protest. Kerr's multiversity thesis switches the focus to the university and in the process suggests that contemporary structures are of overriding importance in shaping behaviour. Of course the two theories are not mutually exclusive and it is realistic to posit some interaction between them. Alternatively, changes may have taken place that encompass, and indeed supercede, both these developments. Technological innovation has brought about a higher standard of living, and this new-found affluence has penetrated most sections of the industrialized society, including young people. The outcome is the growth of a youth culture with, so it is argued, its own distinctive norms which clash with those of the adult world. As elevated a body as the President's Commission on Campus Unrest concluded that it was the presence of this youth culture that distinguished the circumstances of today's students from the past. All the preconditions of student protest had existed before but what had been missing was a catalyst, and now the youth culture was here to set the chemical action in motion.[47] It was in this sense they referred to the youth culture as the *basic* cause of campus unrest. It is interesting that an essentially policy-oriented body should come up with such an academic interpretation of what was going on. It was also a conclusion that made it difficult to suggest policies that could change the cause of events unless it was possible to manipulate the forces that gave rise to the youth culture. Failing this, all that could be hoped for was to control some of the more excessive manifestations of the protest, rather than to eradicate it.

The youth culture thesis can be interpreted in several different ways. In the first place, its homogeneity has to be considered. To talk of a youth culture along the lines of the President's commission suggests a degree of internal consistency that many would dispute. Does it incorporate all individuals within a certain age range, or only some of them? If it is not all-embracing then the criterion of membership has to be decided. Once membership has been settled then the much more important question of the content of the culture has to be resolved, This suggests a possibly different criterion for membership, like Theodore Roszak's counter-culture, rather than simply age being the basis of admission, as implied in 'youth' culture.[48] Counter-culture suggests that there is a set of values, emerging from a distinctive life-style, which is in conflict with the mainstream culture. It is not simply a subculture within mainstream values with the two related life-styles coexisting more or less in harmony. Although a counter-culture, in the true sense, may exist in the United States, the extent of its hold is far from clear. It certainly does not embrace all of American youth or even American students. Lipset has collated a wide body of survey evidence to show that even by the late 1960s many students still held conservative values and adopted conventional life-styles, and Keniston has documented a split between 'the young radicals' and 'the uncommitted'.[49] If the students are not joining the counter-culture *en masse* then its chances of embracing wider social strata are limited, for most American youth are not in a position, socially or economically, to disassociate themselves from established societal values and living styles.

In a somewhat pessimistic interpretation of revolutionary prospects in the United States, Herbert Marcuse has argued that student protest is a consequence of a rather special socio-economic situation.[50] Students are not integrated into established social, economic and political structures like most other sectors of the community, and it is this marginal position that accounts for their radicalism. This enables Marcuse to draw a parallel between students and Afro-American citizens and a contrast with the unionized white working class.[51] So if there is not a youth culture then perhaps at least a student culture exists which is dependent upon peculiar social circumstances and has built into it the potential for political radicalism. In addition to Lipset's and Keniston's empirical evidence that points to internal cleavages other objections can be raised. Students come from somewhere and they are going somewhere so, although their contemporary circumstances may make them marginal citizens, they have past and future socializing experiences that place them in the societal mainstream. Even if student learning experiences are influential they still have to interact with other forces and the extent to which these can be resisted will vary from case to case. At the same time Marcuse's argument smacks of the extended adolescent thesis, so that radicalism is associated with a particular stage in the life cycle, i.e. the student years uuring which the individual lives in a special social situation with its own cultural context. This may be so, but the collorary must be noted: this is a restricted period of time and in the long run most students will find themselves integrated into the wider society in much the same ways as other citizens.

A final point on the youth/counter culture thesis concerns the extent to which it is independent of adult controls. Superficial differences do not provide a sufficient basis on which to build a new and separate way of life. To some extent aspects of the youth culture have been sponsored by established institutions and even the political protest was not free of this taint. Students were a newsworthy item in the 1960s and it was uncommon to read the newspapers, listen to the radio and, most important of all, watch the television without hearing the words of wisdom of one campus hero or another, or of the antics of students *en masse*. Likewise it was in the commercial interest of publishers to promote the books of the twenty-year-old militants as well as their ageing father figures. I am not claiming that student radicalism was merely a product of the media, but that the media had a special interest in it which was hard for the radicals to resist, and as a consequence the protest was in danger of being debased and exploited by such flattery.

What is to done?

Responses to student conflict were naturally dependent upon perceptions of its causes. To see it as a minority/deviant problem pointed to a different course of action from an explanation dependent upon changes in the socialization process. Actual and suggested remedies followed one of three broad tracts: the traditional order was being undermined by evil forces and firm action was needed to root them out; because the protest flowed out of inevitable contradictions in the capitalist system all proposed solutions were no more than temporary remedies and what was required was a new order; and because the confrontations had specific origins and causes, piecemeal reforms could control the more extreme elements, and the aim should be to create a new consensus within the university. Since the latter tactic predominated, and because it has wider implications for socialization theory than the two other approaches, it will constitute the bulk of the discussion that follows.

If the student activists were a small minority of extremists then perhaps the best way to handle them would have been to ignore them completely. But given the explosion in student numbers even a small percentage of students meant several thousand demonstrators. More significant is the fact that this supposedly small minority were capable of causing considerable disruption, and so it was impossible to sit quietly and wait for the storm to abate. The temptation was to propose policies of repression that, it was hoped, would cut out the cancerous minority. Beloff claimed that the liberal society could not, and should not, compromise with the student revolt.[52] Bettelheim saw the answer as compulsory induction into the army or a civilian peace corps for this would remove the feelings of obsolescence by providing meaningful work.[53] Brzezinski, in what seems to be a direct analogy with American anti-guerrilla warfare strategy in Vietnam, proposed explicit confrontationist tactics. He wrote, 'If the initial act of violence is suppressed quickly by established authorities, the chances are that the revolutionary act itself will gain social opprobrium . . . '[54] And to achieve that suppression,

... the use of force must be designed not only to eliminate the surface revolutionary challenge, but to make certain that the revolutionary forces cannot rally again under the same leadership. If that leadership cannot be physically liquidated, it can at least be expelled from the country (or area) in which the revolution is taking place.[55]

These were tactics that invariably played into the hands of some of the more militant students who at times were working hard for open confrontation. Expulsions, temporary rustications and police action with its accompanying arrests and violence created a united student front on several occasions and had the effect of bringing a new range of issues into the dispute. Needless to say it was a course of action that skilful campus policy-makers learnt how to avoid but, given the wider political climate, as well the presence of a certain amount of hard-line opinion on most campuses, the hopes of the confrontationists were sometimes fulfilled.

Implicit in this hard-line strategy of the right is an ambivalent attitude towards student demands in general. On the one hand there is some recognition that the 'militants' have to be separated from the 'moderates', but on the other hand there is a genuine distaste for the aggressive posture of contemporary students. Some of the older faculty have found it difficult to adjust to the fact that students may have grievances and are capable of expressing them forthrightly, and they seem to hanker after a long-forgotten world in which established authority was accorded both respect and deference. Beloff has scornfully referred to the 'so-called moderates' and Brzezinski has shown his scepticism regarding the role of moderates, believing that ultimately they will have to decide with whom they are going to throw in their lot — the authorities or the revolutionaries.[56]

If the view is accepted that student conflict is a manifestation of wider societal forces, it cannot be controlled independently of those forces. Furthermore, if the conflict is a consequence of inherent contradictions within the society it will not be eradicated independently of removing those contradictions. But even the most ardent proponent of this viewpoint faces short-run choices unless he is prepared to stand by and watch history take its inevitable course. In the 1960s the competition for grass-roots student support was fierce, and to counteract the charge of elitism the militants had to show they could carry a substantial percentage of the student body with them. On some occasions it could justifiably be claimed that militant tactics paid off, and some authorities feared this would lead to more demands backed up by further threats of action. The liberal's disaster scenario was an ever-increasing spiral of demands backed by militant action and followed by concessions. But it is clear that concessions split the ranks of the students, especially amongst the rank-and-file. For example, most of the original demands of the Berkeley FSM were eventually agreed to and a sit-in to protest against the failure of the administration to capitulate completely was a disaster. The radical students were only able to re-enervate the crisis thanks to a blunder which involved taking action against certain leaders of an earlier demonstration.[57]

So although the radicals were generally issue-oriented, they did not always have an interest in reaching a settlement. While the demonstration lasted they were at the centre of attention, and given time it was possible that the authorities would commit a blunder which besides exposing 'their true nature' would also ensure that the mass of students rallied to the cause. In addition a demonstration could help to spread 'revolutionary consciousness', and many participants in a sit-in have testified to its solidifying effect. Proceeding along these lines it becomes more important to promote and sustain confrontation than to reach solutions to genuine grievances, and sufficient evidence suggests that this did occasionally occur.[58] This was a viable strategy as long as each particular battle increased the intensity of the overall conflict, leading to a general raising of consciousness and then on to the revolution! A superficial creditibility was lent to this thesis as more confrontations occurred and more students were sucked into the mêlee. The problem is that the conflict was, by and large, confined to the campus and students, and although the black ghettos exploded in this decade, only tenuous links could be drawn between the two events. It was not a united assault on the status quo and, even if it had been, it was still an insufficient basis for a popular revolutionary movement. It is also doubtful whether the radical cause gained many long-term recruits, for when the political climate changed the level of protest dropped off dramatically and now both British and American campuses appear to be returning to their previous stupor.[59]

Both the right and left approaches to student conflict see it as a consequence of fundamental ills in the wider society. Whereas the right would emphasize the increasing disrespect for established authority, stimulated by more permissiveness in the home, school and university, the left would point to the exploitation of the university by the military and capitalists. The main response has been based on a much more complex view of the conflict. The first premise is that the conflict is multi-causal, and the second is that the university has a certain amount of room in which to manoeuvre. This is consistent with the view that fundamental changes have taken place in the learning experiences of young people, but within this context the university is not simply a dependent variable but can chart a course that exercises an independent influence. Central to this strategy is the attempt to build a consensus as to the university's values and the rules by which it is supposed to work. It was believed that the consensus would contain the vast majority of students, and that those who were excluded would isolate themselves (rather than be explicitly isolated by the authorities). To build the consensus concessions had to be made and it was hoped that these would win over most students thus segregating those who had no intention of being pacified, so making it that much more difficult for them to mount a counter-attack.

Building a consensus may sound a vague approach to the problem but in fact it depended upon taking concrete action in a number of different directions. A willingness to discuss a series of academic reforms was expressed and in both Britain and America there have been many experiments with the content and evaluation of courses as well as grading and examination methods. In certain cases this was extended to establishing courses emanating primarily from the students.[60] This may have represented an advance for students but their academic role was also contained, for they have not penetrated, to any noticeable extent, related areas, e.g. the appointment, promotion and dismissal of staff, determining graduation or degree requirements or the content of examinations. The notion that a community is based upon consensus implies a widespread participation in the decision-making process. One of the watchwords of the student movement was 'participation' and it instigated a lengthy debate as to both the form it should take and in what areas it would be permitted. By the end of the decade most universities of repute had student representation on the total range of decision-making bodies. The extent of representation varied according to what was being run or decided. Letting students run dormitories (as in the United States) or their own catering service (as in Britain) aroused little resistance but much greater reticence was expressed when it came to deciding the academic or financial structure of the university. In fact much of the representation is little better than tokenism.[61]

Another major body of internal reforms affected the universities' disciplinary procedures. At Essex and Berkeley the actual disciplinary processes became a greater centre of confrontation than the reasons for the original alleged offences.[62] The outcome has been the intrusion of the full judicial process onto the campus with the accused frequently having the right to a defence counsel, to call and cross-examine witnesses, and to appeal against sentences.[63] At some universities students are now part of the disciplinary body, so the notion of trial by peers has made partial inroads into campus government. Of course the assumption is that these rituals will not be used very often, but if they are put into operation they are meant to show that those who have offended the consensus have received a fair hearing.

The essence of such reforms was to construct an institution that could command the overwhelming loyalty of its members. It responded to demands for academic reforms by granting them, it built loyalty by giving all its constituent parts a participatory role in the decision-making process, and where a breach of the rules was alleged to have occurred it established procedures which it was expected that most would find reasonable. This was by no means an egalitarian community but inequality was legitimized more fully and carefully. The control of faculty over academic issues could be justified on the grounds of their expertise, and that it was a function they were expected to perform by both the university administration and the wider society. Much the same arguments could be used to justify the sphere of influence assigned to the administrative hierarchy. What was important was the attempt to incorporate all groups within the system, which meant that ideally some had to at least acquiesce in their relative powerlessness. In this sense the university came to resemble one model of the democratic polity: a fully legitimate inegalitarian order operating within a broadly defined consensus that secured, thanks to its benevolence and participatory norms, the acquiescence, and perhaps even the loyalty, of its members. This was a powerful strategy and one which worked remarkably well in view of the intensity of the confrontations that arose during this period of time.

Even the university's relationship to the wider society could be included in this strategy. 'Teach-ins' were devised as a method of critically re-examining American foreign policy, especially in relation to Vietnam.[64] After the invasion of Cambodia many universities held teach-ins that drew in other sectors of the society, such as alumni and local residents. This invasion also led to the famous Princeton Plan whereby students were granted a short time period, free of studies, to participate in the forthcoming mid-term (1970) elections. Although this opportunity was not always used in the intended manner, the fact remains that it provided the universities with a safety-valve, and in many respects a successful one. Parallel developments were instigated to counter the charge that universities were part of the structure of institutional racism. More black students, some of whom did not meet the official entry requirements, were admitted; more black faculty and staff were hired; and black studies programmes sprang up so that the historiography of the Afro-American developed into a boom research area. In both these issue areas the course of events was exceedingly tortuous, and obviously something other than simple institutional self-defence was involved, but the trends none the less complemented the wider tactic of internal reform.[65]

The meaning of the student movement

The seriousness of the student movement was grossly underestimated by many politicians, journalists and social scientists, as well as citizens at large. Much of the analysis of what was taking place on the campuses in the 1960s contained either a strong streak of flippancy or outright hostility. This was unfortunate, for besides deflecting attention from the messages of the movement it also hindered the understanding of its meaning. Given the fact that this was a revolt of comparatively privileged member of the society perhaps this negative reaction was not too surprising, but none the less it was regrettable. The student movement reintroduced ideology into the analysis of the American political system. Admittedly it may not have been a very coherent or co-ordinated reintroduction, but for all its inconsistencies it showed that the emerging consensus could be challenged and that ideology was not at an end.

Of course radical/populist revolts are part of the American, and in a different sense the British way of life, but by 1960 mainstream developments in social science pointed to the emergence and strengthening of the consensus society. It was genuinely believed that the major political, social and economic boundaries of the western industrialized nations were now firmly fixed — all remaining problems were of an essentially technical nature and as such could be successfully resolved within these guidelines. Although the revolutionary elements within the student movement were comparatively small, the values of the liberal democracies were widely questioned. If the values themselves were not attacked then questions were raised about the failure to implement them or how obvious atrocities could be justified in their name.

This attack upon the established order was by and large successfully contained within the campuses. By that I mean no broad-based revolutionary movement filtered out from the universities into the wider society. This was partly a consequence of the gulf between students and other sectors of the community, their interest in different issues and the ability of elites to defuse crisis situations. But what the student movement has done is to stimulate other groups into action. In the American South black students played a direct part in the civil rights movement, and on specific campaigns they were actively supported by their white peers. In Northern Ireland it was the students of Queen's University, Belfast, who in the late 1960s led the attack on the status quo that propped up the Stormont regime. With the outbreak of riots in the black ghettos of the northern cities, and the re-emergence of the IRA, the initial student stimulus has been left far behind. Likewise, official sponsorship of equal rights for women has superceded the early campus-based days of the women's liberation movement. So what took place within the universities during this decade acted as a catalyst for various attacks upon the status quo, and in each case there was the question of whether the demands could be met within the established societal boundaries or whether those boundaries were themselves the real constraint on reaching a viable solution. So it was a too simple and narrow-minded judgement to dismiss the campus stirrings as the bleatings of over-indulged and under-worked sheep.

By 1970 the crisis within the universities was being taken very seriously indeed in many quarters, and in no way is this better exemplified than in the establishment of official bodies to investigate the origins and cures for campus unrest.[66] It was the extent and persistence of student revolt that required both policy-makers and social scientists to take it seriously. The response, therefore, was two-pronged, involving social scientists who were concerned with what was happening and policy-makers who were more interested in what should be done about it. At the centre of the storm lay the university, whose function within society was of critical importance to everyone. The conflict forced into the open an explicit re-evaluation of these functions. Over time the university had enmeshed itself in the established societal structures and the ivory tower model as exemplified by the Oxbridge stereotype was long dead. In its place some saw the emergence of a bureaucratic edifice at the beck and call of particular powerful interests. Such an institution was not likely to provide a bastion for a counter-ideology, but could it pursue even the university's supposedly traditional goals of scholarship and critical thought?

This debate about the changing role of the modern university was central to what socializing influences it could exert over students. If the university was simply an instrument of the military industrial complex, or, in alternative left-wing jargon, the ruling class, then its structure and content would reflect an ideology that attempted to legitimize and per-petuate the status quo. The various features of Kerr's multiversity could certainly be viewed in this light. If this is so then the explanation of the student revolt is even more perplexing, for the emerging multiversity clearly failed in its task. A whole range of issues were placed under a critical microscope: the structure of the university, the content of a university education, the ends that higher education served, governmental policies and indeed the very nature of the advanced capitalist state. In fact very little seemed to be sacrosanct. Both the political right and left posed explanations which suggested that students, if not the university itself, were not integrated into the system in the same way as other social groupings and that this marginality was at the root of their rebellion. But marginality was dependent upon membership of the university, for this gave students the freedom from constraints imposed upon most other individuals in the wider society. Those more enamoured of western values could also point to a model of society in which the university traditionally acted a centre of criticism and a stimulant for change. Perhaps the univer-sities were slowly but surely abandoning this task but there was some way to go before all hope was lost. This would place the student move-ment within an established tradition, as another manifestation of the university's critical role. Fears were expressed that this would be taken to the point where the university was 'politicized' and its central task would be to attack the established, i.e. capitalist order. Of course the political left could claim that if this was so then the university was merely performing a different political function from that which it had served in the past.

At about the time the political socialization studies were portraying a compliant and supportive population of schoolchildren, the modern student movement was bursting onto the scene in apparent contradiction of this growing body of scholarly research. What the student revolt illustrated was the importance of relating early patterns of socialization to subsequent experiences. The university was within itself a learning experience that could possibly contradict, rather than reinforce, the attitudes and behaviour acquired earlier. It was also part of a structural context, i.e. it had a particular pattern of relationships to other social, economic and political institutions. As I have briefly discussed, the precise nature of these has been disputed, but there is no denying that this influences the learning experiences that will flow out of a university education. So an intimate link exists between internal learning patterns and structural context, and the situation is made infinitely more complex by the changing pattern of these links. If it is the case that technological developments are constantly reshaping the various aspects of the super-structure, and more especially the way they interconnect, then socialization is constructed upon quicksands. Some decades will experience more rapid changes than others and the last three or four have witnessed more turmoil than most.

Kenneth Keniston has shown the necessity of interrelating learning stages.[67] This provides for possible change within the individual learning cycle, i.e. how attitudes and behaviour acquired in the early years can be transformed by later experiences. For Keniston student radicalism was a moral response on the part of individuals who were disillusioned with the failure of the society to fulfil values that they had been taught were sacred. Without in any way denying the importance of his modifications to our understanding of the political learning process, I would like to stress that the context within which this individual pattern of learning is taking place is also evolving. Institutions do not automatically have a constant structure and content, which makes it impossible to view them as imparting the same messages over time. So two movements, both affecting the political learning process, are taking place side by side. This makes it more difficult to predict behavioural patterns on the basis of socialization processes and more dangerous to suggest that they will aid one cause (e.g. system stability) rather than another.

This potential unpredictability, besides introducing elements of uncertainty into the understanding of how behaviour is formed, also increases the potential for elite manipulation. In the 1960s various policy-makers attempted to channel the direction of student protest. This may have been merely superficial action, in the sense that it controlled only the manifestations, rather than the causes, of discontent, but it is difficult to evaluate this criticism when such contradictory explanations existed. Besides, if you believed that some form of conflict was inevitable in the modern industrial state then this was really no problem — it was something you were always going to face. Certainly the authoritative responses varied from campus to campus and appeared to have considerable bearing upon the course of a confrontation. Even if the peace was temporary many would feel that this was better than permanent crisis. The central response was to create a university community built upon consensus, and to tie into this its most marginal constituent element, the students. The radical right believed that the student militants were so alien to the rest of the community that they could be exorcised without upsetting the apple-cart. The reformist approach saw complex internal fissures rather than straightforward polarization, and so rejected this strategy. No consensus could be wide enough to embrace all the perspectives, and to make it too broad could endanger its credibility, but it was hoped that only a small, powerless minority would be excluded. It was hazardous to try to maintain cohesion while pursuing non-consensual action, so the minority had to be seen to exclude itself, rather than the authorities physically to expel it from the university. This manipulation, much of it fortuitous and unconscious, served the university well in a time of unprecedented crisis. But the new consensus is a fragile inegalitarian order, based upon different forms of participation by its constituent parts, and it remains to be seen how it will stand the test of time.

The portrayal of student conflict as essentially a minority preoccupation, occupying the attention of the deviant few, will find other parallels in this book. It is a convenient explanation, implying that all is basically right with the world and that for the causes of the temporary disturbances we must look into the social and psychological problems of those who are at the centre of the conflict. It devalues protest by casting it as a minor aberration in a tranquil society, which certainly denies that fundamental structural faults could be the motivating force. If protest is a deviant and minority activity then those who engage in it have been exposed to special, or even peculiar, socialization experiences. An excellent parallel from the recent past is the explanation of McCarthyism, which saw it as a movement supported by social margins who had various psychological and status problems.[68] Likewise, the learning experiences of such people would be peculiar because of their need to cope with the psychological problems arising out of social marginality. The alternative viewpoint was to argue that the movement's supporters, far from being abnormal, were in fact part of the political mainstream, viz. the conservative right wing of the Republican party.[69] Most observers were willing to accept that students occupied a special social situation, and as such were both free from, and exposed to, pressures not experienced by the rest of the population. In this case the point at issue is whether or not the activists were different from other students, and, as with McCarthyism, what message the movement held for the political system. As a final point it should be remembered that classifying behaviour in terms of minority and deviant activity suggests that there is a mainstream socialization process which incorporates most of us, and to whose dictates we conform. I have posited a model in which differential political socialization takes place, thus attacking the notion that some socialization experiences are abnormal.[70] This means it is much more difficult to label political behaviour as either acceptable or unacceptable. Where such labelling is used it is usually a political strategy designed to register either approval or disapproval, which may be perfectly reasonable, but is something quite different from trying to understand behaviour.

Notes

1. Lipset has argued that the peace movement on the American campuses in the 1930s was as strong as, if not stronger than, the various student protests of the 1960s. See S. M. Lipset, *Rebellion in the University; A History of Student Activism in America,* Routledge and Kegan Paul, London, 1972, pp. 178–196. Although this chapter will not compare student protest in these two time periods, the distinctions I make in this opening paragraph suggest more, and certainly more intense, activity in the 1960s.
2. For a synopsis of the continuing confrontations at Berkeley see S. S. Wolin and J. H. Schaar, *The Berkeley Rebellion and Beyond,* Vintage, New York, 1970.
3. For an overview of the LSE confrontations see H. Kidd, *The Trouble at the L.S.E., 1966–1967,* Oxford University Press, London, 1969.
4. Students were very fond of the theme song of the civil rights movement, 'We Shall Overcome', and apparently this spread as far as Northern Ireland, where it was sung at some of the demonstrations organized by the Northern Ireland Civil Rights Association.
5. For a discussion of the multiversity thesis see C. Kerr, *The Uses of the University,* Harvard University Press, Cambridge, Massachusetts, 1964.
6. American state universities, with their more or less open pattern of student recruitment, were on stronger ground in making this charge than either the private American universities or British universities in general. After all, the latter do have selective entry standards and they can hardly complain about the character of the students they themselves have selected.
7. D. Bell, *The End of Ideology,* Free Press, New York, 1960, pp. 393–407.
8. The discussion of which Ralph Miliband rightly claimed was absent from most political socialization studies. See op. cit., pp. 181–184.
9. *Political Man,* pp. 340–343.
10. W. Peterson, 'What is left at Berkeley', in S. M. Lipset and S. S. Wolin (eds.), *The Berkeley Student Revolt: Facts and Interpretations,* Anchor Books, New York, 1965, p. 371.
11. S. M. Lipset and P. Altbach, 'American student protest', *New Society,* **8** (1 September, 1966), 329.
12. *Rebellion in the University,* p. 75. It is one of the themes of this book that the protest of the 1960s occurred in the midst of a student body that remained essentially moderate, even conservative, to the very end of the decade.
13. Penguin Education Special, *The Hornsey Affair,* Penguin Books, Harmondsworth, 1969.
14. The least protest-prone universities being the religious institutions located mainly in the American South

15. This is in direct contrast to the German SDS, which showed a profound interest in ideological debates.

16. Quoted by the editors of the *California Monthly*, 'Chronology of events: Three months of crisis', in Lipset and Wolin, op. cit., p. 161.

17. ibid.

18. To many people of Kerr's generation 'communism' was virtually synonymous with the line espoused by the Soviet Union, but in the eyes of most western students 'Soviet Communism' was as discredited as 'American Imperialism'. For a discussion of this point see Lipset's *Rebellion in the University*, p. 8.

19. M. Beloff, 'Universities and violence', Survey, **69**, 1968, p. 39.

20. Of course some universities create a subcultural ethos that attracts certain young people, but as some of these are potential students and others past students the dividing line between these individuals and registered students is not always that sharp. Cultural interests, including politics, would help to create a common front.

21. For a good statement of 'the students as social marginals' thesis see S. M. Lipset, 'Students and politics', in Lipset and Wolin, op. cit., p. 5.

22. W. Letwin, 'Democracy and the English universities', *The Public Interest*, **13**, 1968, 9.

23. Z. Brzezinski, 'Revolution and counter-revolution', *New Republic* (1 June 1968), 23–25.

24. R. Aron, 'Student rebellion: Vision of the future or echo from the past?', *Political Science Quarterly*, **84** (1969), 289–310.

25. B. Bettelheim, 'Obsolete youth: Towards a psychograph of adolescent rebellion', *Encounter*, **33** (1969), 31.

26. L. Feuer, *The Conflict of Generations: The Character and Significance of Student Movements*, Basic Books, New York, 1969; see especially ch. 1.

27. For the adolescent identity crisis see E. Erikson, *Identity, Youth and Crisis*, Faber and Faber, London, 1968.

28. J. Katz and N. Sandford, 'Causes of the student revolution', *Saturday Review* (18 December 1965), 64; S. M. Lipset, 'The student activists: A profile', *The Public Interest*, **13** (1968), 46.

29. Lipset, *Rebellion in the University*, pp. 262–263.

30. Or perhaps they have no identity crisis that needs resolving!

31. For student opinion on the Vietnam war see Lipset, *Rebellion in the University*, pp. 40–47. Lipset notes that student opinion lagged behind the rest of the country in condemning American involvement and in calling for the withdrawal of American troops, but it is equally true to say that some of the most vociferous demonstrations against the war were instigated by radical students.

32. ibid., p. 37.

33. op. cit., pp. 12–15.

34. D. L. Westby and R. Braungart, 'Class and politics in the family backgrounds of student political activists', *American Sociological Review*, **31** (1966), 690–697; Lipset, 'The student activists: A profile', p. 46.

35. *Rebellion in the University*, pp. 181–182.

36. For an elaboration of this theme see K. Keniston, op. cit., ch. 2.

37. Lipset, *Rebellion in the University*, p. 80; R. Flacks, 'The liberated generation: An explanation of the roots of student protest', *Journal of Social Issues*, **23** (1967), 67–68.

38. But like Lenin, to whom he gives the credit, Feuer appears to believe that the end result of such protest is either a failure to finally break from the conservative family straitjacket or its degeneration into a desperate nihilism, op. cit., pp. 46–49.

39. The implication is obvious — experimentation has given way to permissiveness. In fact the label 'the permissive society' was applied to British society as whole in the 1960s.

40. op. cit., pp. 51–55.
41. See, for example, some of the responses Keniston elicited under the theme 'On being a radical': ibid., pp. 25–36.
42. This assumes that radical students have been socialized into the correct value pattern and that they are aware of its internal tensions and inconsistencies.
43. I do not wish to imply that Kerr's foresight should have enabled him to predict the Berkeley confrontation, or even to have enabled him to resolve it. I wish merely to point out the irony of the coincidence.
44. Report of the Committee on Higher Education, *Higher Education*, HMSO, London, 1963; see especially ch. 3 ('The growth of higher education in Great Britain'), ch. 4 ('The future demand for higher education and the places needed to meet it') and Recommendation 1, p. 277.
45. Pressures on British academics to publish have been substantially less, and the prevalence of the tutorial method of teaching results in closer faculty — student contacts.
46. Many of these individuals could be classified as 'off-campus' elements, with a fair portion of them being students who were temporary absentees from the university.
47. *The Report of the President's Commission on Campus Unrest*, Washington, 1970, p. 61.
48. T. Roszak, *The Making of the Counter Culture*, Faber and Faber, London, 1970.
49. Keniston's 'Young Radicals' are committed youth whom he contrasts with the uncommitted. See K. Keniston, *The Uncommitted: Alienated Youth in America*, Dell, New York, 1965. See also Lipset, *Rebellion in the University*, p. 72 ff.
50. For a good review of the basis of Marcuse's appeal to students see Roszak, op. cit., ch. 3. See also H. Marcuse, *An Essay on Liberation*, Allen Lane, The Penguin Press, London, 1969, especially ch. 3, appropriately entitled 'Subverting forces in transition'.
51. Marcuse, ibid., pp. 58–59.
52. op. cit., p. 39.
53. 'Obsolete youth: Towards a psychograph of adolescent rebellion', p. 40.
54. op. cit., p. 23.
55. ibid., p. 24.
56. ibid., p. 25.
57. For a cogent synopsis of the 1964–65 confrontations at Berkeley see the editors of the *California Monthly*, 'Chronology of events: Three months of crisis', in Lipset and Wolin, op. cit., pp. 99–199. For a discussion of the tactical blunder see S. M. Lipset and P. Seabury, 'The lesson of Berkeley', ibid., p. 342.
58. Consider the following quote attributed to Mark Rudd, the SDS leader at Columbia University: 'We manufactured the issues. The Institute for Defense Analysis is nothing at Columbia. Just three professors. And the gym issue is bull. It doesn't mean anything to anybody. I had never been to the gym before the demonstrations began'. Quoted in Lipset, *Rebellion in the University*, p. XXI. Lipset is quoting from M. Levine and J. Naisbitt, *Right On*, Houghton Mifflin, Boston, Massachusetts, 1970, p. 70.
59. Although it would be hard to substantiate the case that no changes of any importance have taken place.
60. The level of sustained interest in curriculum reform was disappointing and the extent to which the university now provides a different educational experience, in the formal academic sense, is not open to doubt — it doesn't.
61. For the importance attached to student participation in the British university see the evidence of T. Fisk and J. Straw to *The Parliamentary Enquiry into Student Relations* (3 December 1968); and Recommendations 40–43 of this enquiry *Select Committee on Education and Science: Student Relations*, Session 1968–6⁹ HCP 64–i.

62. At the University of Essex the Vice-Chancellor used his disciplinary powers to suspend three students who had disrupted the lecture of a visiting speaker. At Berkeley the Chancellor instigated disciplinary proceedings against certain leaders of the Free Speech Movement some weeks after the alleged offences had occurred and immediately after the apparent resolution of the major grievances.

63. For some of the legal wranglings surrounding disciplinary procedures see Kidd, op. cit., ch. 12.

64. The Vietnam teach-ins originated at the University of Michigan, where they were a compromise replacing a proposed university strike.

65. It is important not to overlook the widespread moral disgust within American universities at the course of the nation's foreign policy.

66. The two best, but by no means only, examples being the Parliamentary and Presidential investigations.

67. This is a central theme in his work. In *The Young Radicals* he argued that it is the interaction of early socialized experiences with a wider societal context that produced political militancy in his sample.

68. Of course McCarthyism evoked contradictory explanations. For a review of them that comes down on a different side from that stated in this text see M. Rogin, *The Intellectuals and McCarthy: The Radical Specter*, MIT Press, Cambridge, Massachusetts, 1967, ch. 9.

69. N. W. Polsby, 'Towards an explanation of McCarthyism', *Political Studies*, **8** (1960), 268–271.

70. See pp. 29–35.

Chapter 8

The Political Socialization
of Afro-Americans

The black revolution

The most important socio-political movement to occur within the Anglo-American democracies during the past three decades has been the revolt of black Americans. Significant in its own right, it also triggered off other protest activities.[1] The movement falls into two broad phases: the struggle for basic civil rights, which concentrated upon the southern states, where those rights were most blatantly denied, and the push for social and economic improvement in the sprawling urban ghettos of the North. The two struggles represent an attack upon well-established forms of exploitation and inequality, and as such form a two-pronged drive for full citizenship. Each particular struggle has placed considerable stresses and strains upon the structure of American society, and the two together have at times seemed more than it could bear. It is this telescoping of the phases into a continuous movement from the early 1950s up to the present that has intensified the nature of the problem. T. Marshall has dissected citizenship into three parts: civil, political and socio-economic rights.[2] He has then proceeded to show how the extension of these rights has been worked out over centuries in Britain, and many would claim that it is still far from complete. In relation to black Americans the battle was commenced in earnest only at the end of the Second World War, and since then it has been fought on all three fronts simultaneously.[3]

The push for civil rights was directed primarily at the rural South, while the move for better socio-economic rights has concentrated mainly upon the Northern ghettos. The chronological meshing of the two movements, however, suggests that one has fed off the other. Certainly Martin Luther King recognized that turning his attention to the social and economic problems of the ghettos was an extension of his earlier civil rights programme in the southern states.[4] In fact he had to do this, for he wanted to prove the viability of his strategy in solving related problems within a different context. However, the problems of the rural South and urban North were not all that distinct. Obviously southern blacks were interested in social and economic advance as well as civil and political liberties, and it was not until after the Second World War that most of the restrictions on the civil rights of black Americans in the northern cities were finally removed.[5] Residential segregation within the city, coupled with severe economic deprivation, undermined both the exercise and the power of those rights. An interesting category is those black Americans who actually moved from the South to the northern cities during the 1950s and 1960s when the push for extended rights was so intense. Besides experiencing dramatic changes in their life-styles, they could have been caught up in both the southern civil rights movements and the northern riots.

The racial factor is a peculiar element in this struggle for citizenship which distinguishes it from the related movement amongst the white working class. Race is a unifying mark which even those who want to cannot escape,[6] and it makes it difficult to incorporate the black man's protest within a wider movement. An additional concern, therefore, was with black identity, and whether this could be found and expressed within a basically white America. The responses to this problem will not form a central theme within this chapter, but I refer to it because I recognize its tangential importance to understanding contemporary black political behaviour. In a dated piece of research the eminent Afro-American sociologist E. Franklin Frazier argued that the black bourgeoisie had a stake in perpetuating segregation, because it enabled them to achieve a limited amount of economic power *vis-à-vis* the black proletariat.[7] What is remarkable about recent events is the interest shown by the middle classes in changing the status quo. The civil rights movement was instigated and led by middle-class blacks, and many of its younger members have shown considerable sympathy for the more militant forms of protest.[8] The reason is very simple: moving into the middle class has not been a way to escape the stigma of being a Negro, for the racial stereotyping still remains, and with it the mark of inferiority. The protest movement has consequently held a broad appeal, attracting an educated, articulate elite as well as the black proletariat. Compare this to Britain, where the grammar schools have sponsored individual social mobility, so providing a safety-valve in a class-based society. As long as his racial identity is a sign of general inferiority it is impossible for an individual black citizen to find salvation through personal mobility.

Naturally a strong element in black exploitation is the economic inferiority of the Negro American and much of the protest has been directed at this state of affairs. For both ideological and tactical reasons this part of the struggle has sometimes been interpreted in non-racial terms, usually as an attempt to secure the rights of all poor or deprived Americans.[9] But given the pattern of poverty, its prevalence amongst blacks, Indians and Mexican-Americans, it is difficult to hide the racial variable in an economic label like poverty. It might be assumed in explanations of poverty that inferiority is a natural corollary of certain racial characteristics, or that a racial group is discriminated against simply because it is a racial group. In addition, the black movement was not only concerned with economic rights, or even with the whole range of rights incorporated in citizenship, but also with the notion of individual dignity, which in the case of black citizens had to mean racial dignity. As the radical student protests were contained partially by the fact that it was students who were demonstrating, so much the same is true of the black movement. In both cases the protesters were members of a larger group with distinct characteristics that hindered the creation of common alliances with other groups *seemingly* in a similar position. Contemporary democratic theorists have argued that cross-cutting social cleavages are one of the prerequisites for political stability.[10] It is true that ties binding social groups may help to prevent conflict from breaking out, but once the point of no return has been passed (i.e. violence erupts) then a fragmented social structure may help to contain conflict. Neither the students nor the blacks succeeded in arousing much sympathy amongst the white working class, who were their logical political allies.[11]

Whether one examines the civil rights demonstrations of the 1950s or the riots of the 1960s, one is looking at a revolt against inequality. Over the centuries American blacks have been socialized into inferior roles, resulting in a less than equitable share of the scarce resources of income, power and prestige, and from the 1950s they were unmistakenly voicing refusal to accept this state of affairs any longer. The purpose of this chapter is to explore what implications for the socialization, and more particularly the political socialization, of black American citizens can be drawn from this. I will focus upon the urban riots, because as the most explicit manifestation of rebellion they evoked the most extreme responses — intense fear and hostility as well as great hope. The civil rights movement received considerable white support as well as official sponsorship. Its leaders were fêted at the White House and they were accorded international acclaim and sympathy. The riots, however, were an altogether different matter, and to many whites they seemed an incomprehensible act of rage that did nothing to promote black aspirations and much to thwart them. Even if it were possible to appreciate why the ghettos exploded, it was hard to condone such obvious lawlessness, and even harder to view it as a meaningful form of protest. Yet this is precisely what some observers were prepared to claim, so adding to the general complexity and confusion.

As we have already seen, the major stress in the political socialization literature is upon how learning experiences build support for the political order. One problem then is to re-evaluate this presumed relationship between political socialization and political stability. Certainly the race riots which took place in the 1960s could hardly be regarded as a sign of support for the established political order! But were they grass-roots rebellion aimed at destroying the societal fabric? If political behaviour is the product of a socialization process, then the new patterns of protest should tell us something about the learning experiences of black Americans. Of course the riots could be interpreted in different ways, with each interpretation casting a new light upon these learning experiences. Regardless of what conclusion was reached, it was impossible to ignore the challenge that the movement posed. Students could be scoffed at and their protest dismissed as the rantings of a pampered elite. The plight of many black citizens so blatantly contradicted, in Myrdal's famous phrase, the American Creed, that it was far harder to so conveniently devalue their movement. In spite of this some of the explanations of the black revolt were couched in similar terms to those used to evaluate campus unrest.

The foregoing is not meant to suggest that the traditional role socialization processes were formerly successful at both creating and legitimizing inequality, and that only comparatively recently has this state of affairs been challenged. This is a very sensitive issue in the study of black American history. Until recently it has been claimed that historians have either ignored the contributions of Afro-Americans to the making of the United States or they have portrayed them as a servile people who accepted their unfortunate lot.[12] With the increasing interest in black studies this view has been questioned, until it has become fashionable to talk of black disenchantment with the American experience rather than of their acceptance of a subordinate role within the total system. Both views imply that the absence of explicit opposition to the status quo gives it legitimacy. It was necessary, therefore, for those who wanted to condemn the United States for the treatment of its black population that the Afro-Americans themselves should be working actively to bring down the established order. Slavery provides a classic illustration of the point, for on the one hand it is possible to show how the Africans adjusted to their enslavement (unlike the Indians) by internalizing the values that their masters desired and by rarely mounting a serious rebellion, while on the other hand there is plenty of evidence to show how much the blacks hated slavery.[13] But regardless of where the truth lies — acceptance, compliance, internalization of values or latent rebelliousness — does the behaviour legitimize the institution? Put more specifically, could slavery be considered as a legitimate institution simply because most of the slaves complied (or even more strongly, accepted) its dictates? Even if this appeared to be so was it not still relevant to ask the slaves what they actually felt? Or, as Elkins argues, was the pattern of American slavery so all-encompassing as to embrace the mind as well as the body?[14]

So the radical critique of black American history rightly accepts that interpretations of the black man's experiences in the United States must be based on empirical evidence. But one has to keep in mind the constraints within which behaviour is formed; the absence of rebellion does not mean that general contentment prevails.[15] Furthermore it is important that the rewriting of history should not serve contemporary political ends, even if one is sympathetic to those ends. Undoubtedly American blacks have been subjected to a vicious form of role socialization and there has been a mass revolt against both the form this has taken, as well as its consequences, in the past three decades. The revolt has been so extensive that it is no longer possible to maintain that the black American is contented with his lot in life. So regardless of how past behaviour is to be interpreted, the contemporary period poses new problems for the social scientist, as well as for the historian.

Political socialization and the changing pattern of black political behaviour

The bias in the early political socialization studies in favour of white schoolchildren has meant that research in this field has little to tell us about the political behaviour of black Americans. The paucity of information is such that Lyons were forced to conclude, 'In previous socialization studies one seeks with little reward clues about the political socialization of the slum child, particularly the Negro slum child'.[16] But thanks partly to the research of individuals like Lyons, the field is not quite as barren as first impressions might suggest. It is considerably enriched by looking for further clues amongst the survey data of adult black political attitudes. Daniel Bell has described the 1960s as 'government by commission', and nowhere has this been more true than of the attempts to explain and control the course of black political behaviour.[17] If political socialization is a life-long process then this evidence is of direct relevance in understanding its shape and direction. Even if one believes that the most important learning experiences are confined to the childhood years, it may still be possible to glean from the adult patterns trends that throw at least an indirect light upon the process.

Greenberg has examined the attitudes of both white and black schoolchildren (aged 8 to 15) towards the usual foci of 'political community', 'regime norms' and 'the political authorities'. In spite of high initial supportive attitudes he was ' . . . forced to conclude, that with the exception of a late rally to the national government, black children experience ever decreasing levels of diffuse support for the American political system'.[18] Lyons researched the development of the social-psychological orientations of efficacy and cynicism and, although his findings were somewhat less clear-cut, he was led to a similar conclusion: ' . . . evidence presented here indicates that the high-school years are a more critical period in the political socialization of Negro and white slum children than they are for other children'.[19] They are more critical in the sense that cynicism increases while efficacy fails to improve, so widening the gap between the social strata.

These two socialization studies, both conducted in the turbulent year of 1968, point to a coherent attitudinal basis underlying the participation of black youth in the urban riots. However, the overall attitudinal trends are very much in same direction for both black and white youth, indicating that their respective worlds are not completely polarized. As Easton and Dennis have shown, even white middle-class suburban schoolchildren register a significant decline in support for the political system during the teenage years.[20] The findings of both Lyons and Greenberg substantiate this and it is simply a question of a greater lessening of support on the part of the black adolescents. In view of the course of events in the United States during the 1960s, and more especially the attention devoted to the urban riots and the probable spill-over effect of this, it is scarcely surprising to record this difference in black—white attitudes. Perhaps of greater importance is that structural constraints will bear more heavily upon black than on white youths. As the high-school years draw to a close the individual has to start making concrete plans for the future; a lower rate of college admissions and a much higher unemployment rate must exercise some influence upon the maturing black citizen. In lieu of any clear understanding of what is taking place, perhaps all that is being documented is a universal (i.e. both black and white) life cycle phenomenon rather than a mass withdrawal of political support by America's largest coloured ethnic group. This is absurdly flimsy evidence on which to base such a thesis but the case is hardly any more fragile than one pointing to a growing revolutionary conscience. The latter interpretation requires that the riots should be taken into consideration, for the survey evidence alone will not substantiate it.

Paul Abramson, in a general review of the literature which analyses the political socialization of black adolescents, has argued that 1967 was a watershed in the development of the attitudes of black youth.[21] The pre-1967 evidence is limited to five studies carried out between 1963 to the summer of 1967, hardly a substantial basis on which to arrive at historical watersheds. Two social-psychological variables — political trust and political efficacy — are the common link between the various studies, and again I would suggest that this is a fragile foundation for making generalizations. In fact neither the pre- nor post-1967 data show very substantial racial differences in levels of political efficacy and so Abramson's case rests on the distributions for political trust. Previous research has shown that political efficacy is the best social—psychological determinant of mainstream participation; if this is so, then perhaps Abramson should have arrived at a more optimistic conclusion.[22] I would also argue that his interpretation of the evidence is faulty, for, although differences in black and white trust scores do appear after 1967, the most noticeable feature of the data is the wide fluctuations in percentage distributions from one study to the next.[23]

Abramson suggests that the reason for this alleged divergence in political trust scores after 1967 was increasing black disillusionment with the political system from 1964 onwards. Up until then American blacks felt that the polity was responsive to their demands, but there was a shift which by 1967 was reflected in the declining levels of political trust.[24] He terms this a 'political reality' explanation which he sees as an alternative to the more usual explanation for black discontent — social deprivation. Abramson argues that as the pattern of social deprivation remained more or less constant throughout the period when the surveys were undertaken, but political realities changed for the worse, the latter provides the better explanation of new attitudes. The factual grounds for this line of reasoning are rather dubious. The comparative standard of living of whites and blacks widened in the early 1960s and perhaps narrowed in the latter half of the decade, so the riots could be seen as a delayed response to increasing relative deprivation.[25] After 1964 a Voting Rights Act and the Office of Economic Opportunity were concrete signs that the Federal government was still responding to black political pressure, and at the local level the number of Afro-Americans moving into positions of real political power expanded.[26] A final point to note is that 'social deprivation' is rarely seen as a cause of black political behaviour, for it is much more usual to stress the importance of 'relative deprivation'. This introduces a greater element of uncertainty because it is as dependent upon individual perceptions (i.e. where they think they stand in relation to others) as upon objective facts (i.e. where they actually stand in relation to others).

Up until the mid-1960s an aura of mild optimism surrounded the analysis of trends in black political behaviour. Outside the South the forms and levels of white and black political activity were about the same, once controls for socio-economic factors had been introduced. The various social and economic forces that shaped the pattern of political behaviour influenced black and white citizens in similar ways. The two major distinctions were the overwhelming black vote for the Democratic party and the virtual exclusion of Afro-Americans from positions of formal political power.[27] Both could be viewed as temporary aberrations: as the number of middle-class blacks increased so one could expect a growing allegiance to the Republican party, and the greater protection and exercise of political rights, coupled with expanding numbers in the urban centres, would lead to more formal political representation. But as Jackson has observed, ' . . . by the late 1960s, the predominantly optimistic outlook was tempered by the definite changes that were observed'.[28] The central reason for this growing scepticism was that riots broke out, more or less every summer, throughout the late 1960s, in an apparently ever-increasing number of American cities.

The riots could be interpreted as a sign that black Americans had lost faith in their ability to effect changes through the normal political channels. An additional concern was the disproportionate participation of young blacks in the riots and as their numbers in the urban ghettos continued to expand it seemed as if the violence could only grow worse. Thus a scenario for perpetual violent conflict was perhaps emerging, and even a sober document like the Kerner Commission Report smacks of this at times.[29] The liberals feared a white backlash which would heighten the polarization of the racial communities, leading to an official emphasis on containment and control rather than reform and change.

The most extensive surveys of black political attitudes were undertaken by Gerald Marx in October 1964 and by Campbell and Schuman (as supplementary evidence for the Kerner Commission) in 1968.[30] Both surveys point to a surprising degree of moderation. Opposition to segregation was strong and there were misgivings about the speed of change coupled with specific grievances, e.g. the expected strong black antipathy towards the police force. In spite of these qualms, moderate leadership and conventional forms of political behaviour (including peaceful demonstrations) had stronger support than the more extremist leadership and violent strategies. These general surveys contain some significant sub-sample differences. On a militancy scale, admittedly one that was surprisingly mild, Marx found that black youths tended to be more militant than the older generation.[31] This is reinforced by the later Campbell and Schuman evidence showing greater militancy amongst the younger and better-educated blacks.[32] This parallels Lipset's survey evidence on students, which pointed to a surprising degree of general moderation up to the very end of the 1960s in spite of increasingly radical political behaviour on more and more American campuses. What this suggests is a growing divergence *within* the racial communities with certain categories in the vanguard of the protest movements. It is unrealistic to put this down solely to long-run changes in the socializing experiences of these particular individuals. Their youthfulness implies a combination of differing learning processes, greater sensitivity to social constraints (i.e. these impinge especially heavily upon this age group), and wider opportunities to demonstrate (i.e. family influences are less restraining and young people have the physical ability to demonstrate which is very important when it comes to rioting!).

The political behaviour of black students reinforces the notion of a vanguard of militancy within a wider body of concerned moderation. The very extensive Matthews and Prothro study shows wide support for and participation in protest activities on the part of southern black students.[33] By the late 1960s several confrontations between black students and college administrators had occurred on northern and western campuses (Columbia, San Francisco State and Wisconsin to name some of the better-known) and the Black Panthers had established a number of university-based branches. These developments indicate centres of militancy that tend to be swamped in the general surveys of the type conducted by Marx and Campbell. But once again this black student radicalism finds a parallel in the white world, for in this decade of protest the demands and tactics of white students were as militant as those of the blacks. The parallel is strengthened by the similarities in the backgrounds of these students, both whites and blacks, who tended to come in disproportionate numbers from middle-class families, and who were studying either the social sciences or humanities at prestigious colleges.[34]

The political socialization studies, supplemented by trends within the more general surveys, as well as evidence on student behaviour, point to a growing radicalism amongst black youth. But these various data also suggest certain parallels in the learning experiences of both white and black citizens. Young children, of both races, show considerable support for various aspects of the political system and there is a universal decline in these high supportive attitudes in adolescence. Even the police, who are widely distrusted by black adults, are assessed very favourably by young black children.[35] Likewise, what limited information is available on black student protest illustrates its complementary nature to white student protest. The one major difference, and the evidence to substantiate this is somewhat sparse, is the more rapid decline in black supportive attitudes during the adolescent years. Why this should be so is none too clear, but it seems reasonable to note the pressures that bear down upon black adolescents during these years. They are coming into more direct contact with the wider society and their purported inferiority is now more explicit and concrete. Friction with the police is undoubtedly a very good illustration of this. The same problems are faced by white youths but not to the same degree. It is interesting to conjecture what role the peer group plays in the socialization of black adolescents. Given the greater fragmentation of black families, peers probably play a more significant part in the learning process of black youths. Since opportunities to escape the ghetto are limited, this reinforces peer group structures, for they enable the individual to better survive in an oppressive environment. But again the differences should not be exaggerated, since white adolescents follow a similar, if less intensive, course.

The black experience as an American subculture

The Parsonian foundations of political socialization research have been severely shaken by black political protest. The riots suggest a society in which agreement on basic political values is lacking and in which learning experiences have not successfully inculcated all major segments of the nation state into an agreed consensus.[36] Parsons, as was to be expected, has posited a non-revolutionary interpretation of the black movement. It may be a revolt against inequality, but it is also, in his words, a drive for 'inclusion', to obtain the full rights and obligations of American citizenship that are enjoyed by other ethnic groups.[37] Central to this movement is the reality of cultural pluralism within the United States, whereby the ethnic groups can retain much of their identity and yet still see themselves as American citizens. This requires the groups to make certain compromises, and to these I want to return later, but the important point is that blacks can, again in Parsons' words, be Negro-Americans rather than just Negroes or Americans. In his characteristically optimistic vein Parsons believes that the United States could act as a model for other nations if it succeeds in incorporating Negro-Americans into full citizenship, thus creating a viable culturally pluralistic society.[38]

In a famous modification of Parsons' theory, Merton has argued that not all individuals who have internalized mainstream values are in a position to fulfil them in conventional ways.[39] The objective then is to understand the circumstances which prevent the normal fulfilment of socialized values. This points to the presence of various subcultures within the society which because of structural constraints (e.g. discrimination) have peculiar socialization patterns (e.g. extended rather than nuclear families), so preventing individuals fulfilling their potential (i.e. becoming successful in conventional ways). Many Americans could not remain as optimistic as Parsons in the light of what was happening in the 1960s, and they saw the urban riots as a breakdown in society rather than as a necessary stage in the journey towards the promised land. Rioting was seen as abnormal behaviour and they sought to understand it as such, and quite naturally they turned to the notion that the Afro-Americans formed a distinctive subculture. When the political socialization studies started to look at samples other than white middle-class schoolchildren it was implied that their learning experiences might be abnormal. If the individuals did have different values then this was a consequence of peculiar socialization processes and if these were changed so the values could likewise be altered.[40] So within the political socialization literature there were precedents for analysing black political behaviour in subcultural terms.

The strongest statement of the subculture theme has been formulated to explain the poverty, rather than the political behaviour, of black Americans. One variant of this is Oscar Lewis' 'culture of poverty' thesis, but he has been careful to note that only a minority of black Americans (admittedly a sizeable number) are subject to its influence.[41] The essentials are straightforward: individuals who live in a perpetual state of poverty establish cultural norms which enable them to survive in those circumstances but which also trap them further. In the words of Lewis, 'By the time slum children are aged 6 or 7, they have usually absorbed the basic values and attitudes of their subculture and are not psychologically geared to take full advantage of the changing conditions or increased opportunities that may occur in their lifetime'.[42] If these early experiences are of crucial importance then the initial socialization agents — in particular the family — must exercise a powerful hold on the individual.

For some decades the structure of black families has occupied the attention of both social scientists and policy-makers. With the publication of the Moynihan Report, and the publicity it evoked, a new burst of interest and fury was unleashed.[43] The report could be interpreted to mean that some black families are now firmly ensnared in a culture of poverty. Moynihan's evidence shows that in comparison to white families (and it may be an unfair comparison) the black urban family is more likely to be headed by a female, has more children (several of whom may be illegitimate), and knows only the intermittent presence of a male figurehead, and frequently a changing one at that.[44] More contentions is the suggestion that the level of dependence on welfare is no longer related to unemployment trends. Before the mid 1960s, as unemployment increased so did the dependency of black families upon welfare, and vice versa, but after the mid 1960s the two trends apparently moved in different directions, i.e. welfare dependency increased in spite of declining levels of unemployment.[45] One could surmise that many black families are now trapped in a culture of poverty for they are unable to take advantage of improving circumstances.

Rodman and Rainwater have argued, in a Mertonian vein, that lower-class people are perfectly aware of conventional values but they 'stretch' them to make them fit the realities of their daily lives.[46] The constraints they experience make it difficult for them to follow conventional morality and if middle-class Americans want them to change their ways then they should provide what Rainwater calls 'social logistic support' to make this feasible.[47] The problem is deciding what characteristics of the immediate situation have to be altered before behavioural changes will occur. Moynihan, to his great credit, has stressed the importance of providing decent employment opportunities and a guaranteed family income, while those who still believe in the recuperative powers of formal education may emphasize the desegregation of schooling and the raising of standards of educational attainment. Alternatively the central ingredient in black inequality may be political powerlessness in which case a strong argument could be made out for locally controlled community action programmes.[48]

A related problem is the sensitivity of responses to changing circumstances. Lewis did not conceive of all individuals within the culture of poverty being permanently trapped, but that changes over more than one generation may be needed to escape. Rodman and Rainwater obviously feel this can be speeded up for lower-class people have an awareness of conventional morality and the assumption is that they will act according to its dictates if only the correct conditions are provided. I am not too sure that following conventional morality is the best way to escape poverty but would accept that it is hardly likely to occur if to do so means a self-imposed handicap in the struggle for survival. Although there is this significant difference in their respective time scales, it stems from what they consider to be the most important determinants of behaviour. The culture of poverty thesis looks to the socializing influence of the family and, although this can be manipulated, it takes considerable time to do so. With Rainwater's social logistic support — employment opportunities, higher wage rates and family allowances — change is much more rapid. Whether this within itself can provide permanent, rather than temporary, relief depends partly on the objectives and partly on perceptions of the initial problem.[49] If Moynihan is correct perhaps it is now too late to do little more than provide economic relief, which may enable people to temporarily escape poverty but not necessarily the conditions that are responsible for it in the first place.

Some have argued that the black subculture in the urban ghettos has been formed independently of white society and it is designed to enable the Afro-American to survive in a hostile world.[50] As Rainwater writes,

It is the central theme of this paper that the caste-facilitated infliction of suffering by Negroes on other Negroes and on themselves appears most poignantly within the confines of the family, and that the victimization process as it operates in families prepares and toughens its members to function in the ghetto world, at the same time that it seriously interferes with their ability to operate in any other world.[51]

The view Rainwater expresses here is close to both Lewis' 'culture of poverty thesis' and Moynihan's picture of the black family structure. Moynihan was also aware that the black family enabled people to survive within the ghetto, but his objective was to show that in spite of survival many black families still lived in poverty. After all, some of the inmates of the Nazi concentration camps managed to survive, but this does not automatically jusify the survival techniques and certainly does not make concentration camps any better. It is true that ghetto culture may take a form that is self-, rather than externally imposed, but it does so within boundaries that are set by the wider society. One can scarcely talk of a freely determined culture when segregation decides where you will live, the kinds of jobs available to you, the quality of the education you receive, what local government facilities are available and even the shape of a primary socialization agent like the family. These are not the ideal boundaries within which to establish your cultural freedom.

The subcultural thesis as applied to American blacks makes similar assumptions, as when it is used to explain the behaviour of other groups. I have discussed how Parkin poses a subcultural model to explain how certain British workers manage to resist the Conservatism implicit within dominant values.[52] In both cases, British and American, the subculture is seen as a total experience which the individual cannot escape. Once again we have returned to the over-socialized conception of man, and if one accepts the 'culture of poverty' interpretation the subculture maintains its influence across the generations. Rainwater's view of the black experience is one in which the possibility for change is much greater but it is a flexibility almost entirely dependent upon external (i.e. essentially white-controlled) political manipulation. It is true that the socio-economic reforms may be stimulated by black political protest, including riots, but it is others who have the power to grant or withhold what is being demanded. As long as Afro-Americans are excluded from the main centres of power this will continue to be so. The one possible area of autonomy is the ghetto itself, but the riots indicate considerable disaffection with the consequences of ghetto life, if not with that life-style *per se*, I have also questioned the extent to which this is a meaningful autonomy, given the constraints which the wider society places upon urban blacks and more particularly their residential enclaves, the ghettos.

Individuals trapped in a culture of poverty are not usually in a position to make political demands. In fact their poverty is so all-encompassing that they have little time or interest to concern themselves with anything else other than its immediate alleviation.[53] But the black movement has been essentially a political protest in which the masses have been galvanized into effective protest organizations, and although the urban riots may have been the work of a 'few criminal malcontents' they conjured up a different image from that implicit in 'apathy', 'resignation' or 'anomie', all labels used to describe the political predispositions of the poverty-stricken. Even if the riots were not a political act, and shortly I will consider this case in some detail, they did evoke a political response from some very important quarters. The political behaviour, therefore, of black Americans suggests that there is no general entrapment in a culture of poverty but rather that the poor have learnt how to conduct grass-roots political campaigns as well as to express their outrage more dramatically, and perhaps even more effectively.

Interpreting the urban riots

As with the campus unrest of the 1960s, the black urban riots were interpreted in various ways. Because they involved an oppressed race, rather than a future privileged elite, and because the intensity of the conflict was so much greater, it invited even more extreme reactions. An immediate parallel with the student protests concerns the numbers and kinds of individuals participating in the riots. Obviously riots are a much more viable means of protest if the numbers involved are large, if they include a good cross-section of the community and if they have the active sympathy of the locality's non-participants.[54] The evidence contains a few contradictions, as is to be expected in view of the time span over which the riots occurred and the different cities in which they erupted, but there is substantial agreement on the main issues. Given what takes place in a riot it is unrealistic to expect every man, woman and child in the ghetto to have been involved. In the cities where rioting broke out substantial minorities, in the range of 10 to 20 per cent, were active participants.[55] Although not a perfect cross-section of the community they were sufficiently representative to rule out any notion that this was only the 'riff-raff'. Finally, their support in the wider black environment was quite substantial. Tomlinson succintly summarizes the case:

In sum participation in and support of riots in the Negro community is by no means the position of a tiny minority of malcontents. The riots in the eyes of a large proportion of Negro citizens were a legitimate protest against the actions of whites, and the outcomes are expected to produce an improvement in the lot of Negroes and their relations with white.[56]

Faced with the meticulous social science evidence, much of it collected in officially sponsored surveys, it was inappropriate to devalue the nature of black protest in quite the same way as was true of campus unrest. A more fruitful tactic for the conservatives was to question the viability of riots as a political protest, and even to suggest they had no political meaning but were more in the nature of a criminal act. The very word 'riot' carries connotations of violence, noise and chaos.[57] It most decidedly has little to do with the established forms of political action, and the fact that illegal acts took place during riots increases the discrepancy between them and the more usual forms of political protest. So, although the social scientists established that there was mainstream black participation in, and support for, riots, this merely reaffirmed the prejudices of the conservatives, i.e. that the criminal mentality pervaded the ghettos.

Most social scientists saw the rioting as a form of political protest, but sharp divisions appeared when it came to evaluating its tactical viability. The numerous commissions, as officially sponsored bodies (on which some social scientists sat and to which even more gave evidence) could hardly condone behaviour that was so evidently illegal and was so negatively received by many in the white community. By and large, the commissions offered very persuasive reasons as to why the rioting took place and did not lack sympathy and understanding in proposing how it should be handled, but this is a long way from expressing approval. Matthews and Prothro have written, 'The anomic, leaderless and largely self-defeating riot in the Watts area of Los Angeles in 1965 might seem a bland and gentle prelude compared with what *could* happen in the South'.[58] This neatly sums up one interpretation of the kind of political protest the urban riot was — a minor holocaust!

Others — most prominently Tomlinson and Fogelson — have argued that the rioting was a meaningful political protest and not merely an act of wanton destruction.[59] This forms the basis of their combined disagreement with the Kerner Commission, whose other findings and prescriptions they find commendable. Their central reason for seeing the rioting as a coherent political gesture was that the rioters themselves and other members of the black community considered it as such. But it was impossible for them to see it as otherwise — at least they could hardly have viewed the riots as straightforward criminal activity. A related objection is that the label 'political' may end up being applied to any behaviour that the individual wants to categorize as such. The conclusion is obvious: the behaviour must be evaluated in terms of certain criteria before it can be classified as 'political' or otherwise. It may be difficult to agree upon the specific criteria but there should be defined objectives and some understanding as to how the behaviour will result in their fulfilment. But these are general points and it may be possible to legitimize any behaviour as 'political' within their terms. Furthermore, it means superimposing upon the participants criteria that they may not find acceptable. In spite of the difficulties encountered in constructing 'objective' criteria this could be a less dangerous course to follow than allowing the very positive label 'political' to be applied at random.[60]

The most frequent and damning criticism of the tactical viability of the riots was their self-destructive quality.[61] In a literal sense this was perfectly true, for they destroyed the homes and services of the ghetto residents as well as causing the death and injury of scores of black citizens.[62] On the other hand they drew attention in a dramatic fashion to the black urban community and its problems, and what to do about rioting became a national political issue. Several commissions were created with the ostensible goal of discovering why the riots took place and what policies were needed to prevent their repetition. Some of the less sanguine have claimed that the real purpose of the commissions was to placate the fears of white citizens rather than to solve the problems of the ghetto residents.[63] It is certainly difficult to draw a definite relationship between rioting and specific policies designed to assist Afro-Americans, although there are a few instances of increased funds flowing into a ghetto after a riot. As Tomlinson and Fogelson have shown, the riots made the biggest impression on the residents of the ghettos themselves. They saw them as a meaningful political protest, in the sense that it was their own expression of their dissatisfaction. For the urban blacks the riots were the equivalent of the southern protest movement with its marches, sit-ins and boycotts, and they probably created the same aura of race solidarity. Most decidedly the riots were not *organized* political behaviour for they were far too spontaneous to be that, but they gave the ghetto residents a chance to express what they felt about their plight and to establish some recognition of their importance, both in their own eyes and in the eyes of the external community.

Amongst those who have accepted that the riots were a political protest, the major dispute is what kind of political protest they were. Herbert Gans has written, 'Events commonly described as riots or civil disorders are in reality spontaneous rebellions, carried out impulsively by Negroes disenchanted with the way they have been treated by white American society'.[64] Rebellion smacks of an organized and extreme political movement, which is probably why Gans qualified it with the adjective 'spontaneous' and why most social scientists have opted for the more tentative and moderate description, 'protest'. 'Protest' is an all-embracing term, more or less equivalent to the Kerner Commission's labelling of the student disturbances as 'campus unrest'. Besides this it has political overtones, i.e. the rioters are making a statement about something and they are not simply criminals or relieving their boredom. Finally, and perhaps most significantly, protest is part of the normal political process in a complex democracy like the United States. If this is so then the established institutions and processes should be capable of handling it, if not of successfully dealing with its causes. This is the logic behind the official commissions of enquiry: they will discover the causes and put forward the necessary remedies. Certain of the commissions on both student and black protest laid down guidelines for the law enforcement agencies to follow in confrontations. The implication of this is clear — if reforms fail to end the demonstrations then the society may be called upon to find other means to protect itself. But this is a two-edged weapon, for the theme of the official enquiries is that reforms will work, and if the violence continuous then perhaps the reforms have been more apparent than real.[65]

It was Gans' reality that led him to describe the riots as spontaneous rebellions, but others, with differing perceptions, saw them as a fundamental attack upon the status quo. This explanation took one of two broad paths. Some emphasized the racial composition of the riots, suggesting that they were an expression of black nationalism and thus part of wider struggle to break the chains of white colonialism.[66] This would link the riots to some of the anti-colonial movements in the Third World, and in particular in Africa. Alternatively the riots could be explained in essentially socio-economic terms; not only in relation to the relative or absolute poverty of Afro-Americans but also because of their lack of integration into the established social and economic structures.[67] In both cases the revolutionary intent of the riots would be as much a question of their presumed objectives as of their alleged causes: in the one case the desire for a separate black nation within the confines of the present boundaries of the United States, and in the other case a socialist economy and an egalitarian social order. Both perspectives run up against the disconcerting evidence that the overwhelming majority of the ghetto residents have not expressed revolutionary attitudes and want to opt into, rather than out of the American mainstream. Of course black racial pride has taken a giant stride forward in the past decade and there is a widespread recognition of the need for a general improvement in the socio-economic standard of black Americans, rather than a widening of the channels of individual mobility. But like the Kerner Commission most Afro-Americans feel this can be accomplished within the existing societal boundaries, and a revolution — nationalist or otherwise — is unnecessary.[68]

So far the character of the riots — the numbers and types of persons who rioted, whether they were a viable political protest, and if so what kinds of protest they represented — has been discussed. These are all important issues, but the fact that so much time and energy was expended in analysing them is as much a consequence of the political controversy surrounding the status of the riots as of the intrinsic merits of these issues. As with the student movement, political reasons exist for both devaluing and inflating the meaning of the riots. The parallels between black and student protest in this respect are very similar. The most prominent student protests were frequently viewed as being instigated and led by a few deviants who had precious little to do with the campus in the first place.[69] In the same vein some sought to characterize the black rioters as totally unrepresentative of the ghetto residents and sometimes as little more than outside agitators. Whereas student protest was seen by some as an attempt to resolve individual personality problems, the black rioters were occasionally looked upon as common criminals. In both cases the objective was to refrain from using a political label to describe what was taking place, for to have done so would have suggested the need for a political response, thus according the participants a status that some wanted to deny them. This was the direction of the conservative interpretation of the two movements. At the other end of the political continuum they were conceived in revolutionary terms, which in fact made a political response equally difficult, for what was being demanded was the total destruction of the established order, and few people were prepared to concede this!

More important than the character of the riots are their causes and what can be done about them. The black movement may be a revolt against inequality, but the question of its timing still requires an explanation. Afro-Americans have always been one of America's most deprived ethnic groups, and in the decade immediately preceding the riots considerable advance was made on all fronts. To many it was disturbing to witness such outrage during a period of apparent progress. James Geschwender has argued that five main hypotheses purport to explain the black revolt:[70]

1. The vulgar Marxist hypothesis — deprivation is actually worsening.
2. The rising expectations hypothesis — individual expectations have outrun actual improvements in socio-economic circumstances.
3. The sophisticated Marxist hypothesis — the individual perceives his relative deprivation as worsening.
4. The rise-and-drop hypothesis — improvement in socio-economic circumstances is followed by a sharp reversal.
5. The status inconsistency hypothesis — protest emanates from those who rank differently on a number of status hierarchies, and as there are now more of such individuals so the nation is more protest-prone.

Geschwender's review of the evidence suggests that it is consistent with the second, third and fifth hypotheses, and the link between them is the concept of relative deprivation. This leads him to formulate the following simple model:

$$
\left.\begin{array}{l}
\text{Objective conditions,} \\
\text{especially socio-economic} \\
\text{variables}
\end{array}\right\} \rightarrow \left.\begin{array}{l}
\text{Relative} \\
\text{deprivation}
\end{array}\right\} \rightarrow \text{Rebellion}
$$

In his model relative deprivation can be both an objective fact as well as a state of mind; i.e. the individual perceives himself to be deprived in relation to other groups.

I have discussed Geschwender's article in some detail because it is a good synopsis of the debate, and because it provides a convenient framework on which to hang other points. A central theme in much of the literature, and this is certainly illustrated by Geschwender's hypothesis, is the determining influence of socio-economic forces. In view of the evidence this could hardly be ignored. I would like to suggest the additional importance of a number of political issues. The idea that the demands of black citizens could be accommodated within the established order was encouraged — not surprisingly — by politicians, and they could point to considerable success in passing legislation which guaranteed formal civil rights. But they had far less control over the actual implementation of those rights, and even less say in bringing about a change in social and economic conditions. This was inevitable, but it was impossible to convey this to individuals whose expectations had been raised by the words and actions of politicians. Accompanying the changing disposition amongst politicians was a considerable political mobilization of black citizens, especially in the southern states, at the grass-roots. It was doubly important, therefore, that there should be continuous tangible pay-offs. So political conditions should be added to Geschwender's model and, although deprivation, relative or otherwise, may be less important in this sphere, perceptions of the meaningfulness of political activity and elite promises are probably quite crucial.

Gary Marx has written, 'What we find is that . . . social participation does not have much *direct* effect on militancy. Rather, social participation produces certain psychic states, such as high morale, and it is these which facilitate the development of a militant outlook'.[71] The survey evidence showed an increase in race pride, especially amongst younger black citizens, and these were the very individuals most likely to be militants. The relative deprivation stage in Geshchwender's model should be replaced by a more general psychic make-up stage through which the individual interprets his world and thus makes decisions as to how he should act. A central part of this make-up will be Afro-American racial consciousness, which flows out of the individual's perception of his past and present heritage. While the social scientists have produced statistics to illustrate the 'disintegration' of the black family or the 'social pathology' of black culture so a parallel trend has emerged from the grass-roots, stressing racial pride. This way of looking at the causes of political protest is directly parallel to the explanation of the mainstream forms of political activity discussed in Chaper 4.[72] In both cases, although the psychological variables have the most immediate relationship to the actual political behaviour they do not cause that behaviour. They form the consciousness which interprets a changing world.

Changing the political socialization context

The studies of the political socialization of Afro-Americans in fact tell us very little about the dynamics by which black political behaviour is formed. The stress, as with all the political socialization research, is upon discovering the pattern of political attitudes amongst black citizens, in particular adolescents. Although the authors have emphasized the uniqueness of their evidence, especially the declining levels of support shown for the political system during the adolescent years, I have pointed out their basic similarity to white attitudinal trends. What is distinctive is *the extent* of this drop in black support for the political system during adolescent years. This is a likely consequence of the growing awareness of structural constraints that bear more heavily, although by no means exclusively, upon black adolescents. These constraints are such as to force many adolescents, both black and white, to forget the earlier socialized messages and to commence a process of resocialization that will better fit them for the realities of their adult lives.

The structural constraints may be sufficiently influential to cause the development of well-defined subcultures within which the individual adopts patterns of behaviour that enable him to survive in his isolated world. Although one may not be prepared to go this far in characterizing the context within which black Americans find themselves, there is wide agreement that many Afro-Americans are in a special socio-economic situation which results in their receiving a smaller share of the available scarce resources. Although this may not give rise to a culture of poverty in Lewis' sense, it clearly influences behavioural patterns and for some time various efforts have been made to change this, with the riots stimulating a new burst of activity. Central to the problem is the fact that the collective inferiority of black citizens (i.e. inferior because they are Negroes) cannot be resolved only by individual mobility. As long as one's racial identity is within itself a mark of inferiority then no amount of personal advancement is going to resolve this problem. This is why one of the most important aspects of the black movement has been the attempt to end this dilemma. A solution would break down some of the links that unite the most diverse of Afro-American citizens by fragmenting them along the same lines as other ethnic groups. I am not suggesting that only black citizens show ethnic solidarity or that they are not already internally divided by many socio-economic dimensions. It is partly a question of the extent to which these trends have developed, and more importantly whether the racial identity acts as a unifying force in spite of these fissures. As long as black citizens are considered to be inferior because of their racial identity then this will both slow down internal social fragmentation and smooth over the cracks that may appear.

In a society like the United States which has strong norm approving of individual social mobility, it was obviously desirable that social tension should be resolved by personal advancement through the available channels of mobility. As this was a course in keeping with societal values it consequently demanded the fewest changes. Acceptance of the norm of individual mobility also means that failure is likewise personalized and it is then possible to look for aberrations in the individual's life-style to account for his failure. This would support a subcultural theory of deviance in which norms pertaining to the group are perpetuated across generations by peculiar socialization processes. But before such a case could be made out and defended the obvious reason for black inferiority — the stigma associated with the label Negro — had to be removed.

In the 1950s and 1960s the black movement aimed to break down the barriers of segregation. What was to follow from this was far from clear, although some saw it as a step toward the total assimilation of black citizens. But this has been resisted by both whites and blacks and now the goal is full citizenship along with the retention of a separate black identity. However, many social scientists have argued that the Afro-American has no distinctive cultural identity. Ironically, in their classic analysis of the perpetuation of ethnic life in the United States Glazer and Moynihan wrote,

. . . it is not possible for Negroes to view themselves as other ethnic groups viewed themselves because — and this is the key to much in the Negro world — the Negro is only an American and nothing else. He has no values and culture to guard and protect. He insists that the white world deal with his problems; since he is so much the product of America, they are not *his* problems but everyone's.[73]

More recently Bennett Berger has maintained that

. . . stripped of its mystique, black culture is basically an American Negro version of lower-class culture, and, race prejudice aside, it can expect on this ground alone to meet strong resistance from the overwhelming majority of the American population which will see in the attempt to legitimize it an attempt to strike at the heart of the ethnic of success and mobility, which is as close as this country comes to having any really sacred values.[74]

Berger's message is explicit: even if the black citizen has a cultural identity it is in his best interest to escape its confines as quickly as possible.

In 1961 Milton Gordon wrote that there was no ideological commitment to a separate black identity.[75] If this was true then it is clearly no longer so and the past decade has witnessed a serious attempt to give this identity some substance. The history of the black man's role in the United States has been filled out and re-evaluated; his unique contributions to the society have been spelled out more clearly; and his African origins — and their retentive hold upon him — have been explored in more detail.[76] This is not simply pushing towards the creation of a particular version of a lower-class culture. Many of the cultural symbols — skin colour, hair style, music, dress and food — cannot readily be given a class label. Furthermore, the emphasis on cultural uniqueness was designed to achieve various goals: to raise individual self-esteem, to build racial solidarity, and to establish a base with which to seize control of local political structures and the policies which affect ghetto residents. Other Americans may object to this but this cannot be on the grounds that black citizens are trapping themselves in a lower-class culture from which everyone else wants to escape.

So far I have argued that the creation of a black identity which found recognition within a culturally pluralistic American was the crucial step by which full citizenship could be attained.[77] What bothered many white citizens, and perhaps even Berger, was that this could be interpreted as an attempt to exclude themselves from the rights and obligations of American citizenship. Black citizens have been separated from whites by their primary associations (e.g. little racial intermarriage), segregation has enforced structural and secondary isolation (e.g. residing in ghettos they attended their own schools, churches, etc.), and now they appeared to be embracing alien cultural values.[78] Parsons himself has implied that the boundary between 'inclusion' and 'exclusion' is rather fine: 'By being included in a larger community structure, the individual need not cease to be a member of the smaller ones, but the latter must relinquish certain of the controls over him which they previously exercised'.[79] What these controls are Parsons does not discuss, but in the 1960s the opposite appeared to be happening and to many this seemed like a push for cultural autonomy rather than cultural pluralism.[80] The consequence of this could be not so much a subculture but rather a separate culture in conflict with mainstream values and perhaps competing with them for allegiance. The outcome would not necessarily be a different socialization process but certainly one with a new content, teaching a particular perspective on Afro-Americans.

The focus of white Americans has been upon the various ways in which black Americans have been denied full citizenship. This has resulted in action to either grant full citizenship rights (in the civil or political spheres) or to create the conditions in which full rights (especially social and economic rights) can be more easily obtained. The overall goal was to create an all-embracing consensus within which everyone would have an equal opportunity to be unequal. One difficulty, which Marshall did not stress, is that citizenship rights are not separate entities. Although one may formally have full civil and political rights these cannot be exercised in a meaningful way without a certain amount of social and economic support, nor, undoubtedly, with equal effect as long as there is considerable socio-economic inequality. Given the historical legacy which black Americans had to bear, it was inevitable that equality of opportunity would do little in the short run to improve their lot. Thanks mainly to the inspiration of Moynihan the goal switched from equality of opportunity to equality of results.[81] But the time scale for equality was perhaps as lengthy, for Moynihan stressed the importance of full employment and a guaranteed family income. These would bring families above the poverty line but would not within themselves create socio-economic equality. Even if implemented, equality of results would simply mean that the lines of inequality existing in the wider society would be repeated amongst black citizens. As I have already argued, this is only a viable strategy in a truly culturally pluralist America, where no racial stigma has to be cast off. It also assumes, rightly I believe, that the black movement is not within itself capable of superimposing upon the wider society egalitarian norms, and that the vast majority of black citizens will be prepared, or simply forced, to settle for much the same internal cleavages and inequalities that pervade other ethnic groups.

Alongside cultural, social and economic changes one can see parallel movements to achieve a political equality of results, but still the problem of adjusting to existing realities has to be faced. Political power, like wealth and prestige, is invested in certain institutions and is obtained by following established procedures. The slogan 'Black Power' implied that black citizens should form an independent power base which could be used to secure a more effective control of those aspects of the political system that most directly influenced their lives. This seemed to make sense given the increasingly concentration of Afro-Americans in the largest cities and the decentralization of the administrative apparatus that governed such things as welfare programmes and the schools. Black Power and Community Power had very much the same implications, and received limited official sponsorship through the community action programmes run for a short period of time under the auspices of the Office of Economic Opportunity.[82]

In a federal system political power is fragmented in the United States which is increased by the ethnic diversity of the population.[83] So, although the concentration of black citizens in the ghettos may give them power over their localities, including a number of major cities, they are still a comparatively small minority of the total population which necessitates political alliances at the higher — i.e. state and federal — levels of government. So even a separate political movement would have to come to terms with other political groups or face exclusion from the most important centres of power.[84] The black ghettos are invariably the poorest parts of the city and if they are going to be renovated money has to be pumped in from outside. Again this is most likely to be forthcoming if local political structures are prepared to work within a wider framework. They may wish to retain their separate identity, but the necessity for wider co-operation cannot be overlooked; of course this will inevitably mean making compromises. The price of maintaining one's integrity may mean starving the community of much-needed funds. There is a direct analogy here with Parsons' point that there are limits to cultural pluralism. Just as the group makes cultural concessions so it is forced to make political concessions.

I have outlined some of the major responses to the black movement that arose in the United States after the Second World War. The goal has been to reconcile some of the traditional individualistic norms with the demands of a movement which came to embrace black American citizens as an ethnic group, and to argue that the only viable solutions were collectivist ones. With the breakdown of the 'melting-pot' thesis, which saw American citizens as essentially an amalgam of European heritages, and its replacement by cultural pluralism, the way was open for a reconciliation.[85] This allowed for a collectivist cultural solution to be complemented by individual patterns of social and economic mobility.

But this strategy has to face the harsh realities of economic life. The Kerner Commission reported, 'This is our basic conclusion: Our Nation is moving toward two societies, one black, one white — separate and unequal'.[86] In fact most evidence suggests that the black community is itself moving towards two separate and unequal worlds. Moynihan has summarized the case thus: ' . . . the experience of Negro families living outside the poverty area was one of steady improvement, while the conditions of life in the poverty areas grew *worse*'.[87] In an optimistic interpretation of 1970 data Wattenburg and Scammon arrive at very much the same conclusion and in their terms a majority of black citizens can be classified as 'middle-class', with a sizeable minority improving their position and now approaching the poverty line, and the rest being, as they euphemistically put it, 'left behind'.[88] How these fragile economic gains have been whittled away by the recession of the mid-1970s, and what consequences this is likely to have, it is as yet too soon to say. Certainly unemployment amongst black youth has risen to its previous astronomical level, and this alone makes it hard to be optimistic.[89] As important as this is the impact of the increasing polarization upon the black community. Many blacks may now be trapped in a genuine culture of poverty and for them race pride can scarcely compensate for their poverty. How do those who have managed to escape react to this? Is the ethic of social mobility sufficient to break the ties of racial solidarity? Again we shall have to wait for the answer to this question.

If a genuine culture of poverty is now emerging then socialization processes could trap those within its confines for several generations. If individuals in this situation are isolated from the rest of the society, including their fellow ethnic members, then it becomes easier to treat their situation as arising out of personal failings rather than societal shortcomings. Disparagingly, Wattenberg and Scammon describe the contemporary ghetto as 'a place made up disproportionately of the dependent poor — the female headed families and the elderly — social derelicts: winos, addicts, hustlers, pimps, prostitutes, criminals and bums'.[90] The commissions of the 1960s made concrete recommendations on what procedures the forces of law and order ought to follow in a riot, and many police forces purchased special equipment in case the need should arise. If the character of the ghetto has changed along the lines indicated by Wattenberg and Scammon, control, rather than change, is likely to be the order of the day, if the circumstances are deemed to warrant it. So the socio-economic trends point to both a widening consensus as well as increasing polarization. This may be an American solution, but not one that other multiracial nations would necessarily find congenial.

Notes

1. For example, many students, both black and white, cut their protest teeth in the civil rights demonstrations.
2. T. H. Marshall, 'Citizenship and social class', in T. H. Marshall, *Sociology at the Crossroads and Other Essays,* Heinemann, London, 1963, ch. 4.
3. I do not mean to suggest that it was wrong to move fast, but rather wish to make the point that a certain amount of social chaos was inevitable as a consequence of the extent and speed of the attack upon inequality.
4. M. L. King, *Chaos or Community,* Penguin Books, Harmondsworth, 1968, ch. 1.
5. Note the tardiness of change in the American capital as explicitly seen in this quote: 'As early as 1947 the larger hotels in Washington began to accept Negro guests and by 1956 most of them were doing so. The motion picture houses and theaters followed suit'. J. H. Franklin, *From Slavery to Freedom,* Alfred Knopf, New York, 1967 (3rd edition) p. 612. Admittedly, Washington is not strictly a northern city but its symbolic importance as the nation's capital is of great significance.
6. There is a limited amount of 'passing' into the white world but this is a drastic course of action and an explicit recognition of the racial inferiority of being a Negro.
7. E. F. Frazier, *Black Bourgeoisie,* Free Press, New York, 1957.
8. For an analysis of the leadership of the southern wing of the civil rights movement see D. R. Matthews and J. W. Prothro, *Negroes and the New Southern Politics,* Harcourt, Brace and World, New York, 1966, pp. 180–185; for the involvement of middle-class youth see pp. 429–433.
9. As reflected in M. Harrington, *The Other America; Poverty in the United States,* Macmillan, New York, 1962.
10. See pp. 247–248.
11. This is a debatable point, but if the black movement is seen as a revolt against inequality then potential links with the white working class were theoretically feasible. The problem is that white workers have felt threatened by the movement, seeing it as an attack as much upon themselves as upon the system which also exploits them. The student protest against American involvement in the Vietnam war should likewise have struck a chord of sympathy amongst workers; after all they were providing much of the cannon-fodder. T' gulf between students and workers was so great that it could not ʲ by policy interests that perhaps overlapped.

12. This is a claim that is difficult to either substantiate or refute. Most general historical texts include small sections on the role of the Negro in American history. Undoubtedly their contribution in this sense has been no more overlooked than that of other ethnic groups. Furthermore, several texts have been devoted solely to the history of the black man in the United States. Evaluating the historian's perspective of Afro-American history is more contentious. I would argue that the black man's contribution has been grossly undervalued in much the same way as have the contributions of other oppressed groups. A central problem in relation to Afro-American history is the exclusion of black citizens from political life, and as so much of American history, like British history, is political history this exaggerates the lack of attention paid to them. For a substantiation of the claims in the text see L. Knowles and K. Prewitt (eds.), *Institutional Racism in America,* Prentice-Hall, Englewood Cliffs, New Jersey, 1969, pp. 47–53.
13. For a book which illustrates the extent of the opposition to slavery see H. Aptheker, *American Negro Slave Revolts,* International Publishers, New York, 1952.
14. S. Elkins, *Slavery,* University of Chicago Press, Chicago, 1959, ch. 3. Elkins makes a direct parallel between American slavery and the Nazi concentration camps.
15. See pp. 3–4.
16. S. R. Lyons, 'The political socialization of ghetto children: Efficacy and cynicism', *Journal of Politics,* **32** (1970), 289.
17. D. Bell, 'Government by commission', *The Public Interest* (Summer, 1966), 3–9.
18. E. Greenberg, 'The political socialization of black children', p. 186.
19. op. cit., p. 303.
20. See pp. 6–7.
21. P. Abramson, 'Political efficacy and political trust among black schoolchildren: Two explanations', *Journal of Politics,* **34** (1972), 1243–1275.
22. G. Di Palma, *Apathy and Participation,* Free Press, New York, 1970, p. 48.
23. Under the heading 'Finding About Trust' we find the following distribution in the various studies he collated:

Whites	*Blacks*
Commencing 1965	
1. 79% medium or low on political cynicism	77% medium or low on political cynicism
2. 31% low on political cynicism	29% low on political cynicism
3. 74% believe policemen can be trusted	46% believe policemen can be trusted
4. 65% believe the government in Washington can be trusted	54% believe the government in Washington can be trusted
5. 41% low on political cynicism	27% low on political cynicism
6. 64% medium or low on political cynicism	71% medium or low on political cynicism
7. 79% medium or high on political trust	71% medium or high on political trust
81% felt the police were more honest than most	53% felt the police were more honest than most
Ending 1971	

With the understandable exception of attitudes towards the police force, black and white attitudes appear to be remarkably consistent over time.

24. Abramson gives no indication as to why it should have taken this particular time period (i.e. between 1964 and 1967) for the alleged change in political realities to have had this impact upon attitudes.
25. For a supporting position see T. Gurr, *Why Men Rebel*, Princeton University Press, Princeton, New Jersey, 1970, p. 54.
26. I mention this because Abramson argues that if political leaders were elected by black votes (as was undoubtedly true of the black mayors who emerged in the 1960s) this would increase levels of political trust.
27. For a general discussion of the influence of ethnicity upon political behaviour during this period of comparative calm see R. Lane, *Political Life,* Free Press, New York, 1959, ch. 17.
28. J. S. Jackson, 'The political behavior and socio-economic backgrounds of black students: The antecedents of protest', *Midwest Journal of Political Science,* **15** (1971), 662–663.
29. This is a personal observation, but with chapter titles like 'Profiles of disorder', 'Patterns of disorder' and 'Control of disorder' the message is fairly explicit.
30. G. Marx, *Protest and Prejudice,* Harper Torchbook, New York, 1969; A. Campbell and R. Schuman, 'Racial attitudes in fifteen American cities', *Supplementary Studies for the National Advisory Commission on Civil Disorders,* Praeger, New York, 1968, pp. 1–67.
31. Marx, op. cit., pp. 40–44.
32. op. cit., ch. 2.
33. op. cit., pp. 417–424. See also R. Searles and J. A. Williams, 'Negro college students' participation in sit-ins', *Social Forces, 40* (1961), 215–220.
34. Searles and Williams, ibid., p. 219; Matthews and Prothro, op. cit., pp. 416–419; J. M. Orbell, 'Protest participation among southern negro college students', *American Political Science Review,* **61** (1967), 446–447. Note that Orbell is re-analyzing Matthews' and Prothro's data.
35. M. R. Rodgers and G. Taylor, 'The policeman as an agent of regime legitimation', *Midwest Journal of Political Science,* **15** (1971), 85; E. Greenberg, 'Black children and the political system', *Puplic Opinion Quarterly,* **34** (1970), 340; Campbell and Schuman, op. cit., pp. 42–43.
36. Thus undermining one of the implicit premises in 'the end of ideology' thesis.
37. T. Parsons, 'Full citizenship for the Negro American? A sociological problem', in T. Parsons and K. B. Clark (eds.), *The Negro American,* Beacon Press, Boston, 1967, pp. 715–716.
38. ibid., pp. 749-750.
39. See pp. 13–14.
40. See pp. 15–16.
41. O. Lewis, 'The culture of poverty', in D. P. Moynihan (ed.), *On Understanding Poverty: Perspectives from the Social Sciences,* Basic Books, New York, 1968, pp. 196–197.
42. ibid., p. 188.
43. For the report itself and varying interpretations of it see L. Rainwater and W. L. Yancey (eds.), *The Moynihan Report and the Politics of Controversy,* MIT Press, Cambridge, Massachusetts, 1967.
44. The reason why the comparison is unfair, and certainly misleading, is that families in totally different socio-economic contexts are being compared. Many of the black families are still adjusting to a city environment, and they have to cope with the burden of racial discrimination. Would the differences be so stark if the comparison was made with white families (perhaps the Appalachian mountain people are a good example) who are trapped in similar circumstances?
45. For a different interpretation from Moynihan's as to why this may have taken place see L. Carper, 'The Negro family and the Moynihan Report', in Rainwater and Yancey, op. cit., pp. 466–474.

184

46. L. Rainwater, 'The problem of the lower-class culture and poverty war strategy', in Moynihan, op. cit., pp. 229–259; H. Rodman, 'The lower class value stretch', *Social Forces,* **42** (1963), 205–215.
47. ibid., p. 242.
48. Although it was argued that this deflected attention from the real issues of income and jobs.
49. If poverty is a consequence of deeply ingrained cultural characteristics then such a strategy is at best a short-run palliative.
50. It is possible to recognize the impact of white society upon black culture and yet still believe that the black family structure assists revival in the ghetto world.
51. L. Rainwater, 'Crucible of identity: The Negro lower-class family', *Daedalus,* **1966** 176.
52. See pp. 110–111.
53. For a more general discussion of this theme see J. Davies, *Human Nature in Politics,* Wiley, New York, 1963, pp. 15–23.
54. It is important to remember that the riots of the 1960s had a particular character as they were not interracial conflicts (as had happened so often in the past) but essentially black attacks on property. For an analysis of the rioters see R. M. Fogelson and R. B. Hill, 'Who riots? A study of participants in the 1967 riots', *Supplementary Studies for the National Advisory Commission on Civil Disorders,* Praeger, New York, 1968, pp. 217–248.
55. 8 per cent of the Campbell and Schuman sample were self-reported rioters; op. cit., p. 52.
56. T. M. Tomlinson, 'The development of a riot ideology among urban Negroes', *American Behavioral Scientist,* **11** (1968), 28.
57. Note the opening words in the Pocket Oxford Dictionary's definition: 'Tumult, disorder, disturbance of the peace by a crowd . . . '.
58. op. cit., p. 477.
59. Tomlinson, op. cit., pp. 28–29; R. M. Fogelson's contribution to the Review Symposium on the Kerner Commission, *American Political Science Review,* **63** (1969), 1270.
60. This is now a wider problem. In Northern Ireland and the Middle East the labels 'terrorist', 'freedom fighter' and 'guerrilla' are used to communicate either approval or disapproval.
61. See note 58, above.
62. It is sometimes claimed that the destruction of property was selective, i.e. only white-owned property was destroyed. This may have been true of certain riots but not all riots were that selective as to their target; even white-owned property provided the black ghetto resident with a service and not always at an exorbitant rate.
63. Fogelson, op. cit., p. 1269. Consider this quote by Lipsky: 'To a significant degree, recent commissions have been created to provide reassurance to the public that controversial issues are under control and will be dealt with constructively by government officials'. M. Lipsky, 'Social scientists and the Riot Commission', *Annals.* **394** (1971), 73. Although I accept this may have been one of the consequences of the commissions, it is much more difficult to prove this was a major motivating reason for their creation in the first place.
64. H. Gans, 'The ghetto rebellion and urban class conflict', in R. H. Connery (ed.), *Urban Violence and Social Change,* Vintage, New York, 1969, p. 45.
65. The ethos of the riot commission was that if only the correct reforms were introduced it was still not too late to remedy the situation.
66. This is a continuous theme in Afro-American history, exemplified in individuals as diverse as W. E. B. Du Bois, Marcus Garvey and Malcolm X. The survey evidence points to the importance of the cultural dimension to the ghetto residents. See Campbell and Schuman, op. cit., p. 19.

67. It is this lack of integration that led Marcuse to see them as a potential revolutionary force, in contrast with the white working class. See H. Marcuse, *Counterrevolution and Revolt*, Beacon Press, Boston, 1972, pp. 15–30; and op. cit., pp. 57–58.
68. The survey evidence supports this claim. See Campbell and Schuman, op. cit., p. 61. This may be changing in the 1970s given the faltering of the American economy and the re-emergence of very high levels of black unemployment.
69. See pp. 134–138.
70. J. A. Geschwender, 'Social structure and the Negro revolt: An examination of some hypotheses', *Social Forces*, **43** (1964), 249.
71. op. cit., p. 93.
72. See pp. 70–71.
73. N. Glazer and D. P. Moyniham, *Beyond the Melting Pot*, MIT Press, Cambridge, Massachusetts, 1963, p. 53 (Note the emphasis is in the original text). In the second edition (1970) the stress was placed on the American basis of Negro culture as opposed to the claim that the Afro-American had 'no values and culture to guard and protect'.
74. B. Berger, 'Black culture or lower-class culture?' in L. Rainwater (ed.), *Black Experience: Soul*, Trans-Action Books, New York, 1970, p. 127.
75. M. M. Gordon, 'Assimilation in America: Theory and reality', *Daedalus*, **1961**, 283.
76. This may be overstating the case, but there has been an explosion in black studies and nowhere is this better illustrated than in its institutionalization on a number of American campuses.
77. This is a paraphrase of a quote from Parsons in which he describes 'inclusion' as 'The process by which previously excluded groups attain full citizenship or membership in the societal community', *The Negro American*, p. 715.
78. Gordon has argued that there is more cultural and secondary assimilation than structural and primary assimilation, op. cit., pp. 279–283.
79. 'Full citizenship for the Negro American?', p. 739.
80. The distinction between the two concepts is not clear-cut. I would argue that autonomy follows with the incorporation of a political element into cultural pluralism. Note the vigour of the official response to the Black Panthers, who had an explicitly radical political programme, with the much more muted response to the Black Muslims.
81. See Moynihan's advocacy of 'equality of results' in D. P. Moynihan, 'Employment, income and the ordeal of the Negro family', in T. Parsons and K. B. Clark, op. cit., pp. 134–135.
82. This led to the vogue of community action. For a very sceptical view of its value see D. P. Moynihan, *Maximum Feasible Misunderstanding*, Free Press, New York, 1969. This is a protagonist's view of the community action programmes emanating from the Office of Economic Opportunity's policies, and should be read as such.
83. Of course the power elite thesis would deny the relevance of this pluralism for policy-making at the highest levels.
84. This need for alliances is one of the main reasons why M. L. King objected to Black Power, op. cit., pp. 52–56.
85. For a penetrating analysis of these shifts see M. M. Gordon, *Assimilation in American Life*, Oxford University Press, New York, 1964, ch. 4–6.
86. op. cit., p. 1.
87. D. P. Moynihan, 'Urban conditions: General', *Annals*, **371** (1967), 174. (Emphasis is in the original text).
88. B. J. Wattenberg and R. M. Scammon, 'Black progress and liberal rhetoric', *Commentary*, **55** (1973), 35–44.
89. Rising to over 9 per cent in the summer of 1975.
90. op. cit., p. 42.

Chapter 9

Women and Politics

What kind of problems?

In every society, but perhaps in the western democracies above all, women have a special part to play in the socialization process. Biology determines that women give birth to children and culture reinforces biology by placing the responsibility for the initial socialization of offspring in the hands of the mother. Sex differences may be more a consequence of culture than biology, but it appears to be a universal norm that culture will follow the pattern of differences first established by biology. Without a literate population to question the consequences that follow from this it is hard to see why society should do otherwise. Again, it is almost a universal norm that initial socialization takes place within the framework of the family, and in the western industrialized world, the nuclear family. Within this setting the mother occupies a very special role which has a direct impact upon how she exercises her socialization functions. Naturally the manner in which these functions are accomplished will vary enormously both within and between societies, but that they are generally seen as the mother's ultimate responsibility is beyond dispute. In this chapter I intend to explore what impact these socialization processes have upon the political behaviour of women. This stereotypical picture of the woman's role is under attack and I further want to consider what influence this is going to have upon established socialization processes, and how the changes may influence behaviour formation.

In some senses it is absurd to think of women as comprising a specific socio-political grouping when they are approximately half of the world's population. The size of the group alone means that it must be rent by internal cleavages. Although this is undeniable, the universality of certain functions — I have particularly stressed the part women have to play in the socialization process — provides common bonds.[1] One of the central themes of this chapter is to examine to what extent the political behaviour of women is a special problem. Is their political behaviour a consequence of certain factors that pertain to them as women? Alternatively, do they share characteristics with other groups which result in common patterns of political behaviour? Not surprisingly we will find that the answer to both questions is a modified 'yes'! The fact that comparatively so few women have been able to escape the confines that ensnare the majority makes it impossible to consider their cases independent of general circumstances. The successful woman politician in Britain and the United States is such a rarity that we want to know how it is that those who have attained this goal have been able to defy the established barriers. Obviously the same is true of certain categories of men (for example in the past this could be said of Afro-Americans), but women are half the population, and yet still their presence in some spheres is such a phenomenon that it requires an explanation.[2]

In the 1960s the voice of women's liberation was clearly heard once again. Although it has been, especially in Britain, an essentially middle-class, campus-based movement, it has had widespread reverberations and we have heard some echoes amongst women manual workers.[3] In spite of the exploitation of some of its more bizarre trappings by the media it has raised very serious questions about the role of women in contemporary society. Women are challenging both the tasks they have traditionally performed as well as the wider consequences of their undertaking those tasks. For example, women have been responsible for socializing young children within the framework of the nuclear family, with the consequence that they have been severely handicapped in the pursuit of a career. The outcome (i.e. inequality) cannot be considered independently of its cause (i.e. in this particular example, raising children). In many respects this has more revolutionary potential than most of the demands emanating from both blacks and students. Although some students and Afro-Americans sought the overthrow of the established societal institutions and processes, most pitched their demands at a much lower level. These centred around the need for specific policy changes, e.g. withdrawing American troops from Indo-China, or more generally the desire for greater equality. To meet the demands of the women's movement, however, will require more role interchangeability (i.e. between men and women), and this could mean altering some of society's basic processes, such as how children are socialized.[4] The long-term implications of such shifts are hard to predict, especially if one accepts that stability is partly a consequence of role differentiation and all that goes with it.

Whereas the black movement received considerable sympathy and support from the academic community in its revolt against inequality the attitude to the women's movement has been more ambivalent. The Marxists have been reluctant to admit of any revolutionary consciousness other than that of the working class, and the Parsonians naturally fear a breakdown of society's stabilizing institutions and procedures.[5] Both, therefore, have something to fear from the women's movement and this chapter will explore some of the grounds for the respective fears.

Sex differences in political behaviour

One of the established truths in the study of politics is that the political behaviour of men and women differs quite substantially. Dowse and Hughes write,

Some of the most solidly researched and validated findings in the social sciences relate to the differential participation of men and women in political activities of all kinds . . . Women have been found to vote less than men, to participate in political parties less than men, to know less about politics than men. With very few empirical exceptions these relationships hold even controlling for socio-economic status.[6]

The different strands in this veritable mêlée need to be isolated and where the political behaviour of the sexes parts company must be more precisely documented.

Participatory attitudes

For most of the participatory attitudes British and American women have similar predispositions. Men tend to have a higher level of political interest, a more developed sense of their citizenship duties and stronger party identifications, but the differences are neither great nor consistent between surveys.[7] In terms of political efficacy, however, most empirical studies show a more consistent and higher level of sex differences.[8] But measures of political efficacy are rarely constant and it is difficult to know what precise attitude they are ascertaining.[9] The lower level of female political efficacy may be based on perceptions that are realistic, i.e. political authority is less responsive to their demands than it is to those of men. The reason then why women are less politically active than men is not because they are less politically efficacious but because it has been shown to have fewer positive pay-offs for them.

The differences in the attitudes of boys and girls are very much the same as for adults, but they have been magnified somewhat in the varying interpretations. This is perhaps because more evident sex differences appear in other areas of adult political behaviour, whereas for children political predispositions is all that one has to rely upon. It is also difficult to avoid interpreting the adolescent patterns in the light of what we suspect will happen to them as adults. These differences have led Greenstein to suggest that they are a consequence of a long-term process of more general sex-typing:

Sex differences in political activity, for example, seem to be encouraged by the entire process of psychological sex-typing. Beginning with preschool play activity male children learn to orient themselves to aspects of the environment beyond their primary circle and eventually to politics; girls are subtly or directly encouraged to develop domestic concerns.[10]

But Greenstein's own data showed that the child's level of political information is 'infinitesimal'[11] and that 'the world of adult politics is at the most extremely marginal to the child's existence'.[12] In view of this it is impossible to build explicitly political elements into the sex-role typing during the childhood years and, therefore, the link between sex differences in adult political behaviour and childhood socialization experiences must remain tenuous.

Both Greenstein and Hyman have made some tentative speculations to substantiate the above link. Hyman's review of the literature led him to conclude that boys were more inclined than girls towards the world of politics because of differences in the selection of ego-ideals, in the use they made of their leisure time and in their exposure to the media.[13] Greenstein has argued that on an 'aggressive—passive' continuum boys are much closer than girls to the 'aggressive' pole, and that their choice of toys, reading interests and school subject preferences all suggest non-political orientations.[14] Although these appear to me as reasonable inferences, they do suggest a stereotypical picture of 'politics', i.e. it is an essentially 'masculine' pursuit. If this is so then it is evident why boys become more politically aware than girls; the problem then is to explain why politics has this particular aura and how it is perpetuated.

Changes in the pattern of political attitudes over time throw more light upon the development of sex differences. Easton and Dennis found that boys in grades 3 to 7 (aged approximately 9 to 13) were slightly more politically efficacious than girls, but this was reversed in the eighth grade. However, along other dimensions of political involvement the boys were consistently more aware than the girls, although not to any great extent.[15] Hess and Torney note a somewhat more distinctive trend in their data:

The findings that males are more politically active and partisan-aligned is in line with data on adults. Although these differences decrease by grade eight, they apparently reappear at some time during adolescence or adulthood, perhaps because of diminishing institutional support for political activity by women after they leave school.[16]

This narrowing of the sex differences as children grow older helps to reinforce Hess' and Torney's central theme that the American schools are the major force in the inculcation of civic norms.[17] I would like to suggest that the differences may reappear during adolescence or adulthood not simply because of what girls leave behind (i.e. the institutional support of the school) but also because of the institutional constraints they face as they grow older. Family obligations bear much more heavily upon women than men and they are also of a kind that will remove most women from the political world. Just as black adolescents are increasingly exposed to forces that are likely to induce hostility towards the political system, so women are ever more confined by forces that make it increasingly difficult for them to engage in political activity in the same way as men.

Dowse and Hughes have presented some British evidence that accords with the findings of Hess and Torney. They found that boys and girls had different levels of political cognition but in the affective or normative fields the trends were more ambiguous.[18] They also point to the influence of structural factors, especially as they manifest themselves in marriage and at work, in widening sex differences during the adult years. Structural influences are by no means absent from the educational system, British or American,[19] but during the school years they may result in class, rather than sex, differentiation. Some of Dowe's and Hughes' evidence implies this, for they found that by the age of thirteen grammar-school girls were politically better-informed than secondary-modern schoolboys. Class appeared to exert a stronger influence than sex for there was more affinity between middle-class boys and girls than between middle and working-class girls.[20] This may partly reflect school differences with the secondary modern schools (attended mainly by working-class pupils) directing their curricula towards subjects (e.g. domestic science for girls) that are unlikely to provide institutional support for a growing political awareness.

The major area in which most information on the political predispositions of boys and girls is to be found is in that favourite American research field of attitudes towards authority figures (although these are not strictly participatory attitudes). The two sexes follow a similar course, with the girls showing somewhat greater benevolence. Hess and Torney speculate that 'This suggests that girls compensate for feelings of powerlessness in response to the policeman by seeing him as a benevolent, helpful competent figure'.[21] In Parsonian terms, girls have a much more affective, as opposed to instrumental, relationship to the political system, which leads Hess and Torney to speculate further that 'Girls form a more personal attachment to the political system than boys because experience with their major role model (mother) is a more personal one . . . '.[22] These fanciful flights of the imagination are hardly justified by the small sex differences in attitudes. Furthermore, although contrasting political orientations may be emerging there is nothing in this that would suggest greater female political passivity. In fact if the absence of trust in political authorities is a sign of disaffection this could lead to lower levels of male participation.[23]

Both adult and childhood data patterns show few sex differences in participatory attitudes, but the comparatively minor distinctions may be of great importance. If political efficacy correlates more highly with actual levels of participation than other attitudes then the sex differences in this area assume considerable significance.[24] The fact that boys tend to have a deeper and stronger political cognitive infrastructure cannot but help their future levels of participation. The changing pattern of attitudes points to an increasing convergence between the sexes up to the time of leaving school, with more noticeable class than sex distinctions. Thereafter what institutional supports the schools may have provided to achieve this state of relative comparability are apparently undermined by the inegalitarian burden of structural constraints. These constraints should not be viewed as simply undermining earlier socialized attitudes but rather as providing a new context which reshapes the messages implanted by prior learning experiences. This is a continuous process, but it is likely to be more traumatic at certain stages in the life-cycle than others, formally entering the adult world is one such stage.

Electoral participation

In his general text on political participation Milbrath has written, 'The finding that men are more likely to participate in politics than women is one of the most thoroughly substantiated in social science'.[25] If one's focus is restricted to the Anglo-American politics such as strong generalization is invalid. What is generally meant by political participation is electoral behaviour and more specifically the act of voting. Although British and American women may vote less than their menfolk, the differences are small and have declined over time.[26] In comparative terms British and American women are the very models of political activity, and in tones typical of their book Almond and Verba write,

In summary, we may say that American women and, to a somewhat lesser extent, British women tend to be active and involved in their communities, both in an informal and an organizational sense. They are trustful of their social surroundings, politically informed, observant, and emotionally involved in the political scene. They acknowledge the obligation to participate actively in local political affairs, they feel competent to exercise influence over their government, and they take pride in the political characteristics of their nations.[27]

Their data may not justify such effusiveness, but the comparative dimension illustrates the similarity of many aspects of the political behaviour of men and women in Britain and the United States.

Milbrath's generalization is further modified by internal subcultural variations as well as cross-cultural comparisons. As Milbrath himself has pointed out, sex differences in political behaviour disappear amongst certain strata and voting turn-out is universally high for the better-educated, high-socio-economic-status groups who live in the urban centres.[28] This can be elaborated upon by introducing a wider range of demographic variables such as age, marital status, ethnic origins and even regional traditions.[29] In relation to voting turn-out some social scientists have gone as far as to predict the complete elimination of sex differences. The argument is that those forces associated with low participation are on the wane, while those which stimulate high turn-out are gathering strength: people are moving from rural areas to the cities, the white-collar element in the occupational structure is increasing and educational opportunities have been extended. Such developments will affect both men and women, but as women start at a lower participatory level the changes will benefit them more.

Political orientations

It is widely believed that men and women have differing political orientations, and these affect the kind of influence they exert upon the political system. Robert Lane has an interesting synopsis of the many predictions that were made prior to women's receiving the vote, as to what the impact of the female franchise would be.[30] These ranged all the way from claims that it would usher in Armageddon to predictions of a new dawn for mankind, the beginning of an age of sweetness and light. The contemporary women's movement has given rise to similar fears and expectations. Amundsen, in an otherwise restrained and intelligent book, has argued that if women play their full part in the political arena then much more liberal welfare policies will be forthcoming.[31] On the other side there are those who have seen the movement as a definite step toward the destruction of the family, and with it society's total moral order.[32] Regardless of what may emerge from contemporary events, and personally I can see little other than cautious and sober reforms, the winning of universal female suffrage had little impact upon the pattern of public policy.

It is frequently noted that women are inclined to be politically more conservative than men. At times this claim is taken to absurd lengths, and we can read that 'These authors demonstrated that in France, as in Germany or Italy, only the contribution of the female vote had prevented the establishment of Communist regimes'.[33] For Britain and the United States the evidence suggests far less dramatic conclusions. The voting studies show a slight but consistency tendency for women to vote in greater numbers for the Republican party than the Democratic party in the United States, with in Britain the advantage going to the Conservative party.[34] The major distinguishing feature in this respect between Britain and America on the one hand, and the continental countries on the other, is the presence of religious-based, especially Catholic, parties in the latter and their more or less total absence in the former. European women may be more inclined than men to vote for the conservative parties but to what extent this is a consequence of party policy, rather than feminine religiosity, is open to doubt. Furthermore, Tingsten has argued that it is not altogether fair to describe the Catholic parties as conservative if one means by conservative the political right. In ideological terms he sees them as belonging to the political centre, and the various fascist movements of his day as forming the conservative right.[35] Obviously how a party is viewed depends upon the contemporary political context, and in today's terms most of the European parties with a firm religious basis are both conservative ideologically and on the political right.[36] What is important is that British and American women are in a different political context and this accounts for their party preferences following a similar course to that of male citizens.

The slight preference of British and American women for the more conservative parties is partially explained by class differences in voting turn-out. As with men, those with more formal education and of a higher socio-economic status tend to have a higher voting turn-out, and these are the very individuals who favour the conservative parties. This bias is exacerbated by the fact that working-class men may be stimulated into voting by their work situations (e.g. they belong to a trade union), thereby widening the gap between their pattern of preferences and those of middle-class men. Quite the opposite happens in the case of working-class women who are full-time housewives. Their home-centredness shelters them from influences which induce Labour voting and exposes them to those which encourage Tory voting.[37] This increases the appeal of the Conservative party to women, thus strengthening its support amongst them in comparison to amongst men.

Besides this contrast in party loyalties it has also been argued that women have a different political orientation. Almond and Verba have described this as their greater tendency to be more 'sensitive to the personality, emotional, and esthetic aspects of political life and electoral campaigns'.[38] Women are also more strongly influenced by the candidates in making their voting choices whereas men take more account of the policy issues or follow traditionally party allegiances.[39] When women are swayed by issues invariably strong moral overtones are involved. Tingsten has documented the appeal of prohibition to women, especially in the rural regions.[40] Apparently the passions of women are aroused by allegations of corruption, and if they scent a whiff of it they flock to the polls to oust the offending party.[41] It is all too easy to evaluate negatively these different female orientations, as if they suggest a greater degree of naivety, emotionalism and instability, But it should be remembered that prohibition, for example, was a cause taken up by the churches and that wives can suffer considerably from drunken husbands. The interest in personalities rather than policies may not be all that damning in a day and age when policy positions are both diffuse and tend to overlap. Finally, a preoccupation with the qualities of the candidates seems hardly less worthy than straight-forward loyalty to a party label.

Political recruitment

The most intense form of political activity is the decision to stand for office and whereas voting is a swift and private act, seeking an elected post invariably takes time, money and energy. Besides this, it exposes the individual to the public eye, a situation which gives rise to its own peculiar stresses and strains. By and large, the more national in scope the office the greater is the commitment of resources and the intensity of public exposure. So far I have stressed the lack of evidence to sustain the case that the political behaviour of men and women is substantially different, but when it comes to holding public office the contrast is stark. Kristen Amundsen has concluded,

And so the picture is complete. In terms of formal political power, in terms of their proportionate share of representation on the decision-making levels in federal, state and local government, women are left out or take a back seat even more systematically and dramatically than in the socio-economic realm.[42]

In spite of Richard Rose's claim that local political activists (defined as 'from voting to standing as a candidate for public office') comprise a rough cross-section of the population, the bulk of the empirical studies show that similar biases against women are to be found in Britain.[43] The trend is clear: as one proceeds up both the administrative and elective hierarchies so the presence of women declines, until at the very highest levels either there are no women or they are present merely in token numbers.[44]

The ultimate indignity associated with the absence of women from the higher echelons of political power in Britain is the fact that their representation is in some quarters sponsored. The National Executive Committee of the Labour party — its highest policy-making body — reserves five of its twenty elected positions for women.[45] Both the Conservative and Labour parties on assuming office have appointed one or two women Cabinet members, usually in departments which could be considered particularly appropriate for them, i.e. those covering education, the social services or price control, all areas which Parsons might term 'expressive'.

Explaining sex differences in political behaviour

So far I have stressed the similarity between the political behaviour of men and women. Only in relation to recruitment into elite positions are clear and consistent sex differences evident. But in spite of my emphasis it is none the less fair to conclude that the available evidence shows a somewhat higher level of politicization on the part of men. Predispositions to participate, voting behaviour and political orientations all point to a stronger involvement of men in political life. Moreover, the big contrast in elite membership is of great significance, for the United States and Britain, which are frequently held up as proto-typical democracies, have so-called representative institutions that almost completely fail to represent one half of their populations.

Explanations of the political behaviour of women can be viewed as either part of a wider problem or as resulting from certain characteristics which are unique to them — whether these be social, psychological or even biological. The wider approach would include women as one of a number of social groups in the Anglo-American democracies which participate politically at a lower level than one would either expect or perhaps hope for. Superficially the discrimination against women in their assuming political leadership roles appears to be so conclusive that they must be placed in a special category. But in a political system governed by representative institutions only a very small percentage of *any* social group will form part of the political elite. For example, although ex-public-schoolboys have dominated the cabinets of successive Conservative governments only a very small percentage of ex-public schoolboys have become Conservative Cabinet ministers. Except maybe in representative democracies with small and socially homogeneous populations, the principle of representation will rule out the extensive presence of any social group within the political elite. It is simply that some will be more adequately represented than others. A further complication is that most women have several allegiances, so although they may not be represented as women, their presence is recorded in other ways. Up to now the emphasis upon women as a separate political category has not received much attention, but their emergence as such makes it increasingly difficult to justify their exclusion from elite positions. The fact, for example that women may also be trade unionists and the trade unions sponsor men parliamentary candidates is no longer sufficient to satisfy many women trade unionists, for they are now identifying themselves as a separate interest group.

The explanations of female political behaviour have a bearing upon the strategies designed to meet demands for change. If women are encompassed within a unique social situation then theoretically the problem is specific in its focus and requires well-defined remedies. But even if the problems are specific in focus the links between women and other social groups are both extensive and intricate. So attempts to change the lot of women must have widespread repercussions. Nowhere is this better illustrated than in the part that women have to play within the socialization process. If many women are prevented from fulfilling their full potential, including their political potential, by their socializing functions then reforms have to be directed at changing this state of affairs. Although the reforms may be very limited (e.g. providing more nursery-school places), they could change the character of the socialization process by making it less family-centred and perhaps less dominated by women in its early stages. What the consequences of this are likely to be is not at all certain but it does show the possible extent of the repercussions.

Women as a politically deprived group

Simone de Beauvoir has argued that, like the proletariat, women form a majority of the population and owe their inferiority to an historical process of exploitation and yet, unlike the proletariat, ' . . . women lack the concrete means for organizing themselves into a unit which can stand face to face with the correlative unit. They have no past, no history, no religion of their own, and they have no such solidarity of work and interest as that of the proletariat'.[46] More recently it has been popular to draw parallels between the exploitation of Afro-Americans and women, and certainly the contemporary women's movement could be seen as an outgrowth of the civil rights and Black Power upsurges. An important parallel between the black and women's movement has been the desire of many of their members to retain a separate identity. This causes some ambivalence in how their protest is interpreted by the political left. On the one hand the left sees these movements as another manifestation of the fundamental weaknesses in capitalist society, but on the other hand they have to be integrated into a class analysis of the advanced industrial state, and this may be far from easy. Part of the problem is that women and blacks often have no wish to be subsumed within a wider movement, for they fear that their interests will be subordinated to other considerations. Although in theory a common front may be sound, in reality it could disguise specific grievances and delay desired changes.[47]

The political behaviour of women and other deprived groups can be linked in various ways. Women bear a heavy historical burden of political discrimination; for example, full voting rights were not granted to women until 1920 in the United States and 1928 in Britain. Even today some of the older members of the female electorate were adults before the franchise was extended to women. One would expect a certain time-lag before legal rights are fully acted upon by those who are entitled to them, especially when wider societal forces scarcely encourage their full implementation. After winning the franchise the percentage of women exercising it increased steadily, suggesting a gradual induction into the norm of voting.[48] One would expect similar sorts of processes to influence the voting patterns of the newly enfranchised black electorate of the American South or even the eighteen- to twenty-one-year-olds who have recently received the vote in both Britain and the United States.[49] The importance of the historical circumstances is illustrated by some of the characteristics of working-class Conservatism. As Runciman has shown, it is the older working-class women who tend to vote Tory and they were maturing politically at a time when the Labour party did not exist.[50]

Although there may be historical and legal constraints that bear heavily upon a variety of groups, the pressures of day-to-day living will be especially burdensome to certain women. Many younger married women have the responsibility of running a home and looking after children. This can be so restrictive as to prevent even the simple act of voting, let alone more demanding forms of involvement. Variations in the intensity of these burdens is one explanation of why some women are more politically active than others. Middle-aged women with grown-up children, and of secure economic means, do not have the same demands upon their time as young married women with two or three children and husbands of limited earning power. Many women may experience severe situational constraints on their political participation, but again one must think rather of gradations of participatory opportunities embracing both men and women. Men may be in a better position than most women to perform the simple act of voting but more demanding forms of activity are beyond the reach of all but a few of them. Women are prevented from becoming candidates because politics is a career, while men already have careers, very few of which can be adapted to permit the individual to become politically active.

The isolation of women in the home and family gives rise to their 'lack of solidarity' which makes it difficult for them to develop a collective consciousness. Many women who work are still centred, in a social and psychological sense, in the home. Their jobs are rarely careers, but simply a means of supplementing the family income, or if they are not married jobs are the accepted way of filling in time until they set up home and run families of their own. The failure of women to be fully integrated into the work-a-day world is further reflected in their notoriously low membership of trade unions.[51] Even if these factors were changed it is unlikely that women would develop a separate collective consciousness. What is much more probable is that they would be influenced more strongly by the same kinds of pressure that control the behaviour of men. At least at present they have a separate identity in spite of the fact that their social situations handicap the creation of a collective consciousness.

The dispersal and isolation of women within the home besides making it difficult for them to build a common front also increases their susceptibility to certain influences. Undoubtedly the most important of these is their husbands, for they are among their main links with the wider society. With limited sources of information, and no independent social base, it is to be expected that married women will follow their husband's political lead.[52] Lipset has suggested that those with limited access to information will be less politically active.[53] For this category of women, perhaps equally important is the quality of the political information to which they are exposed, for those who do not work are very much at the mercy of the media. Unlike Parkin I am not at all certain that the media are universal transmitters of the conservative biases within the political culture, especially the media to which most housewives are exposed.[54] It may trivialize the quality of life and be highly conservative in the sense of reinforcing role differentiation, especially the sex roles, but it does not follow that it is politically conservative. What is more certain is that the housewife responds to the media as an individual, or at least without institutional supports. I would suggest that given the media's preoccupation with popular culture, this is more likely to depoliticize those who are dependent upon them rather than to make political conservatives of them.

This fragmentation and isolation of women has highlighted special features of their deprivation which place severe restrictions upon political activity. However, not all the social pressure work to ensure the universally high political participation of men. Certain occupational categories are not heavily unionized, especially in the United States.[55] The absence of participatory pressures will be strong amongst some of the American minority ethnic groups, owing to their past political exclusion and their present concentration in unskilled industrial occupations and farm labour. The transient way of life of certain agricultural labourers inhibits integration into a community structure, thus lowering their political activity.[56] The embourgeoisement thesis claimed that many workers were becoming more engrossed in a home-centred family life-style, freeing them from the ties of the work place and perhaps undermining their collective consciousness.[57] Although this thesis has been discredited, it is widely believed that the political consciousness of the British worker is not all that it used to be. Work looms larger for men than women in as much as they are expected to be the family breadwinners, but it does not follow that it has greater meaning for the individual (e.g. personal satisfaction) and increasingly its significance could centre around its economic rewards and precious little else. What political consciousness, if any, is associated with this is open to doubt. Regardless of these speculations about the future, it is clear that at the moment various social, economic and political forces restrict the political opportunities of some men in much the same way as they do of some women.

Those who can perceive a direct relationship between participation and personal welfare have a great incentive to be politically active. American lawyers are said to have such an outstanding record of political involvement because of the close connection between politics and law — in concrete terms it opens alternative career possibilities (e.g. a judicial appointment) or helps to drum up business.[58] For most people the relationship is not nearly so obvious, a fact which has led some to question the rationality of voting. In view of their position in the home women are particularly unlikely to perceive the link between personal welfare and political activity. Their problems are invariably closely related to the family routine and tend to have a very specific and immediate quality. But no social situation is static and the growth of the women's movement must within itself increase the political awareness of many women. Political issues of direct interest to women have emerged recently. As many women control the family budget they are especially aware of price inflation and both British and American governments have made moves to placate the clamour by containing price rises on food.[59] In addition, successive governments have shown their willingness to bring about greater sex equality by passing progressive legislation.[60] It is somewhat ironic, but perhaps not altogether unexpected, that the potentially politicizing issue of price inflation should be so intimately connected with women's role within the family, the very institution that many see as most responsible for her subordination. The drive for sex equality, especially in relation to job opportunities, is in direct contradiction to this, for it could take women out of the family, and thus undermine its character and functions.

Few citizens will perceive a clear, consistent and strong relationship between governmental action and their own personal political behaviour, and this is true of both men and women.[61] What is more important is the ability to aggregate individual behaviour on a group basis and the social situations of men enable them to do this far more readily than most women. Once the group has shown its ability to deliver the goods then individuals are more likely to be convinced that they can best make their weight felt through collective action. No clearer example is to be found than the British coalminer, but few groups have their degree of solidarity or are so favourably placed to wield economic power.[62] Again, therefore, it is more realistic to think in terms of a continuum of power with women relatively unfavourably placed within that continuum, with perhaps the situation changing somewhat of late.

More important than any one disability in the perpetuation of political inequality is the interaction of discriminating forces. The social situation of women — especially their family duties — means that they encounter constraints making it hard for them to participate in politics beyond the mere act of voting. Once non-participation becomes the norm it is all too easy to rationalize it by accepting the virtual ineffectiveness of individual political activity. This cycle of non-involvement and ineffectiveness takes place within a political culture that attempted in the past — and to some extent still attempts today — to both legislate and legitimate these inequalities. While the legal barriers have progressively crumbled, the female politician is still something of an anomaly, a personality to fill the pages of the colour supplements of the Sunday newspapers.[63] (But with the election of Margaret Thatcher to the leadership of the Tory party one hopes that this will change). For these various forms of discrimination to be effective individuals have to at least comply with their messages and this is precisely what many women are no longer doing.

What, therefore, binds women to other deprived groups is the parallels in the pattern of exploitation. Although in each case these may take peculiar forms they have similar causes. There is the legacy of inequality that has been complied with, if not accepted or internalized. In the past this legacy has been embodied in law, for example the disenfranchisement of both black citizens in the southern states and women in general. As the legal barriers have been removed so structural barriers have assumed greater importance. These evolve around various social and economic constraints that become most intense when institutionalized. For women the classic example of this is their role within the family, while for students it is their position of tutelage within the educational system. Ideally, part of the syndrome of inequality is that people think and behave as if their inequality was legitimate, i.e. they are socialized into accepting it and acting within its boundaries. In the not-so-distant past some praised the virtues of Happy Sambo while others saw the contented housewife as an integral part of a harmonious social fabric. What is perhaps unique about the inferiority of women is its universality, crossing class and national boundaries as well as the widest cultural divides. Even political revolutions, including those made in the name of equality, have not been especially successful in destroying all its manifestations.

Women and the politics of socialized inequality

The argument that women are subject to unique socialization processes underlies the claim that they suffer special disabilities that mark them off from other dispossessed groups. In fact the socialization process and structural handicaps are so closely entwined that it is hard to see where one leaves off and the other commences. This is because for women the family is both the agent within which most of her learning occurs and which acts as her structural straitjacket. For many men the family is something to escape from, and when they eventually return to it they do so as heads of the household and as breadwinners in the wider world. Their status is dependent upon the latter for it provides the reference points (e.g. power, income and responsibility) by which most of their fellow citizens will judge them. To most men the family is an appendage, and sometimes an uncomfortable one at that, which can either bask in the glory of his occupation or sink with his failures. To most women the family is the centre of their lives and it is through the reflected glory of their husbands' or children's successes that they will be judged, and almost certainly judge themselves.

To point to socialization processes to explain female inequality assumes that there is a coherent and separate woman's role in society. The legitimations surrounding this concept of a woman's role are well-founded and they regress from cultural forces back to psychological variables and then into the realm of biological differences.[64] The biological legitimations centre mainly, but not entirely, around the contrasting sexual functions of men and women, in particular the fact that procreation is the prerogative of women. It is widely assumed that the biological distinctions give rise to their own psychological dispositions, for example the supposed 'maternal instinct' or greater 'emotionalism' of women. There is a keen debate as to whether Freud, the most famous exponent of sexual identities, based the differences upon a biological or a cultural foundation.[65] Obviously perceptions of the structure of the male and female body, as well as value judgements surrounding those perceptions, were an important part of his theory. But a perceptual straitjacket — in this case the penis-envy of girls — is very similar to the notion of true consciousness in that, it imposes its own reality upon the world. It may also have the same dire consequences, in this case for the psychoanalyst, his patients, and the wider pattern of male–female relationships. As Kate Millett has brilliantly argued, psychoanalysis was a convenient weapon with which to browbeat the flourishing feminist movement at the turn of this century.[66]

One can think of other attempts to sanction differential learning experiences and subsequent inequality. In Britain alleged differences in intelligence were used to justify elitism in the educational system and the outcome, besides educational inequality, was structured access to other scarce resources, most noticeably job opportunities.[67] But the scope of the legitimation was limited and based upon highly suspect foundations. In contrast the foundations of female inequality have been much more extensive and until recently they have received substantial academic support. This is another reason why the women's movement is such an all-encompassing challenge, and equally why opposition to it is so extensive.

The biological and psychological natures of women have been used to support the claim that they have a 'natural' place within the society and what socialization does (all it does!) is ensure that women fulfil this 'natural' role. The outcome is a perfect model or role socialization: children learn from an early age the importance of sex differences, which is reflected in the way their parents dress them and the kinds of toys they are encouraged to play with, as well as their games. In the latter stages of secondary education this is reinforced by their choice of school subjects, and their perceptions of what the future holds for them. Once they leave school boys permanently enter the work-a-day work while most girls pass the time until they are married and have a family of their own. And so the cycle is repeated. It is sometimes argued that socialization processes maintain an egalitarian balance between the sexes, that they reinforce natural differences without any notion of inferiority or superiority. As de Beauvoir has ponted out, this finds a parallel in the 'separate but equal' doctrine that theoretically prescribed a balance between the races in the United States between 1896 and 1954.[68] In both cases equality has been little more than a figment of the imagination. This was inevitable when men rather than women, and whites, rather than blacks, held such a disproportionate share of power, prestige and money, and the sex differences and racial separation themes were devices used to perpetuate those inequalities.

Talcott Parsons has made the most serious attempt to relate psychological and sociological variables. He accepts the basic Freudian model on individual development but has tried to add an additional dimension: 'But what Freud lacked was a systematic analysis of the structure of social relationships as systems in which the process of socialization takes place. It is this which we are attempting to supply'.[69] Parsons accords the family a central place in both the structure of social relations and more particularly in the way it relates to socialization processes. The family performs two related functions: ' . . . the primary socialization of children so that they can truly become members of the society into which they have been born [and] the stabilization of the adult personalities of the population of the society'.[70] Parsons has great faith in the nuclear family with the mother acting as an 'expressive' model and the father as an 'instrumental' model. What is crucial is that the models are not simply dependent upon intra-familial relationships for the parents have wider societal roles to perform and these influence how they will act as parents. Of course the father is invariably the family's major breadwinner and this greatly adds to his 'instrumentality'. Parsons writes, ' . . . but it is fundamentally by virtue of the importance of his occupational role as a component of his familial role that in our society we can unequivocally designate the husband-father as the "instrumental leader" of the family as a system'.[71]

Besides the usual vagueness of the Parsonian terminology (what is meant by 'expressiveness' and 'instrumentality'?), it is impossible to accept this set of relationships as anything other than a perceptive ideal type. This conclusion is reinforced by the lack of flexibility in his phraseology for he argues as if there were no exceptions, or at least none of relevance, to these established social processes. Even in the United States of the 1950s, the period during which Parsonian theory blossomed, there was sufficient evidence to question his faith in the virtues of the nuclear family.[72] None the less, if you reverse the direction of the analysis by asking how the structure of social relations are to be preserved, and come up with a socialization answer, then this gives Parsonian theory a certain amount of logic and strength, if not palatability. It is correct that one of the best ways to stabilize a hierarchical, male-dominated society is to differentiate as clearly as possible between male and female roles, to ascribe superior qualities (or role characteristics) to the former, and to legitimize this through a socialization process, especially the nuclear family which traditionally contains so many of the features of the required outcome. In this model the social structure conditions the socialization process which determines the personality types. The 'normal' cases are the most prevalent, and the nuclear family is lauded because it maximizes these with greatest efficiency within the cultural context of Anglo-American society. The price for this success is paid by those who fail to conform (the abnormal) or even by those who conform, if the consequences are not that desirable. As Millett has written, 'Despite their stability, many oppressive forms do not function efficiently. The debilitated patriarchy which functionalists describe when they turn their attention to socio-sexual matters operates with enormous waste and friction'.[73] And not to mention unhappiness.

In an attack upon Freudian theory de Beauvoir has argued,

Interiorizing the unconscious and the whole psychic life, the very language of psychoanalysis suggests that the drama of the individual unfolds within him . . . But a life is a relation to the world, and the individual defines himself by making his own choices through the world about him. We must therefore turn towards the world to find answers for the questions we are concerned with.[74]

Although Parsons would agree upon the need to add a social dimension to Freudian theory, he would not — like de Beauvoir — suggest that this replaces the whole psychic life. More realistically he looks for the inter-action of internal and external forces, but in the process creates strait-jackets that bind and hold individuals. This is an especially confining model for women, as the socialization processes that flow from the social structure demand their presence in the home where they are to raise children and provide their husbands with succour and comfort. But part of the history of mankind is how people escape the confines of their environment to build new lives. This is a consequence of individuals making their own choices (as de Beauvoir claims) as well as inconsistencies in the wider society. There is no ideological consensus that superimposes upon individuals patterns of inequality that they must internalize. In other words, besides individuals making choices they also have choices to make. Of course for some the controls are more rigid than others, and the choices that can be made are correspondingly narrower. The restrictions upon women have been particularly severe but as we have seen in the past decade the obstacles are by no means insurmountable.

Changing the constraints: A note on the women's liberation movement

In a few hundred words it is impossible to discuss adequately the women's liberation movement in Britain and the United States.[75] I will, therefore, make some general comments about the implications of the movement for socialization processes and briefly examine governmental responses to the demands that women have made in recent years. In both cases I want to spell out some of the implications for the political behaviour of women, although I realize that the impact will extend way beyond this particular focus.

The threads of the women's movement are complicated, but there is a commonly held view that both Britain and America are male-dominated societies which have to be changed to better ensure that women can play different parts from those traditionally ascribed to them. The woman's role within the family, and the assumption that this is her 'natural' lot in life, is credited with much of the responsibility for past exploitation. Good scientific evidence is available to refute biological stereotyping but it is still a fact that procreation is something only women can accomplish. Although the nuclear family as we know it is not an inevitable conse-quence of this, it seems hard to avoid any form of a family structure at all. The answers range all the way from some sort of communal existence, in which tasks are shared, to the retention of the nuclear family with an extension of such aids as nursery schools and more flexible working hours.

Even mild reforms may have wider repercussions than is generally realized. The family is no longer a unit of economic production (although it is a unit of economic consumption) and most job skills are now acquired partly in school and partly at work. What has been left to the family, especially the mother, is the socialization of her children, during what are usually referred to as the formative years. If mothers were not only to work but also to pursue careers then the family's control over even this function would be seriously weakened. Of course all the nursery teachers that would be required could be women and the child would return each evening to the bosom of his family. Women would still provide the 'affective' role model, but presumably as more mothers became full-time careerists the role model images would assume greater complexity with the types of careers pursued by women influencing this. Traditionally they have been engaged in the fields of teaching, nursing and social work, all occupations that Parsons feels have strong 'affective' connotations.[76] Even if this dubious labelling is correct, there is no logical reason why the scope should remain so restricted.

Given that the differences in political behaviour between the sexes are not great, these developments are unlikely to have much impact upon political life. The one exception, and it is an important one, concerns political recruitment. In the past the exclusion of women from political office was part of their more general absence from the professions of both countries, for there was nothing specific about a political career which placed additional burdens upon them. So if the structural constraints which work against women's occupational advancement are lessened, then we can expect an increase in their political recruitment.

Some have interpreted the changes more from the point of view of what they mean for the political order than for women's rights. Almond and Verba have described the British and American family structures as 'open', by which they mean it is most likely to transmit their ideal of the best context for a political order, the civic culture.[77] They see any trend which increases the number of 'politically competent, aware and active females as a good thing, for that will improve prospects for the transmission of the civic culture. But that this does not also automatically improve the status of women is illustrated by the condescending tone of the following quote:

The significance of the political emancipation of women is not in the suffragette's dream of women in cabinets, parliaments, at the upper levels of the civil service, and the like; nor is it in Duverger's conception of the dependent minor. March has shown that there tends to be a division of labor between husbands and wives in the kinds of issues on which they take the initiative. Greenstein has shown that American boys are more politically aware and informed than girls . . . He also points out, correctly, that there are inherent limitations in the adult female role, which set an outer boundary to political participation for the great majority of women'.[78]

We are now witnessing a concerted challenge to the assumption that the limitations in the adult female role are somehow or other 'inherent'. If they are 'inherent' then it is because of barriers contained within the social structure, and if we are to widen opportunities and, we hope, achieve greater equality, these have to be removed.

It may have been of some satisfaction to Almond and Verba that British and American women were more politicized than their German, Italian and Mexican counterparts. But it can be of little comfort to women to learn that their political potential has to be realized first and foremost within the family, to enhance the civic culture rather than their own wellbeing. This can only mean the perpetuation of the present political power imbalance between the sexes: in fact women are called upon to recognize its inevitability and thus to accept their own inferiority.[79] Perhaps a better definition of the civic culture is a society in which women can exercise their full potential, in political as well as other respects, rather than one in which they act as enlightened socializers working to promote the cause of civic stability and male advancement.

Both British and American governments have been moving steadily, if belatedly, in the past few years to legislate changes of direct interest to women. These cover a broad range of legal, social and economic rights although, as always when it comes to removing discrimination, the legislation is more impressive than the actual changes.[80] It is not simply a question of attitudes needing to be updated before legislation can be effective, for change is also hampered by the fact that well-established vested interests have a great deal to lose. This is very clearly seen in some of the manoeuvres to sidestep the equal-pay provisions enacted in Britain. Although this is very rarely made explicit, part of the motivation behind the officially sponsored programmes is a desire to head off more radical demands. The literature of the women's movement has a strong Marxist streak and in typical style it advocates the overthrow of the capitalist system as the only viable means of achieving true liberation.[81] This raises the interesting methodological problem of how we are to know when we have reached the promised land, i.e. the non-sexist society. If the problem is defined in straightforward quantitative terms then the goal is simple: women should have their proportionate share of every facet of the society, especially of every occupational grouping. But not only does this deny the possibility of group differences and preferences (including perhaps the desire of many women to have and raise children), it is an absurdly mechanistic understanding of equality. And yet if sex equality requires the disestablishment of patriarchy, how are we to know when this has been accomplished? Replacing one set of slogans (e.g. capitalism or sexism) by another (e.g. socialism or feminism) does not solve the problem. The official policy is aimed at creating 'equality of opportunity' in which presumably women would share the same opportunities to be as unequal as men. If Afro-Americans with their far greater solidarity find the temptation of personal social mobility hard to resist so will such an amazingly diverse group as women.

The interaction of social structure, socialization and personality is a dynamic and interrelated process. The end result is that socialization and subsequent behaviour are neither as predictable nor as static as both

Parsonians and Marxists would at times lead us to believe. At best there is a precarious balancing of forces with the scales waiting to be tipped in one direction or the other. Such a situation allows individuals a certain amount of choice in deciding what options they will choose. Of course it is by no means an equal contest, for some have greater power, and thus greater freedom of choice, than others. What the women's movement has succeeded in doing is to redress the scales somewhat. Whereas the student movement was strongly issue-oriented and many in the black movement aimed at securing constitutional rights for all citizens, the women's movement has come closest to adopting a true revolutionary posture by challenging society's basic institution (the family) and the traditional method of securing societal stability (the socialization process). But whether it can withstand the seductions of sponsored reformism, and its own internal contradictions, is more than doubtful.

Notes

1. For a general discussion of the various female roles see J. Mitchell, *Women's Estate*, Penguin Books, Harmondsworth, 1971, pp. 101–120.
2. In this respect note the widespread interest in the emergence of Mrs Thatcher as leader of the Conservative party.
3. One or two factories have experienced strikes by female manual workers in the cause of greater parity of pay, if not equal pay.
4. The direction of change is highly complex. There is a relationship between structures, processes and individual behaviour with the lines of influence flowing in several directions at once.
5. For a discussion of the absence of the women's case from socialist literature see J. Mitchell, op. cit., p. 75; J. Mitchell, 'Women: The longest revolution', *New Left Review*, **40** (1966), 11–37.
6. R. Dowse and J. Hughes, 'Girls, boys and politics', *British Journal of Sociology*, **22** (1971), 53.
7. For sex differences in participatory attitudes see Milbrath, op. cit., pp. 54, 63–64; Almond and Verba, op. cit., pp. 177–178, 209–212; Berelson, op. cit., p. 25; A. Campbell *et al.*, *The American Voter*, John Wiley and Sons, New York, 1960, p. 489.
8. Campbell, ibid, pp. 490–491; Milbrath, ibid., p. 58.
9. See pp. 6–7 and 63–65.
10. 'Political socialization', p. 552.
11. F. Greenstein, 'Sex-related political differences in childhood', *Journal of Politics*, **23** (1961), 369.
12. ibid., p. 363.
13. op. cit., pp. 21–24.
14. 'Sex-related political differences in childhood', pp. 365–368.
15. The child's acquisition of regime norms: Political efficacy', pp. 36–37.
16. op. cit., p. 192.
17. See pp. 28–29.
18. op. cit., pp. 55–58.
19. See pp. 45–49.
20. op. cit., pp. 59–60. But note that the most significant discriminating variable is the type of school attended.
21. op. cit., p. 182.
22. ibid., p. 193.

23. G. Di Palma, op. cit., pp. 44–49.
24. ibid., p. 48.
25. op. cit., p. 135.
26. ibid., p. 136.
27. op. cit., p. 397.
28. op. cit., pp. 135–136.
29. As an extreme case, old black women who live in the American South have been excluded from the political process thanks to their colour, sex, age and place of residence.
30. *Political Life*, p. 16.
31. K. Amundsen, *The Silenced Majority: Women and American Democracy,* Prentice Hall, Englewood Cliffs, New Jersey, 1971, pp. 146–148.
32. Which is how some members of the women's movement would like it to be seen, and would argue the need for a new society and a new moral order. See E. Figes, *Patriarchical Attitudes: Women in Society,* Faber and Faber, London, 1970. ch. 8.
33. This is contained in the synopsis of an article by M. S. Devaud, 'Political participation of western European women', *Annals,* **375** (1968), 61.
34. Again the differences are not especially large in either the USA or Britain. See Berelson, op. cit., pp. 73–74; Butler and Stokes, op. cit., p. 129.
35. H. Tingsten, *Political Behaviour: Studies in Election Statistics,* King and Son. London, 1937, pp. 45–47.
36. The best examples are the Italian and German Christian Democratic parties.
37. Again many men are placed in identical circumstances.
38. op. cit., p. 388.
39. Milbrath, op. cit., p. 54.
40. op. cit., pp. 12, 16, 72.
41. See Lipset; *Political Man,* p. 188.
42. op. cit., p. 80.
43. R. Rose, *Politics in England Today,* Faber and Faber, London, 1974, p. 183.
44. Ranney, op. cit., pp. 94–96 and 198, R. K. Kelsall, op. cit., pp. 176–177.
45. The implication is that if a certain number of places were not reserved for women none might actually be elected.
46. S. de Beauvoir, *The Second Sex,* Jonathan Cape, London, 1968, p. 18.
47. Afro-Americans have faced the same problem in their dealings with the American Communist party. The contemporary women's movement is split in several ways, but one fundamental divide is between those who wish to define women as workers (or see themselves as workers) and others who are more straightforward feminists (a 'women of the world unit' strategy).
48. As important as the rate of induction is induction into an on-going political process with well-defined party structures. On this see Rokkan, op. cit., pp. 72–85.
49. One could think of more rapid political mobilization of such groups if they had specific interests that could be catered for by a party that was geared to cope with them. Without this there is no reason to expect anything other than gradual political induction.
50. op. cit., p. 173. Rather, Runciman implies this for he describes the adherence of these older women to the Tory party as more 'habitual loyalty than a choice of specific policies'.
51. Trade unions themselves have been far from active in recruiting women members, and are responsible for many discriminatory practices in industry.
52. Milbrath, op. cit., p. 136.
53. S. M. Lipset, *et al.,* 'The psychology of voting: An analysis of political behaviour', in G. Lindzey (ed.), *Handbook of Social Psychology,* vol, 2, Addison-Wesley, Reading, Massachusetts, 1954, p. 1130.
54. See p. 110.

55. In both countries it is workers in the unskilled service trades who prove particularly difficult to unionize.
56. The recent militancy of the Californian grape-pickers suggests this is changing.
57. See pp. 113–118.
58. See p. 84.
59. This has included temporary price freezes and/or subsidies on basic foodstuffs.
60. At the time of writing a bill promoting a range of measures to ensure sex equality is being sponsored by the British government.
61. Lipset, *et al.,* 'The psychology of voting: An analysis of political behaviour', p. 1128.
62. The coalminer's power was best illustrated in the build-up to, and the aftermath of, the British General Election of February 1974. But note that it was not until the dramatic increase in oil prices that this power could be realized. Up to then all the working-class solidarity in the world had not prevented the running down of the industry and a comparative decline in the wages of coalminers.
63. See for example, 'The women of our choice', *The Sunday Times Magazine,* 19 May 1974, pp. 42–45.
64. See especially J. M. Bardwick, *Psychology of Women: A Study of Bio-Cultural Conflicts,* Harper and Row, New York, 1971.
65. Few of the women in the field have been able to avoid attacking Freud, but for a defence and review of the debate see J. Mitchell, *Psychoanalysis and Feminism,* Allen Lane, London, 1974, Part 1.
66. op. cit., p. 178. And this is true however one interprets Freud.
67. See p. 46.
68. op. cit., p. 15.
69. Parsons and Bales, op. cit., p. 104.
70. T. Parsons, 'The American family: Its relations to personality and the social structure', in ibid., pp. 16–17.
71. ibid., p. 13.
72. Consider Parsons' own fears (and his smoothing of those fears) in this respect; ibid., pp. 4–8.
73. op. cit., p. 220.
74. op. cit., p. 75.
75. For insights into various aspects of the women's movement see the work of Figes, de Beauvoir, Mitchell and Millett (all referenced above) as well as: G. Greer, *The Female Eunuch,* MacGibbon and Kee, London, 1970; V. Klein, *The Feminine Character: History of an Ideology,* Routledge and Kegan Paul, London, 1971; S. Rowbotham, *Women, Resistance and Revolution,* Allen Lane, The Penguin Press, London, 1972; S. Rowbotham, *Woman's Consciousness, Man's World,* Penguin Books, Harmondsworth, 1973.
76. Parsons and Bales, op. cit., p. 15.
77. op. cit., pp. 397–400.
78. ibid., p. 399.
79. In all fairness to Almond and Verba, their book reflects the mood of the early 1960s and I am making judgements with the experience of hindsight.
80. See V. Hanna, 'Industrial apartheid as firms evade the act', *The Sunday Times,* 21 November 1971, p. 65. The article examines how various firms were evading British legislation which specified there should be equal pay for equal work.
81. Probably best exemplified in the writings of Rowbotham. See her concluding chapter in *Woman's Consciousness, Man's World.*

Chapter 10

The Prerequisites of Political Conflict: Divided Ulster as a Case Study

The ideal case study

In the functional models of the political system socialization was the means by which loyalty towards that system was built.[1] Some of the empirical studies have shown that support is not an inevitable outcome of political socialization processes, since minority groups, such as blacks or the Appalachian Mountain people, are subjected to special learning experiences that result in different political attitudes.[2] Northern Ireland illustrates the power of socializing experiences to perpetuate patterns of behaviour that are far from conducive to the making of a fully legitimate regime. It is realistic to talk of socialization into conflict, rather than the creation of diffuse support which Easton and Dennis considered to be the normal product of political learning experiences.[3] I have already argued that the Anglo-American democracies have differential socialization processes in which citizens are called upon to show their support for the regime in contrasting ways, and that stability depends upon a wide acceptance of this division of political labour. So contrasting socialization processes *per se* do not stimulate conflict, but what makes the Irish situation different is the extent of the conflict within the political messages, how this is perpetuated, and its consequences. The aim of this chapter is to explore these dimensions and to examine in broad terms some of the more recent attempts to control and change them.

A central problem in Northern Ireland is that two large polarized communities live within the same territorial boundaries.[4] In a united Ireland the Protestants would form about one-fifth of the total population, a distinct minority but by no means an insignificant one.[5] The situation would be very different if in either case (i.e. in a united Ireland or in divided Ulster) the minorities were much smaller or alternatively there were more than two groups and each group was a minority.[6] This is not to say that the conflict in the province is essentially the consequence of a demographic accident, but that different group distributions open up the possibility of more complex political manoeuvring and perhaps lend themselves more readily to the making of compromises.[7] Certainly there are a number of nation states in the world that appear to have internal social cleavages as intense as Northern Ireland without the same level of political violence, although in all fairness it must be said that some experience even greater conflict.[8] Where stability prevails in spite of internal social cleavages political compromises have been worked out within which the differences can be accommodated, perhaps even encouraged. In Northern Ireland, however, there is no such political compromise, and in fact political conflict is an intrinsic element within the socialization processes. Another objective of this chapter is to examine the political context within which socialization processes occur and to show how the two relate to each other. Again, this cannot be considered without looking at moves to change this political setting so that socialized experiences are contained and may even be rendered innocuous.

Before its abolition the Stormont regime could claim that it was governing with partial consensus.[9] And surprisingly it was able to maintain this state of affairs for a number of decades. Although the regime was never seen as fully legitimate by the overwhelming majority of Catholic citizens, explicit opposition ebbed and flowed, reaching a crescendo in the years immediately prior to its downfall. This is another of those cases where compliance could create an illusion of tacit, if not explicit support. To assume this was to make a dangerous gamble, since fully one-third of the population could be mobilized to oppose the regime, a percentage sufficiently high to frighten most intelligent ruling elites. From about the mid-1960s attempts were made to place the legitimacy of the regime on a firmer basis. This owed something to the political wisdom of the then Prime Minister of Northern Ireland, Terence O'Neill, and it represented an attempt to head off demands for reform emerging internally from the Catholic population and externally from the backbenches of the Labour party at Westminster.[10] But, as Richard Rose has further argued, there may be only one thing more difficult than fully legitimizing a regime that governs without consensus, and that is repudiating it. In view of this perhaps the attempt to change the basis of legitimation was doomed to failure, and the best thing could be hoped for was a regime dependent upon only partial consensus. Of course it could assume a different form of partial consensus from that which had existed in the past, but none the less was still far short of full legitimation. I mention this because it is the unstartling conclusion that my interpretation of the evidence will suggest, and because it will provide a small argument against the case that political stability is the norm and what is required are socialization processes that ensure that state of affairs.

The community basis of political socialization

Before making generalizations about the socializing pressures that Catholics and Protestants in Northern Ireland experience, it is essential to stress that they are by no means monolithic communities. It is part of the British mythology, certainly aided by some of the more horrifying aspects of the recent sectarian violence, that Northern Ireland consists of two primitive tribes that intermittently go to war with one another. The two religious communities may polarize along homogeneous political lines in a time of crisis (for example, it is reasonable to refer to a universal Catholic abhorrence of internment) but in normal times they experience all the stresses and strains that fragment most large groups in an industrialized society. The level of unemployment may be higher amongst Catholics, and those who have a job are more likely to be unskilled workers earning the lowest wages, but the full range of social classes typically found in a moderately industrialized western state stratify both communities.[11] It is one of the unfulfilled dreams of both reformists and radicals that class politics will eventually replace the sectarian loyalties that currently divide the people. In addition to social class, other demographic variables — for example, age, sex and urbanization — exert their influence within the two religious communities.[12]

Even religion is not the monolithic entity that it sometimes seems to be. The Protestants are not simply Protestants but members of the Church of Ireland, Presbyterians, Methodists, or possibly adherents of one of the smaller sects of which Ian Paisley's Free Presbyterian Church is probably the best-known. One of the charges that Protestants sometimes level at the Roman Catholic Church is that it is an all-embracing institution controlling every aspect of the lives of its members. If this is what the Church attempts to do — and not surprisingly many would dispute this — then one can only comment upon its lack of success. The hierarchy of the Church has steadfastly set itself against those who would achieve political change by violence, yet with regularity some Irishmen with sound Catholic upbringings turn to the gun. A distinction must be made between the Church hierarchy and the local clergy, and since the latter has the task of holding the Church together at the grass-roots it may be forced into making all sorts of compromises. Connor Cruise O'Brien has argued that the Church and the IRA can, indeed must, coexist because they do not compete for allegiance with one another in the same areas.[13] The Official IRA, with its brand of Marxist ideology, posed a threat to the Church, and this is why some members of the clergy may have welcomed the Provisionals with their orthodox nationalism. Certainly protracted open conflict between the Church and the IRA within the communities would endanger them both, so the incentive to reach a compromise is very real. What this suggests is tension within the community rather than a theocracy holding absolute sway throughout its domain. Furthermore, many a distinguished agnostic, as well as backslider, shows that Rome does not have all its own way with its children.

The forces which subdivided the two religious communities into a number of groups give rise to contrasting socialization pressures which help to cement different intra-community patterns of political behaviour. There are plenty of examples to illustrate the truth of this. The Protestants provide us with both an Anglicized landowning upper class, which contains a number of important spokesmen for reforming Unionism, as well as the working-class citizens of Belfast who form the backbone of the various Protestant paramilitary groups. The contrasts are not quite so dramatic on the Catholic side but there is a whole world of differences between the reform-oriented middle class which was a major ingredient in the Campaign for Social Justice and the working-class youths of the Catholic ghettos who appear to form the rank-and-file membership of both wings of the IRA.[14]

In spite of these internal cleavages the fundamental divide in Northern Ireland runs along the religious boundary; it is a boundary that encompasses social, economic and political groups as well as members of different branches of the Christian faith. As much as some may hope for the emergence of class politics, or perhaps a large non-sectarian youth movement that promotes the cause of radical politics, for the time being at least these are dreams that must fade in the light of harsh reality.[15] If it is accepted that religion forms a boundary that also separates individuals along other dimensions, especially their political behaviour, then this implies that greater homogeneity exists within the two religious communities than between individuals who share characteristics other than their religion. In other words, in spite of the potential for internal cleavage that the socio-economic variation could stimulate, the homogenizing forces are that much stronger. Precisely what these forces are, how they counteract disintegrating pressures and who has a stake in maintaining this precarious equilibrium are central factors to any understanding of political socialization within Northern Ireland.

The most obvious feature of the political socialization process within divided Ulster is the polarization of that process both in terms of what people learn and how they acquire that learning. In relation to what is learnt, the differences are most clearly exemplified by what O'Brien has termed the cultists of 1798 and 1690.[16] Richard Rose has argued that the ideal type Catholic and Protestant socialization models are alternative and discordant.[17] It is not simply that they impart different views of the world but that their respective positions are defined in direct conflict with one another; we are what they are not and vice versa. What is striking, however, is that the messages are transmitted in a similar fashion within both communities. So, though the content and product of the socialization processes may differ, the way they work does not, and as I shall argue this is one of some considerable significance.

The outstanding feature of the socialization process in Northern Ireland is the community context within which it occurs. On the basis of evidence from other parts of the United Kingdom social scientists have talked of class, school, sex and even generational socialization patterns but rarely of the kinds of influences that the community structure can exert over individuals. It is not that these other forces lose their ability to shape behaviour but rather they are integrated within a particular community setting, and it is this that determines the way they will act upon individuals. Outside Northern Ireland it is more common to talk of the declining influence of the community, of working-class neighbourhoods eroded by high-rise buildings or by sprawling council housing estates located on the periphery of town, and small market towns adjusting to the pressures of a new, anonymous industrial base.[18] But in the province the traditional community either stands as a bulwark against change or re-asserts itself in the face of pressure for change. The housing estates are invariably of one religious persuasion and the contemporary crisis makes it even riskier to experiment with mixed housing patterns. It will probably be some time before another 'Catholic' Divis Flats is built in a position so exposed to Protestant attacks.[19]

In physical terms the Protestant and Catholic working-class communities look alike: either the huddled-up, back-to-back terraced houses that are such a legacy of our industrial revolution or the more spacious housing estates (some less hospitable than others) that have sprung up in this century. It is within these physical confines that the patterns of social interaction are created and acted out. The power of the community stems from the fact that it is both closed and tight-knit, which enables it to direct behaviour along carefully prescribed paths. The community is an institutionalized response to what it means to be working-class and either Catholic or Protestant in Northern Ireland, and as such it enables people to cope in a routine way with the pressures of their daily lives. There are certain parallels here with the black ghettos and, although in both cases some have pointed to high degree of internal social dislocation (e.g. broken families in the black ghettos and vigilante justice in Northern Ireland), it is possible to interpret these as responses to a hostile external environment which are a means of helping people to survive. I would question the degree of freedom of choice that exists for community residents within both situations. In a sense the community is a grass-roots creation, but it is built within a context where resources that determine the quality of life within its confines are controlled externally.[20]

Parents watch their children grow up making friends with neighbouring children of the same religious faith. The children, like children everywhere, base their gangs and other peer group relationships upon the street and the school. In this case the schools are for the faithful only, whether it be the independent Catholic schools or the Protestant-dominated state apparatus.[21] Within the Catholic areas the Church is at the very centre of this web, casting a net to the extremes of its empire. In a description of Derry's Catholic community Mary Holland has written, ' . . . it is necessary to see the extraordinary nature of the Catholic community in Derry, the tightly knit loyalties built around chapels and schools, the fact that the whole identity of the community, its tribal senses, centre on being Catholic. To this naturally enough, the Church is essential'.[22] On the other side of the fence — perhaps Iron Curtain is a more appropriate description — stands the Orange Order. As the Church provides an institutional framework for all Catholics so the Orange Order serves the same function for Protestants, and like the Catholic Church it will have members who are not altogether in sympathy with its theology. Frank Wright has described the Orange Order as an essentially lower-class institution that exists as 'a defence body for the socialization processes of the Christian Faith, Reformed and Protestant'.[23] As such it has for a long time controlled the political, social and economic horizons of many working-class youths who live within the confines of the Protestant ghettos. Given the fact that families, peer groups, schools and churches interact so intimately with one another within well-defined community boundaries, it is to be expected that social intercourse will follow carefully prescribed paths that individuals fail to follow at their peril.

Besides acting as a central unifying force within their respective communities, the Church and the Orange Order provide the organizational link between communities. In comparison with the rest of the United Kingdom, this provides a degree of cohesion to the socialization process that is quite remarkable. In spite of the internal cleavages there exists this overriding framework to which the individual belongs even if he has no wish to be incorporated. Furthermore, those who make a positive effort to stand outside its confines risk social ostracism and endanger their chances of exercising power. In a sense, therefore, it is difficult to escape from the community and still reside in Northern Ireland. Eamonn McCann has graphically shown how Crossmaglen is to all intents and purposes, in spite of its constitutional status, a part of the Republic of Ireland,[24] and this is probably true of much of the border region. However, these areas cannot avoid being sucked into the mainstream of the conflict for their constitutional status demands the presence of the British army. So even in those places where one would expect less of a siege mentality (apparently Crossmaglen has only one Protestant family) the wider political context intrudes to reinforce community solidarity.

In a time of crisis the ghetto citizens turn in upon themselves for defence and succour, so strengthening the power of community structures. This takes the form of throwing up barriers to keep out strangers, allowing only those with the correct credentials to pass freely. At the same time there is a rallying of support for those who are most able to defend the community, which within Northern Ireland has meant the gunmen. In fact for a period of time certain parts of both Derry and Belfast became virtually self-governing enclaves.[25] Since 1969 Belfast has witnessed significant shifts in the distribution of its population. The mixed areas have declined as people move into what they consider to be safer districts, i.e. those inhabited by their co-religionists. The streets that link the major conflicting ghettos have been rent by both voluntary and violently induced movement until a clear-cut divide, sometimes cutting a street in two, has been established.[26] This detachment from the wider society is something more than a symbolic gesture manifested by flimsy barricades manned by local vigilantes. The freedom from official surveillance has increased for the state has not been able to maintain its normal functions throughout its supposedly sovereign territory. In response to this, numerous community-based welfare agencies have sprung up to fill the vacuum left by the state, so further cementing the ties between the individual and his locality, while rendering him even more isolated from the wider society.

The likelihood of workers acting on class, rather than sectarian lines is something I want to consider in greater detail in the analysis of strategies designed to bring about change, but a few comments are in order here. Most of Ulster's working-class citizens have lived in enclosed environments for much of their lives. Although I have strong reservations about the theory that the vital stage in political learning is early childhood, it is none the less true that some are more susceptible to change in the adult years than others.[27] In view of the strength of the community-based socialization processes during these early years, and given the fact that the individual worker still has not escaped its grasp, one would not expect changes to come easily in these circumstances. In addition, no guarantee can be made that the individual will be exposed to wider influences while at work. On a number of occasions prominent Unionist politicians have urged Protestant employers to hire only members of the true faith.[28] Within some industries certain kinds of jobs or particular skills are reserved for either Catholics or Protestants. A notorious example, in view of the support it receives from the British taxpayer, is Protestant domination of the Harland and Wolff shipyards.[29] Another very real tragedy of the contemporary crisis is that sectarianism, in keeping with the general trend, has intruded more deeply into the work place. Workers are afraid to travel through districts inhabited by members of the opposite religious persuasion, the 'odd man out' is a favourite assassination target, and Catholic and Protestant workers have been murdered as they walked in friendship to the factory.[30] The outcome is yet another increase in immobilism with much greater circumspection in the choice of one's work-mates and where one decides to work. The 'safe' home community looms even larger as a place of refuge.

Central to the study of political socialization is the idea that behaviour is learnt, and moreover it is acquired under conditions that lead the individual to make some choices and reject others. Although there may be controversy as to how much individual choice can occur within this process, no one sees it as entirely free from constraints. In spite of this what frightens many outsiders who look at Northern Ireland is the apparent inability of its citizens to escape their confines. The community pressures are so strong that *individual* acts of rebellion are rare. This runs contrary to much of western liberal mythology in which salvation, of one's body and soul, is a personal act. In the United States Negroes still remained Negroes (and by definition inferiors) regardless of their own personal social mobility. Not until cultural pluralism became more of a reality were individualistic channels of advancement meaningful as ways of relieving black discontent. For the Catholic in Northern Ireland the problem is even more complex: the central dilemma surrounds his citizenship, and nothing short of the dismemberment of the constitutional settlement will resolve the problem of being Catholic and Irish in a British and Protestant state.[31] Although the community norms may inhibit individual behaviour, they do provide a basis for enabling the group as a whole to cope with the daily routine and in a crisis there is speedy improvization. When certain Catholic districts were 'invaded' in 1969 the community response was swift: the invaders were repulsed, barricades were set up and defence committees were organized, proving the community was capable of handling the crisis.

The learning that takes place in the ghettos is a total experience. The individual is exposed to a pattern of influences that consistently reinforce one another and external messages run into this central core of learning. The community basis of socialization undermines the concept of distinctive learning stages, in which primary socialization agents interact with secondary agents that may or may not build upon the initial learning skeleton. Family, school, peer group and Church are extensions of one another, so that the individual lives in a constant milieu. In much the same way no distinctive stages mark the daily process of indoctrination. The child lives within a Protestant family, attends the Protestant state school, joins a youth club associated with the Orange Order, and so on. As socialization experiences they are all one and the same thing rather than contrasting entities in a daily cycle of learning.

It is more usual to think of total learning experiences as occurring within institutions that are isolated from the wider society (both prisons and public schools have been quoted as examples) rather than within urban communities.[32] But these are communities that parallel the total institution in the degree of control they can exercise over their individual members. The individual can escape the pressures by moving elsewhere to live (most assuredly by emigrating) in much the same way as the prisoner leaves jail or the public-schoolboy says goodbye to his Alma Mater. Of course some, most noticeably those who have jobs, have to leave the community daily for a period of time. It was interesting to see newsreels in which part of a barricade was removed in the morning to let the workers out, to be replaced once they had left, with the same ritual being repeated in the evening as they returned from work. This symbolized the hold of the community over these men and women, that they had not really escaped its clutches during the few hours they were physically separated from it.

In a phrase widely used in reference to Northern Ireland, Mary Holland referred to the 'tribal' sense of Catholic Derry,[33] which is a good way of imparting what I mean by community-based socialization processes. However, this is too simplistic a view of the various forces that shape behaviour. In Northern Ireland the traditional primordial relations are facing a challenge from the socio-economic forces associated with an advanced capitalist society. If one can view the communities as having created a pattern of social interaction approximating the kinship model, then the emerging networks would be based upon the class structure of capitalism and its concomitants of income, status and power. At the moment the province appears to be an interesting amalgam of the two models with the traditional forces still exerting by far the greatest influence. The evidence suggests that pressures for changes come from the local branches of international companies. In their hiring, promotion and firing policies they are swayed by the factors that influence most such companies: educational qualifications, proven skill, reliability, and length of service.[34] But the demands of capitalism have to interact with the realities of the local political situation and it may be deemed expedient to comply with certain established traditions rather than risk the wrath that innovation can bring forth. To provide an extreme example: it may be expedient to employ no Catholics rather than to hire a few and subsequently have your factory burnt to the ground.[35] Although the communities are by no means self-sufficient, and only partially self-contained, the struggle to release their hold upon their members will be intense and they will never be as anonymous as their English counterparts.

In his book on divided Ulster Richard Rose has written, 'The most important feature of political socialization is what a person learns, not how he learns it'.[36] In view of the fact that once he had controlled for the religion of the members of his sample survey he discovered comparatively few differences in political attitudes, this is a reasonable statement. The religious chasm was so wide that it obliterated other internal divisions, and provided a highly convenient reference point to explain people's beliefs. If the correlations he discovered had been more complex then there would have been a need to explain the distribution of attitudes within the religious communities. Certainly it would have been necessary to return to the political socialization process to explain this; to have examined the complex interaction of forces to see how they gave rise to particular patterns of behaviour. Even though the essential simplicity of correlations obviated the need for this, there is another sense in which it is as important to know how a person acquires his behaviour as to know what the content of that behaviour may be. The community basis of political socialization in Northern Ireland not only leads to polarized political attitudes but also determines the intensity of commitment to what is learnt. If the individual has no alternative sources of information then it is difficult to challenge the validity of what is being taught. Contact does not automatically bring about enlightenment and co-operation, but the lack of interaction, within the context prevailing in Northern Ireland, will lead to suspicion, hostility and outright conflict. Obviously a person's beliefs are crucially important, but what I am suggesting is that the intensity of those beliefs, the likelihood of his acting upon them and the prospects for changing them cannot be gauged without knowing how they were acquired. So the content and acquisition of behaviour are two mutually reinforcing aspects of one socialization process.

In Northern Ireland there prevails a situation in which the two main religious groups learn an almost totally conflicting set of values and beliefs in more or less identical circumstances. Both communities tend to intermarry, live in segregated ghettos, attend schools exclusive to their co-religionists, form their peer group cliques within the neighbourhood, and have much of this segregated existence organized for them by either the Roman Catholic Church or the Orange Order. Parkin has argued that in Britain there is a conflict between working-class values and dominant values, with the latter prevailing where the structural supports for working-class culture are weak. In spite of Protestant claims to be 'loyalists', and the traditional links between Ulster Unionism and the Conservative party, both communities are essentially outside the mainstream of British values.[37] Like those British working-class communities dominated by 'solidaristic collectivism' they have constructed the most powerful of all bulwarks against dominant values — an isolated community structure with a coherent internal value system. In Northern Ireland two dominant cultures exist side by side. They are not in competition with each other (for they do not complete for wavering souls), but rather they form the pen which keep the sheep within the fold. As Eamonn McCann has said, the battle for the hearts and minds was decided long ago and nothing can change this now.[38]

Perpetuating the system: Those with a stake in community segregation

Connor Cruise O'Brien has characterized the Ulster Protestant's view of the world as a siege mentality.[39] The Protestant sees himself as surrounded by an alien and hostile nation state that lays claim to his territory and desires to destroy his way of life. Worse than this, that nation state harbours armed criminals who, acting under the guise of political freedom fighters, make periodic attacks on citizens and property within his borders. To add to his disenchantment there is a large fifth column, whose way of life is similar to those of the predatory nation state, which harbours those who wish to overthrow Protestant Ulster. Likewise the Roman Catholic in Northern Ireland has his own siege mentality, what O'Brien calls 'the siege within the siege'. As a reluctant citizen of the United Kingdom he sees himself surrounded by Protestants who are not only hostile to his religious beliefs but who also have structured social, economic and political processes that heavily discriminate against him. In theory he has a lifeline consisting of his co-religionists in the Republic, but rarely have they shown the concern for his plight that he feels it merits. Thus, like the Protestants who suspect British perfidy, he sees his salvation as resting in his own hands.

The community structures with their concomitant socialization processes stem from these siege mentalities. An integral part of this is the political basis on which the province rests. With students, workers, women and Afro-Americans, social and economic constraints have been central to their peculiar socialization experiences, and although these are not lacking in Northern Ireland, the essence of the internal differentiation is political. The constitutional settlement partitioned Ireland with Northern Ireland being created and perpetuated as a Protestant state, and this state of affairs continued until well into the 1960s, when Terence O'Neill took the first tentative steps towards placing the regime on a different basis. The economic, social and political discrimination follows directly from the constitutional settlement. The consequence is that most state jobs, especially at the higher ranks, have been given to Protestants. In terms of social welfare facilities, particularly in the very sensitive area of housing, the allocation of resources has again favoured Protestants. In political life there was the unique phenomenon, for a so-called western democracy, of perpetual one-party government. At the local level the Unionist party frequently controlled the machinery of government in spite of the Protestants being in the minority within the local authority boundaries. This was accomplished by a judicious combination of limiting the franchise to ratepayers, permitting some individuals to have more than one vote and patterns of gerrymandering that would have done justice to a southern segregationist.[40] Obviously Northern Ireland was not a paradise for all Protestants and a hell for all Catholics, and indeed some have commented on the similar patterns of deprivation suffered by the working classes of both communities, but even the most deprived Protestant — unless he had a well-developed sense of class-consciousness — could more readily identify with the regime than even privileged Catholics.

The various branches of the Protestant establishment that most benefited from these arrangements had a vested interest in maintaining them. Part of the strategy was the cementing of a united Protestant front and, although it is a gross exaggeration to credit a skilfully manipulative elite with the entire responsibility for the absence of a united working-class movement, it is none the less true that on a number of occasions Unionist politicians took steps to undermine any such development.[41] Many Protestants may have been far from satisfied with life in the six counties, but after all it was their state, and the twenty-six counties with their higher unemployment rate, inferior social welfare benefits and a socially dominant and politically powerful Roman Catholic Church were scarcely like heaven on earth. And the fact that a small minority of the Catholics were periodically intent on bombing and shooting them into a united Ireland could only make the prospect less appealing.

A more interesting set of forces that have a stake in maintaining the status quo are those based within the Catholic community. At the level of rhetoric most Catholics and their organizations stand for both a reformed Northern Ireland and the ultimate reunification of the thirty-two counties. Unionists have been known to claim that Catholics live in segregated communities because they prefer it that way.[42] The Church, with its places of worship, schools and social organizations, must find it easier to carry on its tasks in segregated communities than if its flock were more widely dispersed. The existence of well-defined voting blocs helps those who are politically ambitious. Although the Unionist hegemony may have prevented them from exercising executive power they could always rely on the faithful to secure representation. The political parties which have lost out in the struggle for power are those drawing a smattering of support from the whole spectrum of society rather than those with adherents concentrated in particular districts.[43] The presence of well-defined ghettos also assists the IRA, for it provides them with a base where they can find refuge if not support. Perhaps the subtlest acquiescence in the continuation of the boundary has been on the part of successive governments in Dublin.[44] Their formal commitment to reunification has to be weighed against the practical considerations arising out of their economic relations with the United Kingdom. They also have to consider the bearing this would have upon their own political careers, as well the problem of reconciling a recalcitrant Protestant minority.[45]

The Catholic forces that gained something from segregation could legitimately argue that Catholic inequality was more the work of the Unionist hierarchy than their own doing. To draw a parallel with Afro-Americans, an insistence on maintaining a group identity should not lead to inequality. Is it not possible to be different and equal? The difficulty that Protestants have with this point of view is what the differences contain. If, in Protestant eyes, the Catholic has a perpetual aura of disloyalty then he can do little else but look upon him with great suspicion. The state has to be structured to keep this potential disloyalty within bounds (which means Catholic inequality), otherwise it is likely to destroy the state itself.

Socialization processes, therefore, are repeated within a context that follows from the constitutional settlement, and even those forces wishing to change that settlement are firmly enmeshed in its consequences. The polarization between the two religious groups is stronger amongst the working-class strata because it is they who have borne the brunt of the social, economic and political structures and processes that have flowed out of the constitutional settlement. From the point of view of the Catholic working class this is clear-cut: it is they who experience most unemployment, tend to have the lowest wages and least prestigious jobs, who are hardest hit by discrimination in the allocation of social benefits, and whose votes have counted for least thanks to gerrymandering. The working-class Protestant has no evident economic or social benefits to gain from a united Ireland and his identification with the state gives him a powerful psychological advantage over Catholics, who in socio-economic terms may be his equal or even superior. In much the same way racial stereotyping in the United States has given the poor white a certain psychic satisfaction which may have helped to distract him from his poverty.

The static nature of the respective community structures is reinforced by the powerful vested interests that have a stake in the status quo. In post-war Britain much has been made of changing patterns of political behaviour and the breakdown in established mores which contrasts so dramatically with Ulster's apparent inability to change.[46] In Britain it is realistic to think of competition between contrasting value systems with genuine conversions taking place. A conflict may exist, for example, between dominant values and working-class values, but few workers live in such isolated worlds that they can immunize themselves from this potential clash. Even if the cultured divisions are wide, they are not defined entirely in terms of mutual antagonism for most citizens share some features in common. Most Englishmen have a keen sense of their nationality whatever else may divide them. When it comes to translating these consensual sentiments into concrete behaviour there is obviously a division of labour (even patriotism requires some to die in the trenches and others to plan the battles in safety) and fierce struggles will surround the legitimacy of the resulting inequalities. But in Northern Ireland not even a limited consensus exists within which to conduct the debate on the allocation of the scarce resources of status, income and power.

The few empirical studies of political socialization in Northern Ireland show how successfully the learning processes impart a polarized view of the political world.[47] Protestants and Catholics have differing conceptions of their national allegiance, for the former see themselves as British or Ulstermen and the latter as Irish.[48] These national identities are conveniently and emotively symbolized by their respective flags: the Union Jack, or more recently the Red Hand of Ulster, on the one side, and the Irish Tricolour on the other. To wave the Tricolour in the sight of many a Protestant is much like waving the proverbial red flag in front of a bull.[49] Parades play a big part in manifesting a sense of tribal loyalty and, significantly, they invariably celebrate events from the past in which a resounding victory was scored over the traditional enemy. There is no shared, and little independent, past but rather one that is filled with mutual antagonism, suspicion and conflict. About the educational systems Peter Wilby has written,

The schools themselves reflect the two cultures that make up Ulster. In the Catholic schools, Irish music, language, dancing and games pervade the curriculum. But not, of course, in the Protestant schools. The children have completely different pictures of world they live in . . . The best-known example of the divided curriculum in Northern Ireland is in history. The Catholic text-books concentrate on Irish history and present it as a struggle of oppressed people against colonial rule. The Protestant textbooks present Ulster as an integral, though beleaguered part of the United Kingdom and concentrate on the mainstream of British politics.[50]

Northern Ireland is more akin to the United States (perhaps the closest parallel is the American South) than to Britain in its very explicit com-munication of political education.[51] It is as if the people of Ulster are unsure of who they really are, and what they actually stand for, and only by this ritualistic show of strength can they express their true feelings and ward off the threats of a hostile world. As equally important, Catholics and Protestants in Northern Ireland share a totally interdependent existence, but it is an interdependence built upon conflict, in which one community is the negation of the other, rather than one built upon shared experiences and mutual co-operation. This is not to deny that some Protestants have been very influential in the republican cause, and there have been short bursts of co-operation across the sectarian barrier. The conflicting interdependence is symbolized by the great parades. The resistance of Derry and the Battle of the Boyne were not simply Protestant victories, but also defeat for the Catholic cause.[52] In the same way, though some would deny this, the Easter Rising of 1916 has become a victory for Irish nationalism and a defeat for the Protestants who wished to maintain the link with Britain.[53] Again the best Anglo-American parallel is to be found in the history of Afro-Americans, but substantial black–white alliances have flourished in the past and black Americans have a cultural identity that is in certain respects independent of white America.

Changing the system: Hopes and realities in divided Ulster

In the second part of this chapter I want to explore some of the strategies that have been devised to bring about change in divided Ulster. In view of the central theme of the book I will examine their varying implication for the political learning process.

Economic determination to the rescue

Northern Ireland has experienced its own version of the embourgeoisement thesis with the not surprising exception that it was the Catholics who were expected to mend their political ways. Shortly after resigning the premier-ship O'Neill claimed.

It is frightfully hard to explain to a Protestant that if you give Roman Catholics a good job and a good house, they will live like Protestants, because they will see neighbours with cars and television sets. They will refuse to have eighteen children, but if the Roman Catholic is jobless and lives in a most ghastly hovel, he will rear eighteen children on national assistance . . . He (the militant

Protestant) cannot understand, in fact, that if you treat Roman Catholics with due consideration and kindness they will live like Protestants, in spite of the authoritative nature of their church.[54]

The not unreasonable assumption is that different social and economic conditions will produce new life-styles. The political connotations are more indirect. Does to 'live like Protestants' mean that Catholics will accept the legitimacy of the regime if their living standards are improved? To limit the size of the Catholic family removes a Protestant fear that the constitutional settlement could be undermined by their being 'outbred' by the Catholics. Such is the subtlety of the relationship between socio-economic forces and the facts of political life in Northern Ireland.

Built into the embourgeosement thesis, in its application to the British working class, was the notion that political behaviour was changed by the worker's becoming more home-centred.[55] A different socialization process was created by a rearrangement of the constellation of forces shaping the worker's life, so that as some factors increased in importance so others declined. Although in a more prosperous province the ghettos could become embourgeosified in a materialist sense, in other respects they would remain very much the same. Indeed, making individuals home-centred suggests that they may be even more strongly embedded in the community. It is the very opposite strategy of building up a class-conscious working class which would be dependent upon the work situation for its frame of reference.

Another consideration is ascertaining the extent to which political behaviour is likely to change without new political structures. This is clearly vital if the past conflict has essentially political roots. In Britain this was no problem for it was assumed that the political system was already legitimate and all affluence did was increase support for the Conservative party.[56] Of course political reformism could accompany socio-economic change but this did not solve the problem of the very legitimacy of the nation state. In the 1970s political structures have been substantially modified, including the abolition of the Stormont regime, but still the call for the dismemberment of the state is heard from the hardline Catholics, and equally significantly many Protestants appear to want a return to the days before juggling with the political structures commenced.

Even if political change could have been stimulated by socio-economic amelioration, it is doubtful whether Northern Ireland was a suitable test case. Most of the development took place in the predominantly Protestant region east of the river Bann, while the rest of the province, and the more particularly the city of Derry, languished in poverty.[57] In the 1960s the average standard of living rose in Northern Ireland but a question mark hangs over the relative improvement in Catholic and Protestant circumstances. Furthermore, the general rise in the wealth of the United Kingdom during that decade was, in comparative terms, insignificant and certainly insufficient to make inroads into the kinds of problems that the traditionally depressed regions of Ulster had suffered for so long.

Like O'Neillism the Marxist solutions centre around the determining influence of economic forces and the social relations that emerge from them.[58] Ulster differs from other western industrialized societies by its failure to develop a political system organized along class lines. Although this is not a unique phenomenon other bourgeois states have had more success at mitigating non-class conflict.[59] The necessary accommodation have taken place within the framework of capitalist economies and liberal democratic polities, and radicals within Northern Ireland hope that the sectarian reconciliation will be on a different basis. This usually involves an appeal to the common interests of all workers and small farmers, with the accompanying belief that their needs can best be fulfilled within a united, socialist Ireland. The major obstacles to this goal are supposedly a manipulative Unionist hierarchy that has kept the workers divided along sectarian lines, and British interferences in the internal affairs of Ireland on behalf of its own capitalist interests.[60]

At least the theoretical basis of those who believe a solution lies in a communality of interests between workers and small farmers of all religious persuasions is strong. United political action follows from class relationships to the economic system. But in Northern Ireland these have to take into account the sectarian barriers that up to now have stood so firm. The problem is that so few learning experiences reinforce work relations — in fact, quite the reverse, for outside the factories workers of differing religious persuasions will inhabit mutually suspicious worlds. When you add to this an industrial structure that accommodates itself to sectarianism, then the preconditions for united working-class action are very fragile indeed. All this occurs in an economy with a comparatively high unemployment rate and a fluctuating overall economic performance. Finally, the biases in the employment policies of the state apparatus widen the sectarian breach and so undermine further the prospects of a united working-class movement. The Protestant from the Shankill may not have a great deal of economic security, but he is likely to feel that he is better off than the Catholic from the Lower Falls.

A more fundamental problem with all the socio-economic strategies is that the political dimensions have assumed an importance in their own right. Just as the community-based structures of political socialization are dependent upon the constitutional settlement so no solution to the contemporary political problems is possible without tampering with that settlement. And yet tamperings with the constitutional status of the province is likely to produce an even bigger crisis than already exists. The political history of Ireland, and more particularly Northern Ireland, is a legacy that divides the two communities more than their mutual socio-economic interests are ever likely to unite them, at least for the foreseeable future. Neither embourgeoisement nor appeals to a common set of economic interests can resolve the problem of a divided national allegiance.

Ameliorist political solutions

From the mid-1960s, headed by the Campaign for Social Justice and the Northern Ireland Civil Rights Association, the emphasis in the province amongst those who were challenging the status quo was upon the extension of political rights. The public insistence was upon securing rights that were supposedly the birthright of every British citizen. This was a unique protest movement for Northern Ireland as the minority community appeared to be staking a claim for British citizenship. In a haphazard and tentative fashion most of the initial demands have been conceded ('Too little, too late' could be the counter-claim).[61] The root of the problem of this particular approach was the Stormont regime itself. It had been founded on the assumption of permanent Protestant superiority and for fifty years had implemented that assumption. If formal political rights within Northern Ireland were equalized this would not within itself undermine Protestant power at Stormont because of the solid backing they gave the Unionist party. So all the reforms in the world could not prevent, at the national level, the perpetuation of one-party rule. Eventually the British government reached the conclusion that Stormont had to be replaced by institutions and procedures which assured the Catholics a share of executive power and held out some prospect of their achieving their ambition of a united Ireland.[62]

If the aim was to create mass Catholic support for a new regime in which their representatives shared executive power, then this suffers from the same limitations as trying to change political behaviour through socio-economic strategies. In both cases the community basis of political socialization is left untouched. In the long run new life-styles, and changed political structures, may induce different patterns of political behaviour, but this is of little comfort given the immediate nature of the crisis. An alternative way of looking at power-sharing, and one which gives it greater credibility, is to argue that it implicitly recognizes the impossibility of changing radically patterns of mass behaviour. What is established is a regime in which the two communities each receive their respective slice of the cake, so power is divided between them rather than shared. Citizens can then focus their loyalties upon self-selected aspects of the regime. This was immensely attractive to Catholic politicians as it held out the prospect of a guaranteed place in the executive of the province, whereas previously they had been at best an ineffectual opposition. The added bonus was that they could take power without betraying the ultimate goal of a united Ireland for the Council of Ireland proposal could be interpreted as a first tentative step in that direction.[63]

The failure of the power-sharing arrangements within the framework of a new regime illustrates the point that some are more important than others in deciding the course of political change. Obviously the governments of the United Kingdom and the Republic of Ireland were relying on the ability of the established politicians to carry their respective communities with them. On the Protestant side the old Unionist front was shattered and those who opposed the Sunningdale Agreement, which established the post-Stormont regime, came to the fore and took grass-roots Protestant support with them.[64] Within the Protestant communities opposition to power-sharing was mobilized, culminating in the strike of the Ulster Worker's Council which succeeded in destroying the new regime. This is not at all surprising since anti-Sunningdale politicians gradually took control of the Unionist party, the lodges of the Orange Order were increasingly mobilized against power-sharing and the various Protestant para-military groups lined themselves alongside those who opposed the experiment. At the grass-roots, therefore, the battle for 'the hearts and minds' of the Protestant community was a foregone conclusion. To adapt a phrase coined by Rose, most Protestants became Ultras.

Again the situation is more complex on the Catholic side for the Sunningdale Agreement represented a considerable political advance for them, anl especially their politicians. And yet the Provisional IRA still continued its bombing campaign which ran contrary to the expectation that they would find it difficult to maintain hostilities if Catholic support for the proposals was high, which it was.[65] In Maoist terms the water had been changed but the fish had neither died nor disappeared. This throws some interesting light on the relationship of the IRA (both, or should it now be its various, wings) to the Catholic community.[66] The fact that you may approve, in response to a social survey questionnaire, of a nebulous entity like power-sharing does not mean you will then refuse aid to an IRA member who finds himself in a tight spot. The incidences of the local population turning their wrath upon the IRA invariably relate to specific actions that have directly and adversely affected the ghetto community, e.g. an absurd booby-trap, a careless use of firepower or an unpopular assassination.[67] After the IRA recovered from the shocks of August 1969 it re-established a community base by assuming the role of the defenders of the people, and as such it became an integral part of the community infrastructure. Traditionally the recruitment pattern of the IRA has a strong familial basis, although this has undoubtedly been widened by the recent crisis.[68] Now, however, it may be returning to type with perhaps a wider network than of old. The fish now swim in part of the water and, although what remains may be somewhat impure, it is still far from strong enough to poison them.[69]

Integrating the tribes

Intergrating the tribes suggests a direct assault upon the problem of polarized learning experiences for these would be removed by a straight-forward desegregation of community structures and processes. The central theory is straightforward: if people learn together they are much more likely to understand one another's problems, and consequently live in peace and harmony, than if they learn apart. This is one of the universal liberal dreams and it reappears in many shapes and sizes throughout the world. A central plank in the theory is the need for an integrated educational system. Today's adults may be doomed but tomorrow's hopes rest on the shoulders of the future generation, and no better way can be found to ensure this than a common umbrella of former instruction. Education is also seen as a convenient place to commence the integration of all learning experiences for it is subject to state control and thus its structure is more dependent upon political decisions.

The claim that much of the inter-communal conflict in Northern Ireland is reinforced by the divided educational system, and that integrated schools would do much to relieve the conflict, is one that is often heard. After the partition of Ireland some attempts were made to integrate the schools but since this failure the communities have gone their separate ways and the outcome is as expected: the two systems each educating children of one religious persuasion, Catholic children taught by Catholics (many of whom are priests or nuns) and Protestants taught by Protestant teachers, and a different content to the curriculum and extra-curricular activities. In the course of an eloquent attack upon these arrangements Edwards has written, 'The Irish educational system has perhaps done more than any other factor to make for a divided community in Northern Ireland. It has created two worlds within the earliest years of childhood'.[70] The solution would appear simple and direct — abolish the segregation by ensuring religiously heterogeneous schools.

Whereas Wilby wrote of the schools reflecting the two cultures that make up Ulster, Edwards credits them with a more positive role, i.e. they create two childhood worlds. The two worlds are a consequence of general barriers within the society, and although the schools may assist in their preservation, they are not alone responsible for creating them. If the schools assist the preservation of the two childhood worlds they occupy a middle position between Wilby's, where they merely reflect cultural differences, and Edwards', where they create the two worlds, at least in the early years.[71] Even if the schools are accorded a positive function in the perpetuation of conflict very real practical obstacles prevent their integration. The Roman Catholic Church wishes to keep its flock free from what it regards as potentially undesirable influences, for certainly its control will be greater if the schools remain segregated. Some members of the clergy have argued that the Church retains its own schools in many societies that are free of the political conflicts that prevail in Northern Ireland, the corollary being that the problems must have some other cause. Although I accept that the divided educational system has not created the troubles, one has to start somewhere, and perhaps the Church should be prepared to make sacrifices to help break the cycle of conflict.

Assuming a willingness to integrate the schools, the very delicate task of defining the curriculum has then to be decided upon. The sensitive areas of religious instruction, Irish language and history would pose special problems. These are not insurmountable obstacles, but what is emerging is a picture in which creating an integrated educational system in hope of mitigating conflict only leads to the creation of another conflict arena. This is reinforced by the existence of neighbourhood schools with Catholic schools in Catholic areas and Protestant schools in Protestant areas. How are they to be integrated? Are entirely new schools to be built in 'neutral' parts of town? Or will a mutual bussing programme, in which a number of pupils are daily transported to the schools from their neighbourhoods, establish the desired religious mix? In the Northern Ireland context it is easy to imagine what could take place if it were attempted — a more enflamed reaction than has accompanied the bussing programme aimed at securing a racial mix in the Boston schools.[72]

In spite of all the difficulties there are some attractions in proposing that the first step in creating integrated institutions should be taken in the field of education. A majority of parents, of both religious groups, are in favour of integrated education.[73] The evidence collected by journalists points dramatically, perhaps over-dramatically, to a society of young people filled with considerable mutual hatred.[74] The fear is that the preconditions for future conflicts are being created right now and unless something is done about this the cycle will be repeated. The problem is that once again favourable attitudes are not quite the same thing as actively working for, or even supporting, concrete changes. It is difficult to withstand the pressures that the powerful community-based institutions are capable of exerting. Although personally I am sceptical of the viability of creating an integrated educational system, the motives of those who defend segregation are highly suspect. They sound like apologists for institutional privilege who are staring disaster in the face. But their position does illustrate the point that what is required is a political solution that will accommodate itself to the cultural divide. To create an integrated culture not only takes time but also widens the conflict in at least the short run.

The cause of the integrationists is enhanced by the student protest movement that emanated from Queen's University, Belfast in the 1960s. Late in that decade, in common with students across the western world, the undergraduates of Queen's were in the vanguard of political protest in Northern Ireland. Queen's educates both Protestants and Catholics and there was joint participation in the protest movement. Empirical evidence on the precise composition of the movement is lacking, but if Protestant participation was of token proportions then it contained some remarkable tokens.[75] But it is a long leap to assume that because education across the religious divide works at university it will also work in the secondary and primary schools. The university is far less confined by the community constraints within which the schools have to work. Integration is an accomplished fact at Queen's so no political battle had to be fought in a hostile climate to achieve it. Furthermore, university students, like the institution itself, are under fewer community constraints: they are older than schoolchildren, receive grants, are likely to be living away from home, and may have even broken with their formal religious ties. These are all factors that enable them to define a more independnt or university-based position on how they will respond to the political issues.[76] It is pertinent to note that most teachers are trained in segregated institutions, with many Catholics going to the Republic and the Protestants to various teacher-training establishments in Northern Ireland.[77] It is as if the authorities were intent on keeping their young charges free of the kinds of taints that teachers educated in an institution like Queen's could possibly transmit. So even in its higher reaches the educational system is not necessarily a desegregated beacon of light and understanding.

The New University of Ulster provides an excellent case study of the politically divisive impact of educational innovation. Far from becoming 'the forcing house for British radical liberalism in Northern Ireland' as some had apparently hoped, it has turned into yet another festering sore in the game of inter-communal politics.[78] Against all rhyme and reason the campus was located in Protestant Coleraine rather than Catholic Derry. As the troubles have continued so the university has slowly turned into a white elephant, with student applications from outside the province drying up, and potential local students applying to the mainland to escape the conflict. To add salt to the wound Magee College in Derry, which many had hoped would provide the nucleus of the new university, has been replaced by an Institute of Continuing Education. If new educational projects can go so sadly astray then think how much greater is the prospect of conflict should those settled parts of the system be tampered with.[79]

Variants on accommodating socialized differences

Trying to undermine community-based socialization processes with social and economic strategies is at best a long-term prospect. It is of scant comfort to either Irish or British citizens, who are currently reaping the rewards of the internal divisions, to learn that things may be better in a generation or two. Some members of the British army have claimed that the Provisional IRA were on the verge of suffering a military defeat before they called their truce.[80] But no such military victory will resolve the causes of the conflict, and in fact it could exacerbate the difficulties by increasing Catholic bitterness. I have argued that since the abolition of Stormont successive British governments have edged towards a policy of accommodating community differences within a mutually acceptable political framework. This does not rule out social and economic reforms, but they become part of the political accommodation rather than steps in creating more political support for the regime or means of improving community understanding. In classical imperialist terms positive inducements are offered to those who are prepared to work towards this goal and numerous sanctions imposed on those who are not.[81]

The political steps include imposing on the province the full range of British political rights with a few novelties tailored to meet local conditions: an electoral system based on proportional representation, an executive that has to divide power between Protestants and Catholics, and a recognition that both the governments of the United Kingdom and the Republic of Ireland have a stake in the internal affairs of the province. In 1975 a Constitutional Convention, composed solely of delegates from Northern Ireland, met to thrash out a constitution for the six counties. Although nominally free of all British influence it is expected to keep the above constraints in mind. This is very much in the old imperial tradition of indirect rule, but with a stronger political than moral content to the Raj's prescriptions. Whereas we may have been able to stamp out the burning of widows or sacrificing children we fully realize the difficulty of preventing sectarian murders.

The apparent attempt to divide political power between representatives from the two communities has been reinforced by social and economic trends. I have already pointed out that residential segregation has increased since the start of the present crisis and it will be some time before people will feel secure about living outside their religious enclaves. The control of parts of the province is only nominally in the hands of the official authorities; it is all well and good to suggest that the writ of Her Majesty's government should run throughout the length and breadth of the United Kingdom, but the fact has to be faced that the Royal Ulster Constabulary is less than welcome in some quarters of Northern Ireland. No advanced industrialized economy can readily structure itself to accommodate a sectarian divide, but the incentive not to unduly rock the boat is real enough. Finally, as part of the division of power, state resources, including jobs, can be more carefully allocated along religious lines. This is preferable to the past injustice of a gerrymandered Protestant local council offering most of its jobs to its co-religionists.

The problem with all strategies for change in Northern Ireland, including those that try to accommodate rather than to reconcile differences, is that they cannot possibly placate everyone. More to the point is that those who disapprove of innovation are often in a position to vent their feelings. No longer is it feasible to base the regime on mass compliance, let alone mass support. What is needed is political proposals that will gain the positive approval of contradictory elements. As this is an impossibility the best that can emerge is a divided regime, one which will always face the threat of being undermined by one faction or another. This does not mean that the opposition will be permanently mobilized — after all Stormont experienced some comparatively tranquil years — but that the threat of revolution will never be far away. If one believes that all regimes rely on compliance rather than support then perhaps within every citizenry there is a revolutionary potential. What makes the Irish experience unique is the periodic realization of that potential, so that a revolutionary consciousness is ingrained into the way of life. This exists alongside an explosive social structure — the community polarization — which can call forth this revolutionary consciousness from time to time.

Three main alternatives to the present British strategy have been suggested. The first looks to the complete withdrawal of the British influence with the implication that what will follow is some form of a united Ireland.[82] This assumes that the internal conflict has essentially an external cause, i.e. British interference. This is in direct opposition to the theme of this chapter, which has stressed the importance of internal community differences. It may be possible to get rid of the British troops (although economic, social and political ties will be much more difficult to sever) but in itself this cannot wipe out the legacy of hatred that has been internally generated. The logical conclusion of my view is that if the British withdrew community differences would, at least in the short run, reassert themselves more forcibly with control and territory accruing to those with most firepower. The second alternative commences with precisely the opposite premise: the internal divisions are so great that they cannot be reconciled to the point where orderly government and humane society is possible. The course of action is obvious — separate the tribes by a further partition of the island.[83] Although an incisive policy option this underestimates the complexity of the geographic integration of the tribes, especially in Belfast. Once it was known that the boundaries were again open for renegotiation this could trigger off a full-scale civil war, with each side staking its claim. Thirdly, some (most notably Enoch Powell) have pushed for the full integration of Ulster in the United Kingdom. Presumably community differences would be swamped by the realization of fully belonging to a much larger political unit. This is an exceedingly naive assumption, for even hopeless causes do not lack their martyrs. In fact it could have precisely the opposite effect of hardening opinion in the Catholic ghettos, and so intensifying those forces that have produced Irish martyrs.

The prerequisites for political stalemate

Lijphart has written,

If a society is divided by sharp mutually reinforcing cleavages within each segment of the population living in its own separate world, the dangers of a breakdown of the system are clear — not only to the social scientist but to any reasonably intelligent observer, including the political decision-makers.[84]

Lijphart's study of the Netherlands is meant to show how in spite of such cleavages one nation state has managed to avoid this breakdown. The preconditions for conflict in Northern Ireland, however, go beyond a straightforward segregation of the two communities. In this chapter I have tried to show how different forces interrelate at varying levels to create the community divide, and how this is further intensified by conflicting rather than simply different views of the world. The constitutional basis of Northern Ireland is viewed in an entirely different light by Catholics and Protestants. In an endeavour to secure the permanence of the province's constitutional status the Protestants created a state that served their interests. This meant erecting political, economic and social structures, with accompanying processes, that enhanced Protestant power and blatantly discriminated against Catholics. These two layers (i.e. the constitutional settlement and its resulting structures) were reinforced by socialization processes that sanctioned them in Protestant eyes. So not only is the polarization in Northern Ireland based upon divided learning experiences that flourish in separate communities, it is also strengthened by the societal structures and constitutional status of the province that are so intimately linked to the socialization processes.

Attempts to end the conflict in Northern Ireland have been directed primarily at the second tier — the social, economic and political structures and their accompanying processes. The contemporary crisis has reinforced the hold of the communities upon their members, altogether undermining the few tentative steps towards inter-communal interaction. The aim is to create structures that will accommodate themselves to the community divide rather than bridge it. But they cannot function without the support of both communities, or at least without the opposition of those who are in a position to make them unworkable, and so far the correct formula has not been found. Besides the fact that no amount of manipulation at either the second or third tiers (i.e. the political, social and economic structures and the community-based socialization processes) can overcome the problem of national allegiance contained within the constitutional settlement, a workable solution is made particularly difficult by certain aspects of the socialization process.

Socialization processes in Northern Ireland not only implant conflicting views of the world, but they do it in ways that increase the intensity with which these differing views are held, so that no clear boundary exists between what is learnt and how it is learnt. The fact that neither side may want to make concessions is enhanced by the prospect of their both being in a permanent majority. Within the present boundaries of Northern Ireland this is the position of the Protestants, assuming that unemployment continues to ensure a steady rate of Catholic emigration. Even if the emigration dried up the Protestants could fall back upon their membership of the United Kingdom and no amount of Catholic 'over-breeding' is going to undermine this religious inbalance! However, in a united Ireland the

Protestants would be in a permanent minority, so in both cases the incentive to arrive at a compromise is lessened. Although the two communities are far from homogeneous, the internal bonds are stronger than cross-community links (e.g. social class ties do not cut significantly across the religious barrier). The various members of each community are united by a common associational membership — the Catholics in their Church and the Protestants in the Orange Order. Within each community flourish tightly knit groups which appear to be even more immune to external pressure. These are the paramilitary organizations that claim to stand for the true spirit of their respective communities, and in the furtherance of their interpretation of the cause they are prepared to commit the most atrocious outrages. Perhaps the majority of the citzens would be sufficiently deferential to accept resolution of the conflict by some method of elite accommodation, as appears to work in the Netherlands, but the number of groups who are prepared to actively undermine any proposed strategy that does not meet their wishes is large enough to make this a hazardous gamble. The support given to the general strike organized by the Ulster Workers' Council rather suggests that the squierarchy's hold on the Protestant workers is long dead.

The omens for the future are not favourable. Some fear that the children who have been exposed to the violence of the past few years will grow up so embittered that the conflict is bound to reoccur. It should be remembered, however, that many of today's most active participants in the paramilitary groups matured in the comparatively tranquil years of the immediate post-war decade. Without the conducive context socialized behaviour cannot blossom. This does not mean the causes of the conflict can necessarily be resolved, but that it may be possible to move once again into a situation where compliance, rather than hostility, is the norm. John Stuart Mill once suggested that Ireland rather than England provided a more typical model of the socio-political order.[85] Although my analysis has not been comparative, I have hinted at the peculiarity of the preconditions that structure political life in Northern Ireland. For the sake of the lives of ordinary citizens let us hope that divided Ulster is indeed a unique case study.

Notes

1. See p. 2.
2. See p. 15.
3. It is difficult to think of abnormal socialization patterns when the regime has never commanded the loyalty of a significantly minority of the population.
4. The Protestants outnumber the Catholics approximately 2 to 1 within the boundaries of Northern Ireland.
5. And a minority confined overwhelmingly to one part of the country. Note the parallel with Afro-Americans with their increasing concentration in the urban ghettos.

6. As is the case in the Netherlands. Besides Lijphart's book see A. Lijphart 'Review article: The Northern Ireland problem: cases, theories and solutions', *British Journal of Political Sciences,* **5** (1975), 83–106.
7. A central point in Lijphart's work on the Netherlands. See *The Politics of Accommodation,* pp. 204–205.
8. Of course social cleavages may not be the only reasons for political conflict so without more detailed analysis it is dangerous to make comparisons.
9. Richard Rose, *Governing Without Consensus.*
10. ibid., pp. 120–121.
11. C. C. O'Brien, *States of Ireland,* Panther, London, 1974, p. 285.
12. For the most detailed analysis of their bearing upon political attitudes see Rose, *Governing Without Consensus,* ch. 11.
13. op. cit., pp. 288–289.
14. The class composition of the various paramilitary groups is hard to discern. The Official IRA frequently claim that the Provisionals are made up of 'petit-bourgeois' elements but this is surely a more appropriate description of their ideology than their class composition.
15. Rose, *Governing Without Consensus,* pp. 320–326; I. Budge and C. O'Leary, *Belfast: Approach to Crisis,* Macmillan, London, 1973, p. 248.
16. op. cit., p. 208.
17. *Governing Without Consensus,* p. 328.
18. See Stacey's concluding comments to her study of Banbury, op. cit., ch. 9; P. Willmott and M. Young, *Family and Class in a London Suburb,* Routledge and Kegan Paul, London, 1963. Although, admittedly, both studies also show community resistance and adjustment to change.
19. Located in Divis Street at the end of the Lower Falls Road, the flats were at the centre of Protestant attacks in August 1969. See Sunday Times Insight Team, *Ulster,* Penguin Books, Harmondsworth, 1972, pp. 127–135.
20. See p. 169.
21. For a dramatic view of the polarization in the educational system see Peter Wilby, 'Ulster at school', *Observer Review,* 18 August 1974, p. 21.
22. M. Holland, 'The Church and the IRA', *New Statesman,* 2 June 1972, p. 70.
23. F. Wright, 'Protestant ideology and politics in Ulster', *European Journal of Sociology,* **14** (1973), 251.
24. E. McCann, 'The eye of the storm', *Sunday Times Magazine,* 9 February 1975, pp. 26–43.
25. Even though this 'independence' has been ended the full authority of the state still does not cover these areas. The major controversy surrounds the question of who is to police the Catholic ghettos. Note also the virtual 'independence' of many of the rural areas.
26. For an interesting study of the various patterns of population movement see Community Relations Commission, *Flight,* Belfast, 1971.
27. See pp. 22–25.
28. In 1953 Prime Minister Brooke said, 'Many in the audience employ Catholics, but I have not one about my place. Catholics are out to destroy Ulster with all their might and power. They want to nullify the Protestant vote, take all they can out of Ulster and then see it go to hell'. Quoted in Rose, *Governing Without Consensus,* p. 95.
29. For a discussion of sectarian pressures in the economy see D. P. Barritt and C. F. Carter, *The Northern Ireland Problem,* Oxford University Press, London, 1972, ch. 6.
30. With the pace of such sectarian assassinations gathering momentum in the summer of 1975.

31. An alternative, but a rather drastic one, is to emigrate. But even then the individual can carry the sense of grievance with him, as seen in the continuing financial support of Irish Americans for various Irish causes, including the IRA. Also certain Afro-Americans have likewise rejected their American citizenship.
32. With Afro-Americans again providing the closest parallel.
33. op. cit., p. 70. John Whale, 'Can the warring tribes learn to live together?', *Sunday Times,* 25 November 1973, p. 16.
34. Barritt and Carter, op. cit., pp. 103–104.
35. I cannot document this precise train of events, but the sectarian murders that take place on the building sites or in the factories are sufficient evidence of the dangers that are likely to be involved in such innovation.
36. *Governing With Consensus,* p. 327.
37. Perhaps this is an over-generalization, but it is highly ironic to an Englishman to see Protestant workers organize a general strike as a means of showing their loyalty, and even more distasteful to read that the same loyalty requires some to shoot at police and troops. One can only conclude that they are loyal to essentially different things. Enoch Powell incurred the wrath of many Protestants by claiming that they should show loyalty to the Crown in Parliament. See *The Times,* 7 July 1975, p. 2.
38. op. cit., p. 43.
39. For the development of this siege mentality see op. cit., ch. 6.
40. See Barritt and Carter, op. cit., pp. 120–125.
41. For an excellent analysis of the undermining of a united Irish working-class movement see O. Dudley Edwards, *The Sins of Our Fathers,* Gill and Macmillan, Dublin, 1970, ch. 4.
42. This can crop up in various forms. H. Jackson has argued that gerrymandering was partially a response to the Catholic desire for separation. See H. Jackson, *The Two Irelands — A Dual Study of Inter-Group Tensions,* Minority Rights Group Report, No. 2, 1971, p. 11.
43. Rose, *Governing Without Consensus,* pp. 237–238.
44. Edwards, op. cit., pp. 287–288.
45. ibid., pp. 287–289.
46. Of course dramatic changes have taken place in Ulster since the late 1960s but so much energy has been directed at confirming the traditional lines of cleavage rather than changing them.
47. Rose, *Governing Without Consensus,* chapter 11 (entitled 'Socialization into conflict'); M. Fraser, *Children in Conflict,* Secker and Warburg, London, 1973.
48. Rose, *Governing Without Consensus,* pp. 207–208. Rose taps the greater uncertainty of Protestants as to their national identity. Some commentators have referred to an emerging Ulster nationalism, especially following the strike led by the Ulster Worker's Council that brought down the powersharing regime. But it's hard to imagine this nationalism embracing Catholics, even if they wanted to be embraced by it.
49. Protestant sensitivity being so great as to lead to its public banning.
50. op. cit., p. 21.
51. C. A. Karch, 'Anglo-Saxon ethnocentrism: Its roots and consequences in Northern Ireland and the southern United States', in J. C. Leggett (ed.), *Taking State Power,* Harper and Row, New York, 1973, pp. 419–434.
52. Even though the Pope may have congratulated William on his victories!
53. For the linking of Catholicism and Irish nationalism see O'Brien, op. cit., p. 117.
54. Quoted in Rose, *Governing without Consensus,* p. 301.
55. See p. 113.
56. But it was assumed that the alleged working-class desertion of the Labour party would undermine the party's commitment to socialism.
57. Barritt and Carter, op. cit., pp. 105–106.

58. For Marxist perspectives see the interview with L. Baxter, B. Devlin, M. Farrell, E. McCann and C. Toman, 'Discussion on the strategy of people's democracy', *New Left Review*, 55 (**1969**), 3–19. For a short and biting critique of 'Marxist' interpretations see O'Brien, op. cit., p. 19.

59. See Lijphart, *The Politics of Accommodation*.

60. This is a central theme in C. Desmond Greaves, *The Irish Crisis*, Lawrence and Wishart, London, 1972; Bob Purdie, *Ireland UnFree*, IMG Publications, Red Pamphlet No. 2.

61. But as the crisis has deepened so has the attack on civil rights. This is best seen in the introduction of internment without trial, so ironically reform and repression go hand in hand.

62. The outcome was the now defunct Sunningdale Agreement which established a power-sharing executive. With the collapse of that executive the British government arranged for the election of a Constitutional Convention with the object of working out new political arrangements for the province. As the election has resulted in the domination of the Convention by the Protestant Ultras it is hard to see a broad-based agreement emerging.

63. But some would argue they betrayed the cause by agreeing to power-sharing while the state still retained internment without trial.

64. A period of direct rule followed the fall of Stormont and this was reintroduced after the collapse of the power-sharing executive; at the time of writing this is still the form of government in the six counties.

65. Certainly the Catholics voted in large numbers for representatives of the Social and Democratic Labour Party, one of the parties to the Sunningdale Agreement. See Richard Rose, 'Ulster poll shows a mixed reception for power-sharing', *The Times*, 19 April 1974, p. 16.

66. This aside is an allusion to the splintering that has occurred within the republican movement. Three main factions now exist: the Provisional IRA, the Official IRA, and the Irish Republican Socialist Party. The latter is an off-shoot of the Official IRA.

67 Strong community protest was expressed at the murder of Ranger Best, a local Catholic youth who had joined the British army and was assassinated while home on leave.

68. For obvious reasons it is not easy to ascertain the IRA's recruitment pattern. For a history of the movement that gives many insights into the kinds of persons recruited see T. P. Coogan, *The I.R.A.*, Pall Mall Press, London, 1970.

69. This raises the problem of discerning the level and meaning of support. O'Brien is more stringent in his comments for he argues that the Provisional IRA have totally alienated their local base and depend very much upon external aid (especially from the United States) for their sustenance. See op. cit., p. 297. This is difficult to assess, one way or the other, and I would simply like to point out that withdrawing support from the Provisionals is very different from expelling its members from the community. For a view that supports O'Brien's interpretation, but qualifies the meaning of support, consider this quote: 'The Whitelaw doctrine failed because although the Catholics were won over, The Provisionals proved that they could carry on with only one or two per cent of *active* support'. R. Fisk, 'Ulster is growing tired of political and military stalemate', *The Times*, 25 March 1974, p. 12 (my emphasis).

70. op. cit., pp. 219–220.

71. For a conclusion similar to mine see J. K. Russell, *Civic Education of Secondary Schoolboys in Northern Ireland*, Civil Rights Commission, Belfast, Research Paper No. 2, 1972.

72. See p. 48.

73. See Rose, *Governing Without Consensus*, p. 336.

74. J. Heilpern, 'Children of Ulster', *Observer Review,* 12 December 1971, p. 19; D. Herbstein, 'Some talk of Alexandra, some of Pearse', *The Sunday Times,* 2 December 1973, p. 5; S. Jenvey, 'Sons and haters: Ulster youth in conflict', *New Society,* **2** (July 1972), 125–127.

75. Including, so I have been informed, the son of the Rev. Ian Paisley's colleague, Major Bunting.

76. Although this has not prevented some with further education (for example, the Price sisters) from joining the IRA.

77. Wilby, op. cit., shows the pressures that teachers caught in the 'wrong' school can face.

78. For an analysis of some of the difficulties facing the New Ulster University see Kevin Cahill, 'John Bull's other university', *Education Guardian,* 23 July 1974, p.20.

79. Certain steps can be taken in fields where the barriers have not yet crystallized, e.g. preschool education offers some interesting prospects. See R. Fisk, 'Shared schools could break Ulster's religious barrier', *The Times,* 10 May 1974, p. 22.

80. A parallel with the American generals who were always claiming that the Vietcong were on the verge of defeat.

81. The problem is that some of the sanctions (especially internment without trial) drastically interfere with attempts to build a political compromise.

82. It would be impossible, except in the very long run, to eradicate all forms of British influence, as the Republic only too clearly shows. Note that there is an alternative to British withdrawal and a united Ireland and that is British withdrawal and an independent Ulster.

83. H. V. Hodson, 'A second partition may be the answer for Ulster', *The Times,* 19 June 1974, p. 16. For a more interesting variant of this theme see C. Bell, 'Ireland: The dynamics of insurgency', *New Society,* 18 (November 1971), 1026–1028.

84. *The Politics of Accommodation,* p. 198.

85. This is a slightly strained interpretation of Mill's point. He was more interested in showing the great gulf between Britain and Ireland in socio-cultural terms. See J. S. Mill, *England and Ireland,* Longmans, Green, Reader, and Dyer. London. 1881, pp. 9–17.

Chapter 11

The Anglo-American Political Culture: Legitimizing Political Authority

Political inequality and the democratic polity

One of the central assumptions in western political science is that the United States and the United Kingdom are two stable democracies. Democracies because they are governed by certain procedures and stable because these arrangements are accorded legitimacy by most citizens, and as such both polities have been granted the status of models for others to copy and emulate. So much has this democratic character been taken for granted that some social scientists have assumed that American realities reflect true democracy at work and that where this clashes with the alleged tenets of democratic theory it is this theory rather than the reality that is in error.[1] Two particular consequences of this have been the justification of high levels of political apathy and an accommodation of the political exclusion of Afro-Americans. Apathy was given the positive function of aiding stability and change, while black exclusion was seen as a temporary phase that would give way to the full inclusion of Afro-Americans in American political life.[2]

This view of the Anglo-American democracies created a climate which influenced the social science research of the period. Almond's and Verba's five-nation search for the civic culture is a good illustration of this. Before a single American, British, Italian, Mexican or German citizen had been interviewed it was part of the conventional wisdom of the discipline that the most advanced forms of democracy were to be found in the United States and the United Kingdom. It came as no surprise to read that these two countries most closely approximated Almond's and Verba's understanding of the civic culture. It is not that their findings failed to substantiate such a conclusion but it is hard to see how any other conclusion could have been reached in view of the prevailing ethos.

Bell's 'end of ideology' thesis presumed that the major ideological cleavages in the United States, and other western industrialized democracies, were at an end.[3] Future problems would be technical in nature in the sense that established institutions could resolve them simply by committing sufficient resources. Few contemplated failure and even fewer considered the possibility that the very nature of the problem-solving mechanisms — their structures, processes and values premises — were part of the problem rather than part of the solution. Ideology, more especially Marxism, was at an end partly because of internal economic and social changes that undermined potential sources of opposition to the status quo.[4] This is why certain American social scientists waxed lyrical about the embourgeoisement of European politics which was manifested in apparently increasing working-class allegiance to conservative political parties and a growing moderation within the social democratic parties. As explicit proof one could quote the successive electoral victories of the British Conservative party, implying that this meant the new affluent worker was tired of socialist dogma and longed only for the promised land of consumer superabundance for which the Tories had whetted his appetite.[5] In the United States discontented blacks posed a threat to this idyllic existence but it was presumed that their demands could be incorporated in the same way as those of the labour unions had been met. In any case it was believed that Afro-Americans wanted the same kind of things out of life as white citizens and accordingly did not pose a revolutionary threat. The overall consequence was an increase in the legitimacy of the political order. All that remained to upset the apple-cart was a dying band of outcasts (for example, the 'unattached' intellectuals) who were desperately clinging onto an outdated idealism.[6]

As the 1960s unfolded this view of the Anglo-American democracies became more and more untenable. Both nation states experienced sociopolitical movements whose demands could not readily be met. As the credibility of political institutions came into question so did the legitimacy of established political authority. The first question that needs to be asked is what the nature of this crisis was. Political socialization theory had implied that authority was legitimate because it was accepted as such by most citizens, i.e. they had been socialized into accepting the political order.[7] This immediately raises the problems of in what sense political authority is accepted and precisely what the level of acceptance has to be before it bestows legitimacy. The debate is not without its semantic aspects but none the less is still important. I have seen political authority as gaining its legitimacy through its acceptance (which is obviously learnt behaviour) whereas the socialization theorists have been more prepared to see legitimacy as stemming from socialized support. Others have argued that what is assumed to be support is in fact little more than compliance, and in some circumstances this may be translated into opposition to political authority. Compliance, therefore, is either a reservoir of potential sustenance or a source of latent hostility. One of the strongest themes in the voting studies was that the politically apathetic citizens — those who did not vote — were essentially satisfied with the way the political system worked. Be this as it may, it is still true that many citizens moved from a position of compliance (if not acceptance or support) to one of opposition as the 1960s unfolded. Furthermore, they were of sufficient numbers and visibility to make them politically important.

If the first ingredient of the crisis was the breakdown of compliance, the second thread concerns the quality of the protest. All polities, regardless of what Daniel Bell may have once believed, have value systems that are meant to regulate political behaviour. One reason why Britain and the United States were considered to be proto-typical democracies was that they came closest to fulfilling a set of core values that many theorists had designated as democratic hallmarks. But besides several inconsistencies in the pattern of democratic values, they also have a universalistic quality (for example, the equality of all men before the law, and the granting of the same civil and political rights to all citizens) that makes it difficult to match theory and reality. This has always been so, but the exploitation of the inconsistencies, as well as the perception of the gap between theory and reality, are sharper in an age when literacy is widespread, where socio-political organizations exist to mobilize most sectors of the society, and where the communications network is both national in scope and instantaneous in speed.

A strong theme in all the protest movements is that action was necessary because values had not been fulfilled, and until this was remedied the charge of hypocrisy could be levelled at the official authority figures. In their early days the civil rights movements in both Northern Ireland and the United States were struggling for the extension of established constitutional rights. As the movements progressed their essentially constitutional character may have changed but the initial protest was reformist in scope. This demand for the extension of constitutional rights was a subtle attack because it was one that political elites could hardly ignore. So much of the authority of elites was dependent upon its legitimate foundations, i.e. those exercising power had reached that position by following prescribed procedures that commanded widespread support. The critique could be extended to imply that values were not fully implemented because this would threaten the established order and those who benefited most from it. To fail to act could suggest that either the values had no meaning or the charge of elite hypocrisy was true.

One of the central themes of this book has been to show how socialization processes try to fulfil two somewhat contradictory functions: to build political consensus and to ensure role differentiation within the consensus. It is especially hard in a democracy, with its universalistic value system, to justify an inegalitarian division of political labour, and yet this is an intrinsic feature of both the British and American models of representative democracy. What appears to have been happening in the past decade is an increasing dissatisfaction with the structure and consequence of role differentiation. Or, put in a different way, both the means by which inequality is created and the associated pattern of rewards have come under attack. In a curious way this could reaffirm the consensus within which the differentiation occurs, for if inequality is attacked on the grounds that it offends certain constitutional principles then by implication those principles have a special status. This is a sensitive issue in Northern Ireland where opposition to the state has traditionally been of an extra-constitutional nature. Of course the demand for constitutional rights could be merely a disguise for more fundamental changes, e.g. the destruction of the state. Certainly both the Irish and black civil rights movements have experienced more militant off-shoots, but this is not the same thing as saying that these are an inevitable outcome of the original demands.

An important facet of the various protest movements is the entwining of social, economic and political considerations to the point where it is difficult to analytically distinguish one factor from another. This automatically increases the scope of the protest, making it more difficult to formulate a response that will effectively contain it. In his classic study of citizenship Marshall formulated a sequence in which civil/legal rights are expanded to incorporate political rights, which in turn are complemented by social and economic rights.[8] This pattern is based on British historical experience and even with this particular focus it is doubtful whether it accurately reflects the circumstances of women, who after all form approximately half the population. Although analytically distinct the various rights are in reality intimately related, which results in the same rights having more effective consequences for some individuals than for others. The Anglo-American democracies have established a formal egalitarianism in the fields of civil/legal and political rights but few would doubt that this is effectively undermined by social and economic inequality. It is the awareness of this reciprocity that makes the protest movements of the 1960s so complex.

The threads were most intricately interwoven in the protest movements of Afro-Americans. In the 1950s the drive for civil and political rights proceeded side by side in the southern states. In the 1960s attention switched to the urban ghettos of the North and with it the campaign turned to social and economic rights. But the latter did not exclude a political dimension, for some argued that until the black citizens politically controlled their own communities economic and social equality could not be accomplished. The most idealistic sought to create new structures within which all the varying formal citizenship rights could be more effectively exercised. In different ways the same themes have emerged in both the women's liberation movement and the civil rights movement in Northern Ireland. Obviously student protest is a somewhat different category because it cannot be related to the group's own social and economic inequality.

But students have penetrated the other movements, in some respects acting as a vanguard by stimulating the organizing grass-roots protest. In this sense students have formed an important bridge between the various movements, and frequently have added a political ingredient to the content of the protest.

A final aspect of the character of the various crises was the realization that explanations had to embrace a number of different levels of analysis to have any credibility. This has strong academic implications because explanations could not be contained within particular subdisciplines. I have tried to show how socialization processes relate to structural contexts and how in turn these are contained within a wider framework that has socio-economic and political dimensions. Besides widening the understanding of socialization this view also adds to the complexity of policy responses, for to be effective they have to take into account the interdependence of the differing explanatory levels. Again this is best illustrated by the close parallels between the Afro-American and Irish Catholic case studies. In both examples social, economic and political inequality have been an integral part of a life-style indelibly marking many blacks and Catholics as second-class citizens. The disabilities stem from historically sanctified structures that have either been connived at or actively reinforced by the state. In response to the exclusion from the wider society the black and Catholic minorities have created communities in which they can survive; as long as they remain within the community boundaries, physically and psychologically, they are safe, but once they attempt either to move out or challenge the inegalitarian consequences of their separation they face danger.

The community acts as a potential barrier between the individual citizens contained within it and the wider society, for it creates the framework within which particular patterns of socialization processes are evolved. Where the community structure is especially powerful, and I have suggested that Northern Ireland provides excellent examples, then this enables community residents to resist dominant values. In fact the community values are the dominant values, and in Northern Ireland it is more realistic to think in terms of self-contained community value structures that conflict, rather than compete with one another. In the case of Afro-Americans their world is by no means as isolated; the problems that arise out of the clash between universal and subcultural values systems is correspondingly more acute. In either case the community is a source of nourishment for its members, especially those who see themselves as in opposition to the prevailing regime. This poses a problem for established political elites, since official community spokesmen may have no effective power at the local level, and yet negotiating with grass-roots leaders may bestow a respectability upon them that the authorities would prefer to withhhold.

The women's movement has a more specific focus than the protests of either Afro-Americans or Irish Catholics. This is because central to the woman's place in society are her role within the family and the crucial socializing functions she performs within that structure. The various forms of female inequality, most noticeably in the economic field, flow out of her home-centred role, so, although within her place she may be an honoured citizen, it none the less gives her less command over power, prestige and money. To control the other forms of protest it may be conceivable to introduce change without tampering with socialization processes. In fact in relation to divided Ulster I have argued (somewhat pessimistically) that conflict can only be contained by a political strategy that can accommodate the socialized differences in behaviour. But sex equality cannot be achieved without changing the socialization process. This is of a very different order from merely satisfying the demands for more education, jobs, better social services or even political rights that are so closely associated with the drive for black, and to some extent Catholic equality. For this reason the women's movement can be said to have a greater revolutionary potential and it is certainly more difficult to predict its long-term implications. The legitimations on which female inequality are based still have considerable intellectual support and emotional backing in the latter half of the twentieth century. The female role (as wife and mother) is said to rest upon both biological and psychological sex differences and consequently is a 'natural' role. Some, including reputable academics, still believe in the intellectual inferiority of blacks and Irishmen, and many would accept that students should show deference because they are in a state of tutelage, but these are increasingly fragile reasons for perpetuating inequality. So one can expect the struggle for sex equality to be particularly hard, because its basis is so central to the way contemporary society, almost regardless of its political or socio-economic structures, is organized, and because the legitimations of the female role are so pervasive.

The student movement evoked some of the most simplistic explanations. Because it was not seen as a revolt of the underprivileged, it was more difficult to relate it to structural features of the society and consequently the explanations concentrated upon both personal and cultural peculiarities. These ranged all the way from attacks upon contemporary child-raising methods to the grandiose youth culture thesis. Students themselves, however, frequently saw their protest as an attack upon inequality, for they felt they lacked rights that other members of the society took for granted. Berkeley acted as the fuse for the explosion and it should be remembered that this initial confrontation was fought under the banner of the Free Speech Movement. Pitching the protest at the level of civil rights presented the student movement with comparatively soft targets, for few were willing to deny students those rights simply because they were taking longer to complete their formal education than most. Furthermore, campus-centred changes could be more readily implemented than, for example, the demand for black political equality. The scale and scope of the protest is not only of a different magnitude but also of a different character. What is interesting about student protest is its embracing of wider societal issues. This again can be partly explained in personal terms, e.g. students felt the pressures of the draft regulations, but its range, intensity and character were such as to suggest a need to go beyond this. This could only be done by placing the personal and the cultural reasons within the framework of changing structural constraints. The most obvious example was to link the changing character of the university to developments within the advanced industrial state. So, as with the other case studies, certain explanations interrelated different levels of analysis.

What has been remarkable about the past decade is the reintroduction of ideology (although it was never quite buried, as implied by Bell) into the debate on the nature of the Anglo-American political culture. Not one of the movements discussed in this book was entirely free of the claim that arrival in the promised land depended upon the destruction of the liberal democratic polity and its associated mixed economy. Although one aspect of the protest was its demand for the extension of constitutional rights, each movement contained, and still contains, its more revolutionary prophets. This does not mean an all-embracing view of the origins of protest or their eventual cures, but it does mean that the demands are not simply technical in their nature; this being the case they cannot be readily accommodated by prevailing institutions and processes. An ironical aside is that the challenge has not emanated from the source that Marxists considered to have the greatest revolutionary potential — the proletariat. Indeed it could be plausibly argued that the latter has proved to be one of the foremost counter-revolutionary forces of the past decade, especially in the United States. However, circumstances are not static, and that pragmatic instrumentality noted by Goldthorpe and Lockwood may yet prove more all-encompassing in its demands, and more difficult to placate, than all the revolutionary idealism of the essentially socio-political movements that emerged in the 1960s.[9]

The crisis in political science: Re-evaluating political socialization

In the last ten years western social science has been in a turmoil and much of this is a direct result of the internal crises that have rent the fabric of so many western societies. The political socialization literature was especially vulnerable to the criticism stimulated by these pressures, for it had painted a picture in which the various aspects of the political system were accorded overwhelming legitimacy in the eyes of children, and had argued that the learning process was busily turning out citizens with the correct balance of subject and citizenship orientations. This picture was taking shape just about the time students were stirring on the campuses and young blacks were developing more militant tactics to shake the status quo. Regardless of its empirical content this research would have been in the forefront of the re-evaluation of social science, because in the models of the political system socialization had been classified as a major input variable, the means by which support is created and sustained. In a world in which support seemed to be evaporating, this was an assumption that demanded further consideration.

The initial reactions smacked of panic. In a relatively short space of time a subdiscipline that had concentrated most of its attention upon the attitudes of schoolchildren aged 3 to 13 widened its focus to encompass older age groups, socializing agents other than the family and behaviour in addition to attitudes. This book is part of the expansion, but in the process I have returned to the approach adopted in the 1930s by Charles Merriam in his political education studies. The concern is not so much with how individuals learn their political behaviour but more with how the state structures the learning process to ensure that some things, rather than others, are learnt and acted upon. Incidentally, this interpretation of the functional models that categorize political socialization as a system input is better than the more usual descriptions of the individual learning process. It avoids the danger of assuming that the character of the political system can be inferred from these individual patterns of learning. Of course it contains a parallel danger: a co-ordinated structure of state-sponsored and controlled socialization processes can successfully determine the patterns of individual behaviour. This is the mistake that Miliband has made in his attempt to explore the ideological premises that underlie political socialization processes in contemporary Britain.[10]

My view of political socialization, a perspective that I prefer to call political education, retains the standard claim that all states try to perpetuate themselves and in the process erect structures with this purpose in mind. But it must be perfectly clear from the evidence presented in this book that I consider this to be a very fragile operation. After all, the preoccupation of most of the case studies has been with how opposition to established regimes arose, what course it took and what were its consequences. In the process of examining these aspects of political socialization within the Anglo-American democracies I have steered well clear of the functionalist pitfalls of system maintenance and systems persistence, as well as the equally naive Marxist view of an all-powerful capitalist ruling class.

The extent to which political socialization will be successful in creating legitimacy for a regime and its authorities depends upon the structural context within which learning experiences occur, and what room, and willingness, political elites have to manoeuvre in a crisis. Even where there may be high citizenship support for all the important facets of a political system this may be merely a reflection of a more fundamental basis of consensus — although in such cases political education will probably be one of the means by which such a consensus has been established. In certain cases it is not unrealistic to credit political education with a reverse responsibility — the perpetuation of conflict as opposed to the building of harmony. In both Northern Ireland and the United States community-based socialization processes place Catholics and Protestants, blacks and whites, in at least partial opposition to one another. In these situations the learning experiences are the product of wider tensions. The way members of the two communities acquire their behaviour may not differ very much but what is learnt conflicts, so placing citizens of the same nation state on opposite sides of the fence.

The above example of socialization into conflict undoubtedly describes an extreme situation, but it is meant to act as a palliative against the traditional assumption that learning processes inevitably create political stability by assisting all individuals in the acquisition of good citizenship traits. More commonly it is essential to think of socialization into role differentiation rather than socialization into either conflict or consensus. If individuals accept this differentiation, in which some are accorded more scarce resources than others, then it becomes possible to talk of stability and perhaps even legitimacy. Democratic theory may have created an ideal democratic citizen, but in the Anglo-American polities it is more realistic to think in terms of various forms of democratic citizenship rather than one ideal-type model. Conflict ensues when the consensus (real, contrived or forced) surrounding role differentiation breaks down and citizens push for new roles or for changed role characteristics.

Empirical democratic theory attacked the classical model of democratic man on the grounds that its major features failed to match empirical reality.[11] But in the field of political socialization they created a model that was just as unrealistic — the balanced citizen, the man who from childhood learns to combine a judicious mixture of participatory and deferential norms. This is a model of the individual citizen, whereas the empirical work on voting behaviour has stressed the need to look at the characteristics of the total citizenry before describing the nature of the polity. If the socialization research is reinterpreted to suggest the need for a range of citizenship characteristics (i.e. the balancing of participatory and deferential norms within the citizenry rather than the individual) then the evidence on political participation suggests that such a balance is heavily tilted in favour of some classes and groups and against others. However, this reinterpretation is close to my own notion of differential socialization patterns. But such inequality does not automatically lead to harmony but rather suggests a precarious balancing of roles, waiting to be disturbed by the smallest of shifts in social forces.

I have already argued that one of the major problems of legitimizing inequality in a democratic polity is the universalistic quality of democratic values. An equally important difficulty is that the socialization processes contain irreconcilable contradictions. This is neatly illustrated by the internal inconsistencies of formal education, which has to perform at least the following tasks: to dispense useful skills, to help in social training, to act as an instrument of political control and to stimulate personal enlightenment. Of course elites can attempt to round off some of the more blatant conflicts. In the nineteenth century the state's intrusion into formal education in Britain was undertaken to secure various economic, political and social goals, but at the same time it was fully recognized that this could disturb class relations by undermining working-class deference, and perhaps even stimulating revolutionary fervour.[12] So the values, content and structure of formal education were directed along paths that would minimize these dangers. In practice this meant educating children for their station in life and supplementing their education with considerable doses of Christian doctrine. In much the same way the Soviet regime of the 1920s, realizing that mass literacy was a prerequisite of a modern industrial nation, committed it self to the expansion of formal education, but in the process did its best to ensure that Marxist-Leninist doctrine was part and parcel of the daily lessons. In both cases this is very much like trying to keep a lid on a pot that is continually threatening to boil over.

It is easier to describe the structural conditions that lead to socialization into conflict as opposed to the socialization of stability. The pluralist model of Anglo-American society points to a mitigation of potential conflict thanks to the presence of cross-cutting, as opposed to aggregated, social, economic and political cleavages.[13] Following this line of reasoning, socialization processes create political stability within societies that have cross-cutting cleavages, and conversely one can expect socalization into conflict where aggregated differences are found. In the latter situation the differences are reinforced by the socialization processes. According to this view the conflict that emerges in Anglo-American society would be a consequence of basic structural fractures, i.e. some groups are totally isolated. In an alternative model Lipjhart has argued that in certain circumstances group fractures can be accommodated politically but this is facilitated by intra-group cleavages.[14] In the Lipjhart model inter-group differences are moderated somewhat by the possibility of specific alliances between similar interests within opposing groups. Stability is jeopardized by the presence of totally self-contained groups, for it is this that encourages conflicting perspectives by making it easier to sustain socialization processes that perpetuate the traditional myths. A pluralist model may not suggest that stability is dependent upon a universal socialization process but it does imply that the bounds of tolerance cannot be stretched indefinitely. Again it is easier to point to what is not permitted rather than what is permissible.

Much of the past research into political socialization has been based on the premise of a normal learning process which taught future citizens the desirable combination of subject and citizenship roles. The pluralist model does not have the same implications, but I think it under-estimates the extent to which Anglo-American society encourages differentiation as well as consensus. I have already referred to the pattern of role differentiation and the inevitable tension between this and democratic valus (i.e. the consensus within which role differentiation is structured). The structural isolation of some groups, for example Afro-Americans and Irish Catholics, has been part of the means by which stability was ensured in the past, and it received the explicit sanction of elites who controlled the governmental machinery. Now that this is no longer a viable means of maintaining stability new strategies have to be devised. The modern pluralist society also creates its own inner tensions. At a time when most of their peers are engaged in full-time work students are still completing their formal education. For them the dependence of adolescence extends into the adult years, for in spite of a legal equality students are still in a state of economic tutelage. During this time they are members of an institution which, with varying degrees of rigidity, controls admissions, and, not surprisingly, this results in the selection of individuals with characteristics not shared by the population at large. While in higher education they are freed from many of the pressures that other citizens face, and at the same time exposed to special internal learning experiences. Of course students are not an isolated, homogeneous social group, but they do show how the modern industrial state can sponsor social fragmentation. Certainly in recent years many citizens have looked upon students as a self-contained and pampered elite. So, although some social structures are more conducive to creating conflict than others, even a pluralist society has its own tendency to encourage fragmentation.

So far I have argued that both the structures within which socialization processes are worked out and the processes themselves contain a number of inconsistencies that will heighten social tension. This perpetual fragility ensures the importance of individual actors in the political process, for some are more strategically placed than others to affect the stability — one way or the other — of the established order. The socialization research complements the building of mass support by elite recruitment. The functionalists saw leadership as a central ingredient in all political systems, so it was natural to look for clear patterns of elite recruitment. In this broad sense a division within the socialization process was built into the models, for elites would have a different relationship to the political system than other citizens. Throughout this book we have seen elites responding to political crises in ways which have implications for both system stability and political socialization. And yet both the recruitment and socialization of elites is a problem in its own right. The institutional apparatus within which a great deal of politics is conducted in Britain and the United States is characterized by elaborate internal socialization processes. Following the rules is not within itself the path to institutional power, but without accommodating himself to them it is difficult for the individual politician to pursue his career very far — mavericks may arise from time to time but they abuse their institutional base at their peril.

What is evident about political institutions is their ability to create a barrier between their members and the citizens they are supposed to represent. This is another source of tension within representative polities, in this case brought about by the very specialized socialization experiences of the political elite. In a democratic polity the tension is heightened by the fact that the representatives are accountable for their actions to their constituents. So they are acting as representative of the people while undergoing a socialization experience that separates, even isolates them from the people. It is ironic that as political institutions in the Anglo-American democracies have become more subject to democratic controls, and in a demographic sense more representative of the total population, so the gulf between elites and the people has probably widened This is partly a consequence of the professionalization of politics (the emergence of politics as a career) as well as the increased institutionalization (to use Polsby's phrase) of the centres of power.

What the various crises analysed in this book have shown is that the traditional understanding of key political actors needs to be widened. The power-sharing arrangements that were part of the Sunningdale Agreement were essentially a procedural tactic to guarantee a mixed political executive in Northern Ireland. It was assumed that just as the original working-class MPs accommodated their class enemies within the House of Commons, so Catholic and Protestant politicians would be able to amicably divide power in a radically revised Stormont.[15] But the Sunningdale Agreement was destroyed because powerful individuals within the province were able to mobilize grass-roots opinion against it. The conflict within the American cities threw up community figures who were not part of the traditional black establishment, and given the strength of their base it was dangerous to ignore them. As long as the community-based spokesmen (whether they are the IRA or Black Panthers) remain outside the governing institutions the task of arriving at an accommodation with them will prove difficult. They may want some form of official recognition but they must be careful not to alienate their local bases. The Constitutional Convention devised by the British government to work out arrangements for Northern Ireland following the demise of the Sunningdale Agreement, and the community action programmes sponsored by the Office of Economic Opportunity, can be viewed as attempts to co-opt local leadership and place it in an institutional framework which exposes it to a wider range of pressures. In both cases, however, this is clear recognition of the importance of local, officially illegitimate, power centres.

Political socialization is both a process through which individuals acquire their political behaviour and a framework within which some things are learnt rather than others. Miliband is correct to emphasize that whether one looks at socialization from the point of view of the individual or the state, ideological premises still have to be taken into consideration. But to say this is not to say everything and one still needs to know how socialization processes are structured and how their messages are internalized by individuals. The reason why political scientists have not explored the ideological biases within Anglo-American political learning patterns is that so much of it appears to have non-political features — it is acquired in the early years, learnt from parents within the framework of the family, and involves a transference of images from parental to political authority figures. There is clearly a whole world of difference between political socialization processes within Britain and America and, for example, countries with recent revolutionary experiences. We can rely on the family to transmit the correct messages and we can feel more sure of the eventual outcome in spite of the indirect and implicit nature of the political learning process. Certainly some of our past security is vanishing and the demand for more explicit political education is heard. In this respect Britain appears to be approaching the United States where there has been a greater willingness to use the educational system to promote the cause of American democracy, but in comparative terms neither nation state has a broadbased strategy of political indoctrination.[16] I have outlined some of the basic problems associated with such a policy, but perhaps there is another reason why it is not needed, and that is because most citizens tacitly support the quality of political life. After all, compliance may be translated into support as well as opposition.[17]

Explaining and explaining away conflict: Right, left and centre responses

The various conflicts analysed in this book stimulated a wide range of responses from all sectors of society. I have categorized them in three ways: the devaluation of the seriousness or even the legitimacy of the challenge coupled with a desire to maintain the status quo, an acceptance of the justice of many of the demands accompanied by the belief that these could be handled within the prevailing societal order, and the claim that they flowed out of certain inconsistencies within liberal-democratic, capitalist societies and until that kind of society was destroyed the seeds of the conflict would remain. All three interpretations have important implications for the theory of socialized support.

One consistent reaction to the protests was that they commanded only minority support, and somewhat esoteric support at that. This theme is most prevalent in the literature on students but in different guises it emerges in all the debates. This is a central issue because all parties tacitly accept that support for protest activities is a measure of the level of dissatisfaction. If turn-out for a demonstration is high this not only gives it numbers but also gives its claims some substance, and correspondingly if turn-out is low, the movement can be dismissed with derision. Analytically this is a veritable minefield, for it is far from easy to define support and not much easier to measure it. In a specific event, such as a demonstration, the numbers turning out can be counted, but for every person who actually shows up there may be ten sympathisers. Daniel O'Connell, one of the leading lights in the Provisional IRA, has introduced the concept of anticipatory support.[18] He accepts that the 1916 Dublin rising did not command any significant support from the Irish people, but because of what the revolutionary movement subsequently did (and, perhaps even more to the point, how the British authorities reacted!) those who led the 1916 revolt are now considered to be martyrs. Presumably the Provisional IRA can justify its present strategy because in the long run it will be vindicated by the course of events and likewise will then enjoy the adulation of the Irish people.

The alleged esoteric character of support is usually a more explicit devaluatory tactic than questioning the extent of the support itself. One can attack either the leadership or even the whole movement on the grounds that it fails to represent the group it claims to be leading. This can lead to very abusive labelling running from 'thugs' and 'criminals' through 'hippies' and 'layabouts' to 'naive spoilt fools'. Part of this tactic is to use labels that imply the protest has an essentially non-political character. This takes several forms: the protest is a way for its participants to solve their personality problems, it is a disguised form of social activity, or they are committing criminal offences for personal gain. On the other side of the fence the protesters and their admirers have invariably stressed the political nature of their movements no matter how outrageous their behaviour may be. Withholding or granting political status can become part of the conflict, so to designate an act of violence as 'political' gives both the act and its perpetrator a certain status. This poses real problems for the mass media, especially when, like the BBC, it is an indirect part of the machinery of government. The difference between the use of 'terrorist' as opposed to 'urban guerrilla' is more than symbolic. It should not be assumed that all the negative labelling has been an establishment response to quash genuine reform movements. I have shown how some social scientists tried to explain away the phenomenon of working-class Toryism by illustrating, to a large extent correctly, how working-class Tories held a special position within the class. This can be as much a devaluation of the working-class Tory as the claim that student radicals originate from mother-dominated upper-middle-class families can be a devaluation of student radicalism.

The argument that protest emanated from a small, unrepresentative minority was linked to the view that all was right with the world and that to restore order a show of strength was required. This could take different forms: parents should take a firmer line with their children, universities should discipline students (and faculty) who broke the rules, the police should keep demonstrators in line, and the army should be given a freer hand in rooting out those who forcibly attacked the state. In each case the traditional authority structure was urged to flex its muscles to ensure that the troubles passed away. I have argued that this was a strategy that could heighten rather than lessen conflict, but at the same time it must be recognized that alternative approaches might require changes that the advocates of a hard line are not prepared to contemplate.

Some parallels can be drawn between an explanation that sees protest as arising out of a dangerous minority movement that needs to be swatted and one which bases it upon contradictions within capitalism that cannot be resolved short of overthrowing that system. Both explanations see the movements as having revolutionary, although not necessarily political implications. Individuals within both camps were inclined to adopt a contemptuous attitude towards reformism. Many of those who were fighting change saw reformism as mere weakness in the face of pressure, which far from satisfying the 'extremists' would simply lead to further, more exaggerated demands. On the other hand the radicals viewed reforms as mere sops that were no answer to the genuine revolutionary demands rising from the grass-roots, or at best short-run palliatives that could not forever hold back the rising flood of protest.

I have discussed some of the similarities and differences between these movements and have analyzed their internal divisions. Although each movement represents a rejection of past inequalities, there is considerable internal conflict as to what the new order should look like. In a formal sense — redefining boundaries, imposing new regime norms and replacing political authorities — it is obvious that the strongest revolutionary movement flourishes in Northern Ireland, and correspondingly this has been met with the greatest amount of force by the state. In fact as the character of protests change in Northern Ireland so did the response of the state. Or was the process reversed? Although the black protests — especially the urban riots — aroused fears that societal collapse was imminent, in retrospect it can be seen that even if they were revolutionary in intent the likelihood that they would fundamentally change the character of the American polity was severely limited. They may have helped to carve out for Afro-Americans a significantly different niche within American society, including perhaps some form of separatism within many of the major cities, but they lacked the means with which to carry out a wider revolution. Afro-Americans are a comparatively small percentage of the total population, they are rent by internal cleavages, only a minority have adopted a revolutionary posture, and they lack firm allies amongst many other sectors of the community — especially the white working class.

Both the black conflict in the United States and the religious polarization in divided Ulster were present before the full development of capitalist economies within those countries. Although in both countries economic development has superimposed itself upon the traditional divisions one could also argue that capitalism has been forced to accommodate those barriers. So the contradictions are something other than inconsistencies within a capitalist economy. In fact in both the United States and Northern Ireland some of the most intense conflict occurs among members of the same class, e.g., working-class Irish Americans took the streets to protest the integration of the Boston schools by bussing, and in Ulster the paramilitary groups, based mainly on the working class, either shoot their own members or at one another.[19] I have no wish to deny the revolutionary potential within certain of these movements, but I want to argue against any simple-minded theory which will devalue much of their meaning and certainly much of their complexity.

The mainstream social science and political response looked upon the various protests as demands for changes in the system rather than as attempts to destroy the system. If these were movements for change then they could be explained and handled without calling into question basic values, structures and processes. Stresses were emerging within society not simply because of past failures but also because of present successes. In the field of higher education, for example, many of the problems arose out of the rapid expansion of facilities and numbers which changed the character and purpose of the university. Likewise it was possible to castigate the United States for its appalling record on race relations, but the race riots of the 1960s were not only a reflection of this past but also a manifestation of rising expectations that had been stimulated by the improving socio-economic opportunities of Afro-Americans, as well as the successful drive for legal and political rights. In its early days even the protest movement in Northern Ireland could be seen in this light, for internal and external pressures were aimed at extending rights enjoyed by other British citizens to the Catholic minority.

A common thread in the explanations that viewed the protests in this way was to point to the pressures placed on the traditional patterns of socialization by wider social, economic and political movements. In this decade the major agent of socialization — the nuclear family — declined considerably in influence. New attitudes towards the family emerged as reflected in divorce rates, cohabitation without marriage, illegitimate births and abortions. The hold of the family over its members, especially its children, was loosened. Children spent longer periods of time outside the family and they had greater economic independence with which to pursue their own, rather than parental wishes. Even within the family the parents had to compete with the television for attention. The fact that so much protest came out of the institutions of higher education may reflect the freedom that students enjoy in comparison with their fellow citizens. This decline in the importance of the family occurred alongside an increase in the power of certain community structures which can act as a more effective barrier to elite manipulation than the isolated nuclear family. This was particularly significant in the case of urban blacks in the United States and working-class citizens of both religious persuasions in Northern Ireland.

This could be seen as an especially unsettling period that would calm down once the socialization processes had stabilized within their new context. In the meantime the state had to hold the arena whilst the various storms blew themselves out and a new period of stability re-emerged. The transition could be aided by following a consistent policy of accommodation that would meet the major grievances and at the same time tie the protesting group to established institutions and procedures. In economic terms this meant extending more widely the blessings of the mixed economy. In concrete terms this has taken a number of directions: providing more jobs, retraining people, ensuring minimum incomes, legalizing equal pay and establishing new welfare programmes. The educational system was to impart the skills required to progress in an advanced technological society and to help reduce inter-communal tensions by providing an institutional context within which individuals could interact. Political reforms consisted of increasing participation in political life. Formal restraints on mass participation (i.e. voting) were abolished and attempts were made to diversify decision-making bodies, which in Northern Ireland extended to guaranteeing the minority community formal representation in the executive. In fact community politics developed into a new vogue within the discipline of political science.

In spite of the need to fulfil short-run objectives (i.e. to stop the immediate conflicts) the reformist strategy contained long-term implications for the socialization process which consisted of espousing the virtues of the traditional agents, and the family in particular received considerable attention. The alleged breakdown of the black family was widely seen as a central cause of the Afro-American's comparative impoverishment. Again the parallel with the Catholic family in Northern Ireland is striking: both are extended rather than nuclear family structures and, thanks to comparatively high male unemployment and mobility in search of work, the mother is frequently the head of the household. It is pertinent to note that Terence O'Neill saw the Catholic family as the link between socio-economic amelioration and new patterns of political behaviour.[20] The women's movement has been feared by some because of its potential for undermining the structure of the family, together with the feeling that this would lead to social chaos. Already some had blamed the student revolts upon the permissiveness of the middle-class family environment.

Although it may have been felt that long-term solutions were dependent upon new socialization processes (e.g. stable family structures and integrated schools), the pressing nature of the conflicts demanded more immediate solutions. These took the form outlined above, which in some respects further eroded the influence of the family, so, although many saw the family as a stabilizing agent, political realities prevented its full-scale resurrection. In Northern Ireland events reinforced the hold of the community upon its members, while the women's movement motivated governments to pass legislation that would make it easier and more worthwhile for women to work than be full-time mothers and wives, the universities tried to make students a somewhat more powerful, and, it was hoped, responsible constituent party within their governing apparatus, and in the case of Afro-Americans socio-economic changes appear to have left a significant segment of the urban black community as disintegrated as ever. Political manoeuvring has replaced consensus-building as the main tactic in securing stability, which increases the need for skilful elite manipulation and is just one indication that the social order is as fragile as appearances suggest.

No permanent support, no permanent opposition

No political system is assured of complete legitimacy in the sense that all its citizen show diffuse support for the community, its regime norms and political authorities. In most cases the norm is one of general compliance and whether this is translated into support or hostility depends upon various circumstances.[21] In the past it was assumed that in the United Kingdom and the United States compliance was latent support, but the events of the past decade have thrown considerable doubts upon this. These events point to a more delicate model of the political order, in which a constantly fluctuating pattern of role differentiation exists with a vague and shaky consensus that requires constant care and attention. No final security lies ahead for as past tensions are resolved so new conflicts emerge within the changing structure of society. Many would have predicted the black urban riots of the 1960s but few would have guessed at the scope and intensity of student conflict. The former was the manifestation of an old legacy entering a different decade while the latter was a direct consequence of change that has occurred in the advanced industrial state since the Second World War.

In certain respects the United States is in a better position to adjust to internal conflict than the United Kingdom. It has a more democratic heritage with sufficient built-in inconsistencies to smooth the way in matching theory and reality. In this respect it is interesting to note how its egalitarian heritage has been translated into equality of opportunity in which all supposedly have the same chances to be unequal. Superimposed upon British citizenship is a class structure, and as long as the inequalities implicit in this were accepted it enhanced stability but since the legimatons have started to break down so it has proved to be a cumbersome legacy. In cultural and political terms the definition of what it means to be British have traditionally been very wide, but the immigration of the post-war period has raised the problem of reconciling 'Britishness' and 'Blackness' and some have argued that the two cannot be successfully combined. Again the United States has an advantage in this respect. In the past the definition of the American identity was more clear-cut and this undoubtedly led to considerable intolerance towards what was regarded as deviant behaviour. But over time the understanding of what it means to be an American citizen has expanded to the point where cultural, if not political, pluralism is seen as a positive virtue. This represents a real accommodation of the minority ethnic groups. Given Britian's past willingness to tolerate eccentricity within a cultural consensus the same course may be followed, but as the boundaries have been so strongly defined by white Anglo-Saxon Protestants the minority groups may prove to be especially sensitive about their own identities. Certainly the revival of Welsh and Scottish nationalism does not augur well for the future, for if after centuries this accommodation has not been resolved, what hope can there be of successfully incorporating the new immigrants? The WASPS have dominated in the United States but not to the same extent as in Britain and, although the American cultural boundaries may have been rigid, the substance has always been an amalgam. Still it should prove interesting to watch Britain try to move from a class-constrained to a culturally pluralist society. Whether the basic political norms can in the process remain intact has yet to be decided.

The theory of political socialization put forward in this book has attempted to explain socio-political conflict within two advanced industrial states that have liberal democratic political institutions. Such conflict emerges out of the inevitable failure to legitimate inequality. As reforms are advanced to placate one set of demands, so technology brings about a new set of pressures, or as old contradictions disappear, so new ones are spawned. In opposition to the political left I would see this as an inevitable feature of any advanced industrial society, regardless of its political, economic or social structure. Obviously the pattern of inequality, and thus the demand for change, will vary according to the characteristics of those structures. Furthermore, this is a healthy sign, and what we have to fear most is a society in which inequality is defined away, where the unequal may not even know that they are unequal. Britain and America are modified, conflict-ridden pluralist societies — pluralist because there are a number of power centres, conflict-ridden because the distribution of scarce resources is constantly under challenge in spite of sophisticated processes of political education, although the conflict is modified by the uneven distribution of power. What needs to be achieved is a substantial degree of further modification in the distribution of power, which will, one hopes, lead to a more vigorous form of conflict pluralism. A tyrannical consensus of the left or right, maintained by all the instruments of state power — not least of which is political education — must not come to pass.

Notes

1. See pp. 10–11.
2. See p. 167.
3. Bell, *The End of Ideology*, pp. 393–407.
4. And partly because of the debasement of Marxism by the Soviet regime. But this assumes that the Soviet regime has been guided by Marxism, a highly debatable point.
5. See p. 113.
6. See p. 133.
7. See pp. 1–10.

8. Note also that the Marshall thesis stresses the individuality of rights, i.e. they pertain to people as individuals, whereas I have stressed the importance of rights as collective entities. There may be a distinction between civil and political rights on the one hand and socio-economic rights on the other hand. The latter only have meaning in so far as individuals can express them collectively, while the former they exercise as individuals.

9. For a discussion of this instrumentality see pp. 114–117. I allude to the difficulty of trying to control inflation in the United Kingdom by limiting wage demands.

10. See pp. 14–15.

11. See p. 60.

12. See pp. 42–43.

13. Lijphart, *The Politics of Accommodation*, ch. 1. This is an excellent review of the debate and his final chapter gives his amendments to this debate.

14. ibid., p. 205.

15. It may seem strange now, but when Labour MPs first entered the House of Commons some were afraid their presence would disrupt parliamentary proceedings. Whether this was due to their socialist ideology or lack of social graces is not altogether clear!

16. I am using political education in the wide sense of the term, i.e. to incorporate the media, youth clubs, service training, etc. My interpretation is debatable but what is more interesting is the ability of individuals to resist even stringent forms of political education — note the periodic attacks in the Soviet Union upon various forms of deviancy.

17. Something that is often overlooked in the rush to explain that it may equal only compliance.

18. In an interview with Tom Mangold in the BBC 'Midweek' programme (reported in *The Listener,* 13 June 1974, pp. 751–752) O'Connell further argued that support for the IRA was shown by its ability to survive while 'other organizations have gone by the board'.

19. Besides, of course, shooting at the members of the various instruments of control available to the state.

20. See pp. 222–223.

21. For a discussion of what these circumstances may be see Rose, *Governing Without Consensus,* ch. 1.

Index